KEEPING KIDS DRUG FREE

D.A.R.E.®

OFFICIAL PARENT'S GUIDE

Glenn Levant

President and Founding Director
D.A.R.E. America Worldwide

D0950661

San Diego, CA

pp. 29–30 Parent-Child Dialogue and pp. 39–40 "Children decide if"
reprinted with the permission of Simon & Schuster from GOOD
PARENTS FOR HARD TIMES by JoAnne Barbara Koch and Linda Nancy
Freeman, M.D. Copyright © 1992 by JoAnne Koch and Linda Freeman,
M.D.

The following pages from the *D.A.R.E. Student Workbook Grades 5 to 6*
have been reprinted or adapted in this resource: 4–6, 13, 26.

Cover design by Cheryl Ann Harrison
Book design by Lee Ann Hubbard

Library of Congress Cataloging-in-Publication Data

Levant, Glenn Al, 1941–
    Keeping kids drug free : D.A.R.E. official parent's guide
/ Glenn A. Levant.
        p.   cm.
    Includes index.
    ISBN 1-57145-625-2
    1. Teenagers—Drug use—United States.
    2. Drug abuse—Prevention—
Study and teaching—United States.   I. Title.
HV5824.Y68L484   1998
362.29'17'0973—DC21   97-37097
                                             CIP

1 2 3 4 5 98 99 00 01

Dedication

To Jayne, my love and inspiration for 37 years.

To Ellisa and Melanie, our wonderful daughters.

To Matthew and Emily. Papa Glenn loves you so much.

To Allison, Caitlyn, Kimberly, Madison, Brandon, Cameron and Andrew. God bless you. You are our future.

To the 30,000 D.A.R.E. instructors in law enforcement and to 5 million classroom teachers and educators. Thank you for your caring and encouragement.

To the 33 million children and teens each year who are learning and resisting daily, and to their parents and other adults who support them. You are our real heroes.

Contents

Acknowledgments vi
Author's Preface viii
Foreword xi
Introduction: The Threat Is Real 1

Part One: It's Up to You 7
  1. Why Kids Get in Trouble 8
  2. It All Starts With You 25
  3. Parenting to Build Self-esteem 39
  4. Violence in the Home and Community 51
  5. How the Media Sells the Allure of Drugs
     and Violence 73
Part Two: Drug Information 86
  6. Spotting the Signs and Symptoms 87
  7. Gateway Drugs: Alcohol and Tobacco,
     Avoiding the First Serious Steps 97
  8. Marijuana: Pot Today Is More Dangerous Than
     You Think 119
  9. Inhalants: Danger Right Under Your Nose 129
  10. Raiding the Medicine Cabinet 142
  11. Steroids and "Sports" Drugs: A No-Win,
     Fast Way to Lose 155
  12. Illegal Stimulants: Cocaine, Crack, Meth 171
  13. Designer Drugs, Heroin, and Hallucinogens 181

Part Three: Problem Solving 197
  14. "My Kid Is On Drugs. What Should I Do?" 198
  15. Strategies and Smart Ideas for Raising
     Drug-Free Kids 225
Appendices
  A. Glossary of Drug Terms 241
  B. Resource Guide 266

Chapter Notes 271
Index 272

Acknowledgments

Without exaggerating, there are hundreds of people who brought this book to life, and I am grateful to each and every one of them. Many spoke on the record and used their names freely in the hopes their words might help. Others asked for anonymity for reasons important to them. But here is where I would like to name names of people who were so giving of their time, talent, insights, and experiences.

Tara Catogge of Advanced Marketing Services, who had the original idea for this book and presented it to the powers to be. My editor at Laurel Glen, JoAnn Padgett, for working day and night organizing, fact-checking, trimming, patching, hand-holding, and doing all the other things caring editors do to help first-time authors survive the process. My publisher, Allen Orso, who green-lighted Tara's idea and gave JoAnn the time and support to make it happen.

I want to thank my longtime friend and writer, Chris Barnett Godchaux, who contributed his research, reporting and interviewing skills and was my sounding board on the book from start to finish.

I am especially indebted to the dozens of kids and parents who openly and honestly recounted how they stayed drug free or how they coped with drugs and dealt with the pain and disruption to their lives.

To the parents and caregivers who read the manuscript and gave us valuable feedback that helped us strengthen the final book: Karen Boyle, Tara Catogge, Cheri Johnson, Sheri Johnson , Norman Dowling, Richard Kirchoff, John McGee, Cathy Miller, Dave Ranta, Amy Simon, Sydney Stanley, Lisa Vargas. Your time made a difference.

The inspiration for this book came largely from the vision and energies of William J. Bennett, former secretary of education and national drug czar, and Joseph P. Califano, who heads the Center on Addiction and Substance Abuse (CASA) at Columbia University. This book, indeed D.A.R.E. as a drug prevention program, would not have been possible without the open-mindedness of Dr. Harry Handler, former superintendent of the Los Angeles Unified School District, and the drive and diligence of Dr. Ruth Rich, a curriculum specialist at LA Unified, who structured the first D.A.R.E. curriculum. Dr. Katherine Van Giffen, a professor at California State University, Long Beach, and Dr. Leonard H. Golubchick, principal of PS 20, Anna Silver School in New York City, have been cherished and stalwart supporters of our work.

I was fortunate to be able to draw on the collective wisdom of the members of the D.A.R.E. America Scientific Advisory Board, particularly our chairman, Dr. Herb Kleber, executive vice president and medical director at CASA; Mark S. Gold, M.D., Department of Neuroscience and Psychiatry, University of Florida Brain Institute; Elizabeth (B.J.) McConnell, executive director, The Wellness Community of Greater St. Louis; and Sue Rusche, executive director, National Families in Action. Members of the D.A.R.E. America Board of Directors, chaired by Ron Burkle; the D.A.R.E. Regional Training Center Advisory Board; and the National D.A.R.E. Officers Association offered superb comments.

Others who contributed inspiration and crucial information include Mitchell S. Rosenthal, M.D., president of Phoenix House; Martha Gagne, director of the American Council on Drug Education; and Dr. David Moore, executive director of Olympic Counseling Service of Tacoma, Washington. The Partnership for a Drug-Free America was exceptionally generous with its information and findings.

I am particularly thankful to Thomas A. Constantine, administrator of the Drug Enforcement Administration, and his colleague Bob Day. And to James J. McGivney, DEA's chief of public affairs, and especially to Rogene Waite, senior public affairs officer, for her ongoing counsel and access to DEA's most senior drug specialists. Bless you, Rogene.

My entire staff at D.A.R.E. headquarters was incredibly supportive, especially my patient assistant, Jan Appel, press liaison Ralph Lochridge, Mia Strike, Susan Arakaki, and Mark Stine, A special thanks to Pat Froehle who was with us at the beginning. Bill Alden, who logged 30 years with the Drug Enforcement Administration before joining us to head up our Washington, D.C. , office, was an invaluable reality check and navigator every step of the way. Misty Church of Strategic Communications, possibly the best researcher in Washington, responded quickly, accurately, and cheerfully to our nonstop requests for facts and experts. Sarah Cooper, the savvy Washington, D.C., conference manager, generously donated her office and her dedicated staff to act as our unofficial "research command post" for nearly a year.

To Sergeant Ed Arambula, a master trainer with LAPD's D.A.R.E. division; Caroline Buguey, principal of Spreckels School; Daryl Grecich of the Institute for a Drug Free Workplace; Susan Driscoll; Erik Godchaux; Debbie Stone; Selby Lighthill; Bob D'Alessandro, who directs the Center for Prevention Research and Resource Development; Butch O'Neil, substance abuse consultant in Boston; and all my coworkers at the Los Angeles Police Department who are now my colleagues and have believed in D.A.R.E. from the start—thank you.

Author's Preface

Almost thirty years ago, amid great fanfare, President Lyndon Johnson declared a national war on drugs. It was the end of the 1960s, and the love affair with marijuana was spreading to include hasnısh, LSD, and other hallucinogenics. More than 40 million Americans out of a population of 170 million were using drugs monthly, and the numbers were climbing.

I was working the streets as a young sergeant with the Los Angeles Police Department. My job provided a front-line education on how drugs tear apart families, lead to domestic violence and child abuse, and trigger property thefts, robberies, and violent crime. Later, serving in a narcotics command assignment, I realized we were waging a war we had already lost ten years earlier. By the time LBJ had marshaled his forces, America had been overrun by drug users and suppliers.

In the late 1970s, things got worse. The public attitude toward drug use was, in a word, "tolerance." Heroin shooting, PCP or angel dusting, acid tripping, and cocaine snorting were in vogue then in every city and not just the inner city. Films and songs often glamorized drugs. Timothy Leary's anthem of "turn on, tune in, and drop out" seemed to have become our national slogan. In spite of the best efforts of community, city, state, and federal law enforcement agencies, society was losing. No matter how many shipments were seized, no matter how many drug kingpins were arrested, no matter how many dealers were busted and gang members jailed, it didn't make a difference on the street. Drugs were getting purer; dealers were getting richer and more brazen. Locking up lawbreakers for crimes committed under the influence of drugs choked the courts and cost taxpayers up to $50,000 a year. From my vantage point, arresting, jailing, treating—all vitally important—had no lasting impact. Regardless of many excellent efforts by dedicated and talented people, all government drug-fighting policies and programs, fed-

viii

erally funded research efforts, and political pledges to tackle the drug scourge are frustrated by the same fate: not enough time to make a difference. Most are based on elections, budgets, terms of office, or grant cycles and cannot provide an uninterrupted effort to solve a problem that spans generations.

Meanwhile, I didn't want to end my career as a casualty of the drug war, as someone who spent a lifetime in law enforcement without making a dent. I was convinced there was a solution. And if you believe in the law of supply and demand, it is the only solution—eliminate demand. You can't sell something no one wants to buy. This was the inspiration behind D.A.R.E.

An obvious approach was to get to children before their first exposure to drugs and to give them the educational tools and personal skills to make smart, healthy choices—the right choice. The most effective place to reach them was in the schools. This wouldn't be yet another police drug-fighting squad, but a researched-based, community outreach educational program. The concept for D.A.R.E was presented to Dr. Harry Handler, then superintendent of education at Los Angeles Unified School District. He embraced the idea and directed one of his top specialists, Dr. Ruth Rich, to develop a classroom health curriculum to keep kids from ever getting involved in drugs.

Professional educators made a surprising recommendation about the program. You couldn't ask just teachers to sandwich drug education in between reading, math, and science. For one thing, not one state requires school teachers to take any courses in illegal substances as a requirement for getting a teaching credential. But if you put a streetwise, specially trained police officer into the classroom to teach a curriculum developed by professional educators, kids will pay attention. Officers have credibility when it comes to drugs. They can answer a fifth grader's question about the difference between "crank" and "crack" and explain what it does to a young mind and body. Launched in 1983, the first D.A.R.E. classes were taught in fifty Los Angeles elementary schools by ten D.A.R.E. officers who received eighty hours of intensive teacher training. D.A.R.E. started as an unbudgeted experiment—a partnership between parents, schools, and police officers. Yet it had to be sustained so it wouldn't die from a lack of funds like so many other promising drug prevention programs. Because it needed a nongovernmental source of financial support, I founded D.A.R.E. America as a nonprofit organization that would pay for all educational materials and training.

Thanks to many visionary, devoted colleagues and supporters in the city of Los Angeles, the Los Angeles Police Department, the Los Angeles Unified School District, and especially the street cops who got passionately involved, D.A.R.E. was an immediate success. From the first fifty schools, the program has spread to 10,000 municipalities in all 50 states, or 75 percent of the school districts in the United States. Law enforcement organizations and schools in 44 foreign countries have joined forces to teach the program. Less than 1 percent of D.A.R.E. America's operating budget comes from the federal government; 99 percent comes from grass roots sources at the community level, plus corporate sponsorships. This breaks the funding cycle dilemma and ensures the program will continue operating for generations.

While the curriculum has been enhanced nine times since 1983, D.A.R.E. was never designed to be a silver bullet that would win the war on drugs and sweep the streets of dealers and youthful users. It is, instead, a continuous course of prevention education. Instruction goes from kindergarten through fourth grade, with a full semester in the fifth or sixth grade, reinforced with ten more antidrug lessons in middle school or junior high and another nine weeks of curriculum in high school.

The goal of D.A.R.E.—the mission of this book—is to create a generation of young people who choose not to smoke, drink, or take drugs during their childhood and adolescence. To give kids—your kids—a chance to enter the adult world with healthy coping skills and a minimal amount of emotional baggage.

As adults, they will make decisions and live with the consequences. As children, they need your time, your guidance, your understanding and your love—now. Good luck.

Glenn Levant

Foreword

From popular culture to peer pressure, kids today are bombarded with prodrug use messages. As a result, young people are becoming more accepting of drugs and less aware and concerned about the consequences of drug use. In 1990, 40.4 percent of young people ages 12 to 17 believed that using marijuana was dangerous; by 1996, that number fell to 32.6 percent. As attitudes have changed, youth drug use has increased dramatically. Today, over 50 percent of America's 12th grade students have tried an illicit drug; nearly one in four are current users.

The most important reason for this increase in youth drug use is that kids are not hearing the facts about drugs. In 1991, 40.3 percent of young people grades six through 12 reported that their parents talked regularly with them about drugs; in 1996, only 29.6 percent said they talked regularly with their parents about drugs.

The 1997 National Drug Control Strategy established educating our young people as the nation's top priority in combating drugs and drug use. Working with parents, teachers, and mentors of all types, we have to inform our children about the perils of drug use.

Keeping Kids Drug Free provides the facts about drugs that all of us need to know in order to talk honestly and directly to our kids. The Guide can't make you sit down and talk about this tough but important subject; however, it can make the conversation easier and more valuable.

Barry R. McCaffrey
Director,
Office of National Drug Control Policy
The White House

Introduction:
The Threat Is Real

Drugs and kids. It's a reality every parent must face—head-on. You can't deny it. You can't ignore it. But you *can* raise drug-free children. As parents or other concerned caregivers, you are your children's greatest resource.

This Book Will Help You:

- Keep your kids healthy and safe from drugs and violence.

- Understand the pressures on young people to use drugs.

- Know about specific drugs and their major effects.

- Educate your kids about the responsible use of alcohol, tobacco, and other drugs.

- Recognize signs and symptoms of drug use/abuse.

- Encourage positive self-esteem in your child.

- Develop close, open relationships with your children.

- Communicate and teach family values.

- Set rules and establish family guidelines.

- Be a positive influence in your child's life.

- Deal with problems related to drugs and violence.

- Know where to go for help.

Resources Provided

- Drug information: method of use, source of drug, effects, signs and symptoms of use and abuse, dangers, penalties for possession and use
  - Guidelines on how to discuss drugs with your children, including what to tell them and how to get through to them
  - Resistance techniques to avoid drugs and violence
  - Proactive, preventive tips for parents
  - Ways to monitor your behavior and be a good role model
  - Guidelines for setting family rules and communicating family values
  - Techniques to help build your child's self-esteem
  - Role plays to help you and your child practice effective communication skills
  - Tips on how to monitor and control negative messages about drugs and violence from advertising, movies, music, and television
  - True stories as "wake-up calls"
  - Inspirational stories of real families who overcame problems
- Glossary of drug terms
- Evaluation of various drug treatment options
- Information on where to turn for additional help and support, including a Resource Directory
- Practical aids for raising a healthy, happy, drug-free child

"Your child does not have to be a statistic. Your family does not need to suffer the horrendous pain of losing a kid to drugs, gang intimidation, violence, or death."

Most significantly, this book will teach you how to really listen to and communicate with your children and help them with important aspects of their lives.

I've spent over thirty-five years facing the drug epidemic every day, including fifteen years of working directly with

D.A.R.E.* and helping to teach thirty-three million kids worldwide how to resist drugs and gangs and how to avoid violence. I know firsthand that responsible, concerned parents can make a difference. You are the solution. You have the greatest power to shape your children's attitudes, values, and behaviors. Regardless of your social, economic, or educational level, you as a parent play the single most important role in determining whether your children will be snared or saved. Your child does not have to be a statistic. Your family does not need to suffer the horrendous pain of losing a kid to drugs, gang intimidation, violence, or death.

"Responsible, concerned parents can make a difference."

Drugs and Violence in the United States[1]

- 23 million Americans abuse drugs.
- At least three million kids use illegal drugs.
- One out of four fourth graders is pressured by friends or classmates to use drugs or alcohol. Most succumb.
- One out of five high-school students smokes cigarettes daily, which make them prime candidates for lung cancer, heart disease, and graduation to more dangerous drugs.
- One out of five high-school students smokes marijuana at least once a month, usually more frequently.
- Two out of three high-school students drink beer, wine, or hard liquor at least once a month. Many are addicted daily drinkers.

---

*D.A.R.E. (Drug Abuse Resistance Education) is offered to schools through a partnership between a city's school district and its chief of police or sheriff. Any child who has parental permission is eligible to attend the program if the school offers it.

- Over 1,000 drug-related murders occur each month. Most victims are young people—their lives snuffed out before their prime.
- Gunfire is the third biggest killer of children under 18.
- 1,000 people die each month in traffic accidents triggered by drug and alcohol abuse.
- The "War on Drugs" is the longest-running war in U.S. history.

Drug abuse has immediate consequences for your family, relatives, and friends. Ultimately its cost and impact is much greater. Drug abuse impacts the entire community, especially employers, social workers, clergy, educators, and those in law enforcement, medical, and legal professions. No one escapes the impact. Americans will spend $16 billion in 1998 to fight illegal drug abuse. The amount of the annual economy that is spent on expenses directly related to drug abuse works out to a $2,000 drug tax for every American citizen, a sum that's largely spent on healthcare costs and lost job productivity.[2]

In a speech introducing his 1997 National Drug Control Strategy, President Clinton acknowledged that "drug abuse by children continues to rise for the fifth consecutive year.... America's youth increasingly must reject dangerous drugs, including cigarettes and alcohol." Clinton suggested that the nation's counter-drug efforts could be compared to the fight against cancer. Confronting the problem "requires prevention, education, treatment, compassion, and a willingness to commit resources intelligently."

How to Use This Book

The central message and a recurring theme throughout this book is that parents need to get involved in keeping their kids drug free. A lot of effort has gone into making this book user friendly so that it can serve as an illuminating read as well as a handy resource and ready reference. Each chapter is arranged in a systematic order and includes an overview of the problem (both who and what), the dangers, signs and symptoms, solutions, and activities. Key points are highlighted or arranged in easy-to-reference lists throughout.

Part One: It's Up to You, contains invaluable parenting information as well as discussions about influences your child is exposed to of which you may not be aware. If you are just dipping into the book on a need-to-know basis, I would urge you to take the time to read *Chapter 2, It All Starts With You,* and *Chapter 3, Parenting to Build Self-Esteem.* The parenting advice contained within these two chapters is vital to implementing specific solutions offered in this book. If you are concerned about a particular substance abuse problem, you can reference the specific chapter in *Part Two: Drug Information.* Each chapter in *Part Two* stands alone, although there will be echoes throughout of key points from *Part One.* Finally, in *Part Three: Problem Solving,* we review key points, offer strategies for dealing with your child's drug use, and tell parents how to evaluate counselors and treatment options.

> **"The number one goal of the National Drug Control Strategy is to teach America's youth to reject illegal drugs, alcohol, and tobacco."**

This book is reality based. The insights come from my years working with the police force and the D.A.R.E. organization, and from parents and kids who shared their personal stories—both triumphs and tragedies—and the wisdom that they gained as a result. We'd love to hear from you, especially if you faced a challenge and found a way to overcome it. Be an advocate for all children and all parents.

Part One

It's Up to You

1

Why Kids Get in Trouble

Your Worst Nightmare

The phone rings.

- A doctor informs you that your son was rushed to the hospital's emergency room for a drug overdose and the hospital needs your written permission to provide treatment.
- The school principal calls to report that your 10-year-old daughter was caught sniffing paint thinner on the playground with some friends.
- A store manager calls to tell you that your child was arrested for shoplifting. Later you find out that he was stealing to finance his drug habit.
- The highway patrol has arrested your son for drunk driving. He registered two-and-a-half times the adult legal limit for sobriety. Since the minimum legal drinking age is 21 in all 50 states and D.C., teenage drivers should have *no* alcohol in their blood. That means he now has a police record. And you thought he was attending a soccer game with his buddies.
- A police detective calls and asks you to come down to the station and pick up your daughter. She was caught with some friends smoking marijuana in a fast-food restaurant parking lot. She confessed that they all get high regularly.
- The shopping mall security office calls to say that your son and his friends have been banned from the mall for harassing and bullying other kids. In addition, they were caught

8

tagging (spray-painting) graffiti on mall buildings; you will be liable for the damages and clean-up costs.

No One Is Immune

Every day, families like yours have their lives disrupted or ruined by drugs, alcohol, and violence—or all three. The availability of guns, the use of drugs and alcohol, and the presence of violence in the home are key risk factors. Kids are injured physically and emotionally, often permanently. Suddenly, your world is turned upside down. Overnight, you must confront issues that you never thought you would have to deal with—therapy, counseling, the juvenile justice system, detoxification, and possibly rehabilitation programs.

This does not just happen in ghettos or inner cities. It does not just happen to poor kids or kids from broken homes. It happens everywhere in America to families in circumstances exactly like your own and to kids of every age, gender, race, and social class.

Discovering that your preteen uses drugs is a tremendous jolt to any parent, but particularly to a mom and dad who had no reason to believe they might have to face this problem.

Patti and Al's Story

Patti and Al F. are a typical suburban couple. Both have demanding careers. Patti is a field engineer for an office equipment company and travels one week every month. Al works long hours and weekends as a real estate agent. The parents' high-pressure jobs left their two children with too much unsupervised time. The youngsters, Meredith, 9, and Lee, 11, are at the age where they are curious, adventurous, and vulnerable.

At school, their daughter Meredith made a new friend, Andrea. Andrea's mother also works full-time, and the two girls would go to Andrea's house after school to watch TV or to listen to CDs. Andrea knew her mom smoked marijuana. Andrea told Meredith , "It helps my mom relax, and she says it isn't dangerous." Andrea also knew where her mother kept the marijuana and the pipe she used to smoke it. One day Andrea suggested, "It would be fun to try it and see what it felt like. We won't use much. My mother will never know."

Although Meredith was tempted, she remembered what her brother Lee had told her about marijuana. A D.A.R.E. police officer had visited Lee's school to talk to his class about drugs. The police officer told the kids, "There is no such thing as a harmless drug. Drugs are bad, and smoking them is totally uncool." Meredith worried that, regardless of what Andrea's mother said, smoking marijuana was not a good idea. So, using one of D.A.R.E.'s eight ways to say no, she made an excuse that she had to do her homework and she went home.

At dinner, Meredith told her parents and her brother what happened at Andrea's house. Her mother and father were shocked. They thought their daughter was too young to be exposed to drugs. They never considered that drugs existed in their community because they lived in a nice neighborhood in the suburbs and all the children went to a "good school."

They didn't know Andrea's mother, a college graduate and computer programmer for a major local employer, nor did they have any idea that she used drugs. It was a loud wake-up call for Patti and Al. They agreed that if one parent was traveling or had a business meeting, the other would be at home, no matter what. "We had a close call," says Al. "Meredith could have given into Andrea's friendly pressure and taken that first puff." Instead, they were grateful that they were a family that communicates and talks about personal problems and personal feelings. "We felt terribly ashamed and guilty," added Patti, "that our 11-year-old son Lee had assumed the role of family leader because Al and I were so wrapped up in our careers and never considered that our young nine-year-old child could have a close call with drugs in our neighborhood."

All children probably will be tempted to use drugs, no matter where they live or what school they go to, but not everyone will give in to the temptation to experiment with drugs. The solution is prevention—meeting children's needs before they seek dangerous alternatives.

Why Good Kids Make Poor Choices

Kids who smoke cigarettes, who use alcohol and drugs, or who join gangs do so for a myriad of reasons.

Explanations heard most often from school children in D.A.R.E. programs:

◆ **Afraid to say no**
Either they do not know how to refuse or they are afraid of the consequences of refusing.

◆   **To please a special friend**
A friend, usually their own age, wants them to join in, adding heavy pressure by saying "I'm not going to be your friend any more unless you do it with me."

◆   **To fit in because everyone else does it**
They give in to peer pressure. Everyone else is doing it and they do not want to feel like an outcast. They want to be accepted.

◆   **Need to feel cool and older**
Many kids view drinking, taking drugs, or joining a gang as adult behaviors that will make them appear more grown up.

◆   **Curiosity**
To find out what alcohol or drugs are like. Are they as bad for you as everyone says they are?

◆   **To feel good**
For some kids who do not feel good about themselves, it is a quick way to boost low self-esteem or to escape their worries. They get high to ease the pain, anger, boredom, or frustration in their lives.

◆   **To get back at a parent**
Their mom and dad don't want them to smoke, drink, or try drugs.

◆   **Too much stress or pressure caused by:**
  Problems at home
  Arguments or fighting
  Feeling overwhelmed because of too much to do
  Being embarrassed in front of friends and schoolmates
  Trouble with schoolwork and tests
  Feeling lonely and depressed
  Problems with siblings

◆   **For fun**
Drugs and alcohol are romanticized as an escape hatch. Kids think that other kids are experiencing something that might be fun and exciting and they don't want to miss out.

Key Reasons for Substance Abuse

You do not have to be a child psychologist to see that all of the preceding reasons are rooted in one of two categories:

1. **low self-esteem**
2. **peer pressure**

Parents, family, and friends play a key role in shaping a child's self-esteem. Self-esteem is covered in depth in Chapter 3. The remainder of this chapter will focus on ways to address peer pressure as a factor in substance abuse.

Peer Pressure

Peer pressure, clinically defined, is a "force or influence from others who are about their own age." According to research conducted by the U.S. Department of Education,[1] as children move toward their teen years, "fitting in" is a dominant influence in their lives. The onset of puberty is like a rebirth. Children need to let go of the past and find their own unique identities.

Getting invited to a party, associating with a popular boy or girl, eating lunch at a certain table at school, or being picked to join the winning team are just some of the ways that peers influence a child's self-esteem. Being shunned, ridiculed, or not being accepted by these same peers are ways that their self-esteem is undermined.

Types of Peer Pressure

Peer pressure can be divided into four categories—and all of them can have a powerful influence on your child, especially on preteens and teenagers. Combating these pressures can seem overwhelming to kids who do not have the experience or tools to resist.

1. **Friendly Pressure:** A friendly offer to try something made in a friendly way. This can range from anything from a first cigarette to beer or wine to a marijuana cigarette or to sniffing solvents.
   "Would you like to try some?"

2. **Teasing Pressure:** A strong pressure in which people tease to get children to try a drug.
   "Come on, don't be a chicken. Try it."

3. **Indirect (or Tempting) Pressure:** A pressure to use drugs without a direct offer.
   "My brother has a stash of marijuana in his room."

4. **Heavy Pressure:** The strongest pressure used to influence a young person to do something.
   "I won't be your friend if you don't!"

Resistance Techniques to Teach Your Children

D.A.R.E. has identified eight resistance techniques or "eight ways to say no." Any one or combination of them should get the youngster out of a dangerous situation. Discuss, practice, and role-play them with your children, and reverse role-play. Be creative. Set up simulated situations that would be appropriate for your family circumstances. It will help them be prepared the next time they face an uncomfortable situation and feel pressured to do something they don't want to do. Some of the eight ways to say no work better than others for resisting certain kinds of peer pressure. Review the techniques suggested for each type of pressure with your children.

Pressure	Ways to Say No
1. Friendly pressure	Saying "no thanks," giving a reason or excuse
2. Teasing pressure	Repeated refusal, cold shoulder
3. Indirect pressure	Avoiding the situation
4. Heavy pressure	Avoiding the situation, walking away, strength in numbers

Regardless of the method chosen, saying "no" has certain traps that your child can fall into with heavy pressure. For instance, using long-term health consequences as an excuse or reason for saying no is rarely effective. However, giving an immediate or short-term consequence can cut off further discussion. Here is a suggested strategy for your child to use:

Pressure: "Hey, do you want a beer?"
Reply: "No thanks."
Pressure: "Oh, come on. One beer isn't going to hurt you."
Reply
(short-term consequence): "I don't want to get into trouble."

8 Ways to Say "No"

1. **Saying "No Thanks"**
    "Would you like a drink?"
    "No thanks."
2. **Giving a reason or excuse**
    "Would you like a beer?"
    "No thanks. I don't drink beer."
3. **Repeated refusal, or keep saying "no" (broken record)**
    "Would you like a hit?"
    "No."
    "Come on!"
    "No."
    "Just try it!"
    "No."
4. **Walking away**
    "I have some cigarettes. Do you want one?"
    Say no and walk away while saying it.
5. **Changing the subject**
    "Let's smoke some marijuana."
    "No. Let's watch my new video instead."
6. **Avoiding the situation**
    If you know of places where people often use drugs, stay away from those places. If you pass those places on the way home, go another way.
7. **Cold shoulder**
    "Hey! Do you want to smoke?"
    Just ignore the person.
8. **Strength in numbers**
    Hang around with nonusers, especially where drug use is expected.

Where Kids Get Drugs

Perhaps the biggest mystery to parents is where children get drugs. Forget the image of the sinister adult drug pusher hanging around elementary school playgrounds. It is simply a myth. Preteens generally get their first exposure to drugs from other kids, peers and playmates, during unsupervised free time.

Parents or older brothers and sisters have cigarettes, cigars, liquor, prescription medicines, household chemicals, and maybe even illegal substances around the house where they are accessible. For example, a ten-year-old kid knows his older brother smokes marijuana to get high, and the youngster knows where his "stash" is kept. He takes some of the pot or a few prerolled joints and goes over to a friend's house where they both light up and listen to music. Essentially, it is occasional use based on convenience and availability.

This book shows you how to maintain clear communications, establish rules and family values when they are young, and give them love and help now without waiting one minute more. The wisdom that *an ounce of prevention is worth a pound of cure* is absolutely true—and effective—in helping you to keep your kids healthy, safe, and away from drugs, alcohol, and violence.

ACTIVITY

My Stress Level

The following stress level test is part of the D.A.R.E. classroom curriculum. It can be a useful exercise to have your child take periodically because stressors change. Having your child take this test and discuss it with you, may give you valuable insights into what is troubling him/her and an opportunity to discuss problems before they get out of hand. Consider taking the test yourself to see how much you know about your child's day-to-day life. Compare your answers with your child's.

Directions: Answer the questions below. Add the number of checks in the "yes" column, then compare your child's score with the scale.

In the last month, have you	Yes	No
1. Taken a test?	___	___
2. Had an argument or been in a fight?	___	___
3. Been late for something?	___	___
4. Had something exciting happen to you?	___	___
5. Felt lonely or depressed?	___	___
6. Had to speak in front of classmates?	___	___
7. Met someone new?	___	___
8. Had problems with a family member?	___	___
9. Tried hard to win a game or race?	___	___
10. Had too many things to do?	___	___
11. Had trouble with schoolwork?	___	___
12. Failed to complete an assignment?	___	___
13. Helped plan a special party or event?	___	___
14. Had to be the first one to do something?	___	___
15. Been embarrassed?	___	___

Stress Level
0-5 Low, 6-10 Medium, 11-15 High

ACTIVITY

Considering Consequences

1. Ask your child why s/he thinks young people use alcohol, drugs, or tobacco.
2. Have your child come up with a consequence for using drugs, alcohol, tobacco, or joining a gang.
3. Ask the child to identify whether the consequence is negative or positive.
4. Use the following D.A.R.E. Drug Fact Sheet to discuss the effects and harmful consequences with your child.
5. Explain the laws regarding the purchase and/or use of these substances by minors.

D.A.R.E. Drug Fact Sheet

A drug is any substance other than food that can affect the way your mind and body work. Certain drugs, called mind-altering drugs, can change the way a person thinks, feels, and acts.

Drugs that speed a person up are called **stimulants.**

Drugs that slow a person down are called **depressants.**

Drugs that change the ways a person sees, feels, and hears are called **hallucinogens.**

Drugs most commonly abused by young people include:

***Nicotine* is a highly addictive and habit-forming stimulant found in cigarettes.**

- Nicotine increases the heart rate, causes the blood vessels to narrow, and makes the heart work harder.
- Chewing tobacco also contains nicotine. It makes teeth loosen and causes gum disease, white patches in the mouth, and tooth decay.
- Smoking tobacco, chewing tobacco, and snuff give you bad breath, smelly hands, and stained teeth.
- Tobacco can also cause cancer, heart disease, and death. In fact, cigarette smoking is the most preventable cause of death in the United States. The number of people who die each day from the effects of smoking is the same as if two full jumbo jets were to crash every day.
- Even breathing in someone else's smoke can be dangerous to your health. This is called passive [secondhand] smoke. Passive smoke pollutes the air and studies suggest that it is as harmful as smoking itself.

Alcohol is a depressant drug.

When a person drinks alcohol, it is absorbed directly into the bloodstream from the stomach and intestines. Drinking alcohol can cause:

- Drunkenness
- Loss of coordination (balance)
- Increase in violence (destructive acts)
- Inability to learn and remember
- Changes in personality
- Increase in accidents
- Trouble with other people

Use of alcohol can lead to drug dependency, addiction (habit-forming), disease (cirrhosis of the liver), and death. Because of the risks and dangers involved in using alcohol (especially for young people), it is illegal for people of a certain age (18 or 21, depending on state law) to drink.

Marijuana is a mind-altering drug.

Marijuana has many slang names. Some of them are "pot," "weed," "grass," and "herb." Someone who uses marijuana has:

- Slow reflexes
- Poor memory
- Short attention span
- Inability to think
- Changes in sense of time and space

Students who use marijuana may have difficulty remembering what they have learned, are slow, are dull, have little ambition, and may become psychologically dependent on the drug.

***Cocaine* is a highly addictive stimulant.**
It is usually snorted through the nose but can also be smoked in the form of "crack" or "rock." It can also be injected.

When used on a regular basis, cocaine causes a person to become:

◆ Confused
◆ Disoriented
◆ Short-tempered

It may also cause:

◆ Damage to the lining of the nose
◆ Breathing problems
◆ Heart attacks
◆ Death

***Inhalants* are chemicals that are used for sniffing or "huffing" to get high.**
Glue, gasoline, and about 2,000 other dangerous chemicals can be used as inhalants.

Inhalants can:

◆ Be habit forming
◆ Be flammable or explosive
◆ Cause liver damage
◆ Cause brain damage
◆ Cause death

Abusing any chemical inhalant is dangerous. They blur the thinking process, cause dizziness, and can be fatal on the first try.

ACTIVITY

Review each of the following situations with your child and ask him/her to suggest how to handle it. If your child is having problems crafting an appropriate response, review the four kinds of peer pressure and discuss which category each situation falls into. The suggested answers were provided by a D.A.R.E. officer.

Situation: Your child and his pals are playing in a friend's garage. There is a second refrigerator in the garage to store beer and soft drinks. The "host" wants to feel grown up and says to his friends, "Come on, let's drink some beer." *(Friendly Peer Pressure)*

Response: "No. You know what? My aunt is picking me up to take me to meet my cousins at her house and I've got to meet her in front of the grocery store.

or: "Hey, you know I've got a new CD. Why don't we go to my house and listen to it."

Situation: A boy is walking home through a park after soccer practice and sees a bunch of his schoolmates sitting on a bench. One of the kids extends a joint and says, "Don't be a baby, man, take a hit. It's only a joint." The other kids laugh, egging him on. *(Teasing Peer Pressure)*

Response: "No thanks. I'm not chicken. I just don't do it. See you guys later."

He should just walk away. If he stays and tries to answer their taunts, the pressure will escalate and he could wind up in a fight. It's also time to find some new friends.

Situation: Your child and her friend are aware of a party at Bill's house next Saturday night when his parents aren't home. The friend says. "The party will be so cool. There will be a lot to drink and smoke." (*Indirect or Tempting Peer Pressure*)

Response: "I can't go to the party. I'm grounded this weekend."

She should immediately talk to her parents and explain what happened. And her parents should contact the host's parents and tell them what's being planned at their home while they're out of town. They should reinforce to their daughter that she did the right thing because with all that underage drinking and dope smoking, someone can get hurt or arrested. She doesn't need that.

Situation: Your child and three other school friends are behind a trash dumpster at school during lunch period and someone brings out a paper bag and gasoline-soaked rag. The other boys put the bag to their face and inhale the fumes. Then it's passed to your son. "Come on and take a huff. If you don't do it or if you tell, we'll get you after school." (*Heavy Peer Pressure*)

Response: "If you were my friend, you wouldn't ask me to do that."

If the child is threatened physically, he should immediately walk away and tell someone in authority—a school principal or teacher—what happened. The goal is to nip the threat in the bud and avoid the kid who threatened him. He is not tattling on the other kid. He is protecting himself.

2

It All Starts With You

Parenting is the most influential and important job you will ever hold. In order to help children survive and thrive, you must help them grow up to be independent and responsible. Although there are many factors beyond your control, you create the environment in which your children grow.

"Be an active, involved, and concerned parent who sets a good example."

Parents are responsible for:
- **Providing a safe home environment**
- **Ensuring that your children receive a good education**
- **Teaching morals and values**
- **Teaching children to be responsible and accountable for their actions**
- **Setting a good personal example at home and in your community**

Are you worried that your child is vulnerable to the temptations of alcohol, tobacco, and drugs? Get involved now! If you are not involved in your children's lives—at school, in church or temple, in extracurricular activities—you are out of touch with the temptations they face. You must be an active, involved, and concerned parent who sets a good example.

Direct your children toward constructive activities and get involved in these activities. If you know your youngster has already taken that first step by smoking cigarettes, using alcohol,

25

trying marijuana, or using other drugs, do not waste a minute in showing that you care about his or her health and future. Disconnected parents create an environment that is prone to abuse. **If you are too busy to focus on your children, they *will* get in trouble.**

The Parent As Role Model

A parent's behavior is critical in giving a child information to draw on. You are your child's primary role model until puberty.

Monitor Your Behavior

Children believe what they see you do more than what they hear you say. Parents who light up a cigarette without a second thought are undermining their own efforts to steer kids away from addictive tobacco. The same is true when a parent comes home at night and immediately has two or three drinks to "relax." Kids emulate their parents and want to do the same things that they see adults do. If you tell your children that smoking and drinking are bad for you, yet you smoke or drink, you are giving a mixed message. In a child's mind, the message is, "Adults smoke and drink, so smoking and drinking must be okay." That is a child's logic; consequences are rarely given a second thought.

Answering Questions About Your Behavior

What do you do when your child asks:
   "Why do/did you drink?"
   "Why do/did you smoke?"
   "Why can't I drink, too?"
   "Isn't drinking fun?"
   "Did you ever smoke pot? Why shouldn't I try it if you did?"

1. Be honest and frank.

Explain that everybody makes bad decisions, even adults. Tell them why you do not want them to make the same mistakes that you did. Do not be defensive. A personal story from a parent can make you seem more human. Discuss any lessons you learned from personal experience.

Examples:

Explain why you quit smoking.

- You were concerned about your health.
- You were not setting a good example for them.
- Your friend/relative who recently died, passed away due to a smoking-related disease.
- Your doctor told you to because...

Explain what happened when you drank too much.

- Got a ticket for drunk driving (explain the consequences)
- Drove your dad's car into a ditch
- Lost a friend due to a drunken argument
- Drank too much at a party, made a fool of yourself through what you said and did, including throwing up in front of everyone

Tell them that there is nothing cool about drugs. Explain an incident with drugs that you experienced or witnessed. If you were a child from the mid-sixties on, you probably had a personal encounter with drugs—either directly or indirectly.

- Tell them about people who were "busted" (arrested) for either possession of or selling marijuana.
- Tell them if you went to a party where someone "spiked" the punch with LSD and how some kids were sent to the hospital because they were freaking out due to a bad "acid trip."
- Tell them about the kid in school who everybody thought was cool until his parents found him dead from shooting up.
- Tell them about a friend who spent all of his money on his cocaine habit and who now has no job, no home, and no family.

2. **It may seem like a cop-out, but children need to understand that there is a difference between being a minor and an adult.**
   There are different rules and responsibilities for different ages. Parents can make decisions and develop habits that are for adults only. Be sure to add that adults who make these choices must also accept the responsibilities and suffer the consequences of their choices.

3. **Explain how smoking, drinking, or using drugs can hurt them physically.**
   Use the D.A.R.E. Fact Sheet in Chapter 1 or the information about drug's effects in Part Two. You could also use examples of celebrities who have had bad experiences with drinking and drugs: John Belushi, Drew Barrymore, River Phoenix, Kurt Cobain, Robert Downey, Jr., etc.

4. **Discuss the difference between moderate and excessive behavior.**
   Even children should be able to distinguish between healthy and unhealthy practices. People consume many things—fried foods, chocolate, meat, ice cream—that if done in excess would cause health problems. Talk to them about judgment and moderation in terms they can understand. Having one glass of wine with dinner is different than drinking an entire six-pack at one sitting.

5. **Explain that adults are trying to help them manage their lives, not just boss them around—although it may seem like that at times.**
   If your child wants a deeper explanation or another opinion—and chances are s/he will—ask them to seek the advice of their teacher, their D.A.R.E. officer (if they are currently enrolled in the program), their coach, or another adult authority figure. After they talk with someone else, initiate another discussion about what was said.

Parent-Child Dialogue

In *Good Parents for Hard Times,* authors Joanne Barbara Koch and Linda Nancy Freeman provide an excellent dialogue that would help a young child gain a realistic view of alcohol.

◆ ◆ ◆ ◆ ◆

Child: Why do you drink, Mom?

Mother: Well, I like the taste of a glass of wine. It seems to make a good meal taste even better. And wine has a certain effect which is pleasant, makes me feel a little more light-headed, a little more relaxed. Yet many people can't take just one glass of wine or one glass of beer. Do you know any people like that?

Child: I'm not sure.

Mother: When we get together on Thanksgiving, did you ever notice how much Uncle Richard drinks? First he seems silly. Then he seems kind of mean. He's had lots of problems with his drinking. And the family worries about it. As an adult, I found I could take just a little bit of wine or beer. I decided I could do that once in a while.

Child: Why can't I have wine?

Mother: First of all, you're not an adult and so it's against the law for you to drink. When you get to be older, twenty-one years old like cousin Anne, you will have to make a choice. You may choose not to drink anything, and honestly that's the safest choice. I hope you will never drink too much. Remember that time you ate all your Halloween candy on one night?

Child: I threw up.

Mother: Your body is smart. It lets you know. Don't overdo it. With alcohol, your body also lets you know. But some people get so attached to alcohol, they can't stop, even when they know alcohol is making them sick. Even though we sometimes see a movie or TV program where drinking seems to be fun or something to laugh at, it's not fun. It makes people throw up and have headaches.

Child: Then drinking isn't fun?

Mother: Not unless people can stop when they've had only a little, not if they get drunk or what we call intoxicated. And worst of all, people who drink and try to drive often hurt themselves and others. We have a friend whose daughter was jogging one day. A drunk driver drove up on the jogging path and hit her. She is paralyzed. She can't use her arms or legs. Drinking is a dangerous thing. For lots of people, it's a terrible problem.

◆ ◆ ◆ ◆ ◆

Teach By Example

Modeling good behavior is more likely to produce good behavior in your child.

The best way for you to help your child understand good values and behaviors is for you to practice them yourself. Teaching through modeling will have a profound influence on your child, positively and negatively. When a child observes parents

- being loving,
- acting responsibly,
- solving problems without recourse to violence,
- honoring commitments,
- caring for their bodies,
- respecting others,
- reading,
- studying,
- or a myriad of other behaviors,

the child is learning standards of behavior.

Set Rules About Cigarettes, Alcohol, Drugs, and Other Substances

Many parents are reluctant to discuss alcohol or drug abuse with their children. Part of it stems from denial—"There is no way my child would get involved with or use unlawful substances!" Often parents do not know what to say or do until they are forced to cope with the issue.

One prevention strategy is universal: Every family should set and enforce rigid rules against the use of cigarettes, alcohol, and other drugs. This is a primary parental responsibility to protect children at this vulnerable time of development.

Guidelines for Rules

1. Be Clear
For a child or preteen, you need to explain rules in basic terms.

- Drinking alcoholic beverages is not allowed, either inside or outside the home, until you are of legal age.
- Never get in a car with someone who has been drinking.
- Medicines and common household products contain chemicals and drugs that can be helpful when used correctly or harmful, even deadly, when used incorrectly. (Identify some: cough syrup, pain relievers, glue, bleach, paint thinner)
- Never touch, taste, or smell any medicine, household product, or unknown substance without permission.
- Never take anyone else's medicine.
- Always keep out of cabinets or other places where alcohol, medicines, and household products are stored.

2. Spell Out Consequences
Consistent rules and clear limits provide your child with a framework for making behavioral choices. When children experience the consequences of their behavior, they learn decision making and self-control.

- Drinking and driving is dangerous. Drinking impairs your motor coordination, alertness, and concentration. If you drink and drive you could kill others—and yourself.
- Medicine should only be taken when given by your parents, doctor, nurse, or another trusted adult.

3. Be Firm and Consistent

Make it absolutely clear that your child cannot use cigarettes, alcohol, drugs, or solvents at any time, no exceptions, regardless of where they are.

4. Be Reasonable, Not Tyrannical

If your child breaks a rule, don't make threats like "Your father will kill you when he gets home and finds out what you've done." Remain calm and stick with the punishment that was discussed as a consequence for breaking the rule. Explain to your child why s/he is being punished and that you will not tolerate behavior that could be harmful. The child who knowingly breaks a rule might lose his or her allowance, get a time out, be grounded, be restricted from using the computer or watching a favorite TV program, or be assigned extra chores.

Guidelines for Social Occasions

- *Make sure* there is adult supervision. Ask the host if another chaperone is needed; volunteering will give you a chance to meet your child's friends. Ask the parents about their house rules. If they sound permissive or uninvolved, don't allow your child to attend.
- If your child does not drive, provide transportation or know exactly who is driving.
- Set a reasonable curfew.
- If you're hosting a party, make it clear that drinking alcoholic beverages and smoking are not permitted. If there is an infraction, have your child tell the offending party to stop the unacceptable behavior. If there is any indication of drinking or signs of intoxication, arrange a safe ride home for the child involved and talk to his parents.
- If your kid is going to a sleepover, talk to the hosting parent. Will an adult be in the house the entire time? If kids will be supervised by an older sibling, have you met that kid?

Patrick's Story

Patrick W., a B+ seventh grader in Sioux City, Iowa, is a bright, college-bound student from a great family. He has plenty of friends and loves sports. His stay-at-home mom and his dad, a bank manager, seem to have it all together.

One afternoon, Patrick's dad was returning from lunch when his wife called. "It's about Patrick. We need to meet his vice principal this afternoon. I don't know why, but he wants us there today."

Patrick's parents were confused when they arrived at the school. A hundred things were running through their minds. Had he been hurt playing baseball? Was he in a fight? Was he caught cheating on an exam?

When his parents walked into the vice principal's office, Patrick was sitting there with three other students, kids who did not look like any of Patrick's friends, or even the kind of kids he would associate with. Patrick buried his face in his hands when he saw his parents. Once his parents were seated inside, Patrick broke down and cried as the vice principal explained the reason for the call. Patrick and the other kids were smuggling liquor onto campus using lunch box Thermos bottles, medicine bottles, water bottles, and other ingenious techniques. They had been caught drinking in the boy's bathroom. According to the vice principal, the kids had been bringing liquor from their homes on an almost daily basis and had made a game out of who could be the cleverest smuggler. Then the vice president dropped the bombshell: Patrick was going to be suspended and referred to counseling. He would not be readmitted to school until his parents presented a certificate proving that they had completed a family counseling program.

Why had Patrick, a seemingly model youngster, gotten himself involved in such a self-destructive scheme? During family counseling it came out that Patrick wanted to rebel and shock people, he wanted to take risks, and he thought that drinking was a grown-up thing to do.

What Could the Parents Have Done Differently?

It was driven home to Patrick's mom and dad that their conversations about alcohol at home centered around dad having a drink with a client, mom meeting her girlfriends for a drink, and what kind of alcohol, wine, or beer would be served at the family's next party. Patrick's parents realized that *they had never discussed the use and abuse of alcohol with their son, nor did they have a family policy on liquor.* As an impressionable 12-year-old, Patrick, in the absence of any rules, had made up his own.

Patrick's parents were incredibly lucky. These revelations were a turning point in their lives, and the incident opened up the family's communication channels. They discussed the consequences of drinking and set up and enforced specific, consistent, and reasonable rules prohibiting their son's use of alcohol and other drugs. Best of all, Patrick bounced back and is doing well.

Jenny and Leon's Story

The Surprise in the Stash Can

Jenny and Leon C. of Orlando, Florida, had the shock of their lives when they found out that their son, Alex, age 12, had another life.

The discovery was made one day when Jenny was cleaning Alex's room. She found a sealed soda can in his closet. When she picked it up it felt empty and something inside rattled. She twisted off the bottom and cigarette papers, a baggie of marijuana, and a package of firecrackers fell out. It was a stash can.

"I was stunned," says Jenny. "My son is a straight-A kid, and we had plans to send him to a good college. When I found the marijuana, I didn't know if he was smoking it, selling it, or what."

She was in a panic when she called her husband Leon, who left work immediately so that he could be there when Alex got home from school. Jenny and Leo composed themselves and confronted their son directly. Alex made a typical denial: "It isn't mine. A friend must have left it in my room. Why would I leave something out that was so easy to find?" Then he got belligerent and yelled at his parents, "Why were you searching my room?"

They prevailed upon Alex to tell them the truth. Alex tearfully admitted that the marijuana and firecrackers were his, that he had gotten the marijuana and cigarette papers from a friend along with the firecrackers, and that he had bought the stash can at the local mall. As his story unfolded, Alex confessed that he and his friend were in the habit of going to a nearby field, smoking marijuana, and using the firecrackers to blow up bottles and cans.

Jenny and Leon immediately contacted a family counselor who was experienced in drug interventions. It turned out that

Alex had tried the marijuana out of curiosity and was excited
by the danger of it all. Jenny and Leon had not established any
drug prevention rules in their home because they just
assumed their brilliant, college-bound son would never try
pot.

What Could the Parents Have Done Differently?

- Make your child aware of peer pressure. Explain to your
  child that s/he should not feel the "need" to get into
  drugs.
- Be very vigilant about your children's friends. Who, specifically, does your child see after school?
- Do not woorry about "respecting your child's privacy" if
  you suspect drug use.
- Know the behavior patterns to look for:
    — falling grades
    — erratic school attendance
    — withdrawal and isolation
    — unusually passive or rebellious behavior

In Summary—Tips for Proactive Parenting

1. **Be an excellent role model.**
2. **Establish a clear family policy on drug and alcohol use.**
   Do not assume your children know that you don't want them to use alcohol and drugs.
3. **Exercise parental authority.**
   Teach your children right from wrong. Set family guidelines for acceptable behavior. Establish consequences for breaking the rules.

Studies show that by asking your child to get a beer from the refrigerator, to light your cigarette, or to mix your drink, the child is more likely to experiment early with drugs. While this may seem cute to some, encouraging this type of behavior in a youngster compounds the risk of trouble with drug use and abuse later on. Probably the most damaging thing you can do to a child's self-esteem—apart from doing drugs with them or in front of them—is to encourage them to drink at home. It may start with giving your seven-year-old a glass of wine at a holiday Christmas party. This often leads to telling your 16-year-old , "It's okay to have a drink at home, but just don't do it after the high school football game."

"Every family should set and enforce rigid rules against the use of alcohol and other drugs."

But the facts say otherwise. A survey conducted by researchers at the University of Washington found that ninth-grade children whose parents supervised their drinking at home were more likely to have used marijuana than kids of parents who did not permit it. Again, drinking at a young age opens the door to a child's early drug problems and closes the door to healthy personal development.

Katrina M., a former psychiatric nurse who works with children and teens in an exclusive drug and alcohol rehabilitation hospital in Dallas, Texas, says, "The most heartbreaking stories came from kids whose parents openly abused drugs or liquor in front of them. About 65 percent of the youngsters in rehabilitation programs had parents who were abusing drugs, drinking, or both—and these were professional people who could afford to send their kids to this hospital. But they wouldn't or couldn't stop," says Katrina. One father would "reward" his two sons with puffs on marijuana cigarettes whenever they brought home good report cards.

Children who "graduated" from the rehab hospital would try to get their own parents clean and sober, but, sadly in many cases, their pleas fell on deaf ears and the parents would not change their behaviors. "Unless the youngster had tremendous willpower, they would end up using again, and the cycle would start all over again. Kids need parents who are role models, and a drug or alcohol abuser is a lousy role model."

Your Responsibilities As a Parent

Children can be adversely influenced by peer pressure. You are responsible for seeing that your children abide by the laws, drive safely, and stay away from guns and other weapons. You must take responsibility for learning to recognize the signs and symptoms that your child may be abusing drugs and alcohol, involved with gangs, or participating in other illegal activities, and you must deal with these problems as soon as possible. More help for dealing with these issues will be provided in later chapters.

3

Parenting to Build
Self-esteem

The Importance of Self-esteem

Nothing is more powerful than strong self-esteem in the battle against drugs and violence.

Self-esteem is how a person feels about himself, how much s/he likes himself, a sense of self-respect and self-worth. Why is self-esteem important to your child? Because your child's self-esteem has a direct impact on how he lives his life. It is the basis for every choice he makes: the friends he chooses, the way he handles success and failure, success in school, how he gets along with others, his success in life. The importance of self-esteem cannot be overemphasized.

As kids go through the physical, emotional, and hormonal changes of puberty, they are trying to build a sense of self-worth, their self-esteem. They are simultaneously struggling with a tremendous need to belong. The battle between self-esteem and the need to belong can be a monumental job depending on the child's background.

During the years between age 5 and 12, children decide

If they are smart or stupid
If they are popular or unpopular
If they are athletic or clumsy

If they are bullies or victims, leaders or followers
If they are pretty or ugly or just okay
If it's good to be who they are
If they can say "no" when they want to
If they will be influenced by some peers to smoke, drink,
or take drugs
If they will follow suggestions of ads to drink or smoke

In thirty-plus years of law enforcement and nearly twenty years of working with kids to help them avoid drugs, I've seen how emotionally secure, self-confident youngsters can look temptation or taunting square in the eye and walk away. If your kids feel good about themselves, they are less likely to bend to pressures to make them feel "cool," or to seek acceptance through wrong channels, such as gang membership.

With both parents working, children do not get as much parental attention or supervision as they did in generations past. It takes a parent's involvement to build a child's self-esteem.

Parenting Styles

There are basically three parenting styles:

1. **Harsh authoritarian parents**
   Authoritarianism encourages dependency and discourages independent thinking. It has a crippling impact on self-esteem.
2. **Permissive, almost anything goes, overly lenient parents**
   Overly permissive parenting creates self-centered, demanding children who fail to consider the rights of others; abdication of power does not encourage self-discipline or responsibility.
3. **Authoritative parents**
   An authoritative parent encourages a child to develop his or her autonomy within limits and standards.

Luis and Juan's Story

Brothers Luis L., a ninth grader, and Juan, an eleventh grader, have parents who speak only Spanish, and both adamantly oppose drugs, alcohol, and tobacco. Younger brother Luis has largely avoided substances harmful to his mental and physical health, while Juan has not. "I tried cigarettes once or twice," says Luis, "but I didn't like the taste. I tried a beer in one of those big bottles. I didn't like it. Never tried marijuana, and I don't want to."

Big brother Juan says, "I picked up cigarettes in the eighth grade and started drinking at parties during my freshman year in high school." He reports that school friends started him on cigarettes and that half of the kids on campus smoke and one-quarter drink on weekends or use marijuana or both. Juan uses marijuana with his buddies.

Their parents set excellent examples at home. Their father smokes an occasional cigar, and their mother does not smoke. Dad drinks socially and only with male friends. He neither drinks nor keeps any liquor at home. Their father knows Juan drinks on the weekends with his friends. "I try to tell him to be careful, but he is almost a man now. The boys are growing up and they will have to make their own decisions. Still, I think they pick up most of their bad habits from their friends at school. They are a lot less innocent than when I was growing up."

What Should the Parents Have Done Differently?

As an eleventh grader, Luis is only sixteen years old, hardly a man of legal drinking age. By being overly permissive instead of authoritative, Luis and Juan's father isn't effectively parenting his sons about drug and alcohol use.

The parents should have:
+ Asked their son why is he is drinking.
+ Explained the laws about alcohol use by minors.
+ Discussed the harmful effects of alcohol.
+ Set rules about the use of alcohol with consequences for breaking those rules.

*"*The two things children say they want most from their parents is time and attention.*"*

Essential Ingredients

The two things children say they want most from their parents is time and attention. Don't short-change them. High self-esteem is taught through the everyday interactions of parents and children. You are responsible for providing your children with structure and guidance. If kids feel ignored or believe that no one cares, why should they?

Make your children feel like part of the family.

Give them tasks or household chores and recognize them when they complete them. Be complimentary when appropriate. One child can do a good job raking the leaves while another can be recognized for cleaning up her room. However, simply heaping on undeserved accolades has no positive impact on the child's self-worth because s/he knows when they are not earned. Instead, look for ways to recognize your child's ways of being useful, thoughtful, or helpful.

Make the time to give your children your undivided attention.

Spend time with your kids when they are the center of attention—not when you are making dinner, doing household chores, or working. Schedule time each day to talk with one another. Do not try to solve problems. Just share your thoughts and feelings. Put your arms around your child and let him/her know how happy you are to be together.

Encourage and support your child's special hobbies, sports, or other interests.

Take an active role in your children's activities. It is not enough to carpool your child to a soccer match. Volunteer to coach the team. Be a regular and enthusiastic spectator. Don't sit on the sidelines reading a book or conducting business on your cell phone.

Monitor your children's grades and attitudes toward school.

Are they bored, mismatched with their teacher, or intimidated by classmates? Get involved, investigate, and support your child's education.

Are You Talking With Your Children?

Open a line of communication

Do You Know How Your Child Is Doing in School?

A ten-year study of over 20,000 youths and their families conducted by the U.S. Department of Education found that students do poorly academically when mom and dad are too busy to take an interest.

According to a student survey:[1]

♦ 33% believe parents have no idea how they are doing in school.
♦ 18% believe their parents do not care whether they earn good grades.
♦ 50% believe parents would not be upset with a report card full of "C's."
♦ 25% say they could bring home a "D" or worse without repercussions.

This is the fundamental first step. Building self-esteem starts with a two-way dialogue. Above all, just talk. Most kids really want to feel safe, secure, and loved and are willing to share their feelings if they know you care. Sharing and caring through honest communication are superb ways of fulfilling your job as your child's main role model.

Talking to Your Child About Problems

1. Ask your child if s/he is willing to discuss the problem with you and to hear your point of view.
2. Ask who, what, why, and how questions, then show genuine interest in what the child says, thinks, and feels.
   "Who are you having a problem with?"
   "What is the problem?"
   "Why do you think this is a problem?"
   "How do you think you want to handle the problem?" or
   "How can I help you solve this problem?"
3. If your child is not willing to talk with you, ask if s/he wants to discuss it with another adult—a teacher, coach, scout leader, clergy, grandparent, aunt or uncle.
4. If the child does not want to talk about it at all for the moment, perhaps s/he needs a cooling off period to reflect on the situation privately. Tell your child that it is okay if s/he does not want to talk about it right now, but emphasize your concern and willingness and tell the child that you will check back later (within a day's time) to see if s/he is ready.
   "What is bothering you?"
   "Nothing."
   "If you don't want to talk about it now, that is okay. I just want you to know that if you do, I will listen."

Practice active listening

Be attentive when your child talks to you, it shows that what s/he is saying is important and that you care about his or her feelings. Be alert to problems and concerns your child expresses. If your child becomes unusually quiet, sullen, or moody, take the time to talk, to listen, and to understand his or her feelings. Find out what is bothering your child, but without criticizing or being judgmental. Make your child feel safe enough to talk to you about what is happening without fear of punishment. Especially listen for "hidden" messages.

> *"Making your children feel good about themselves is your single biggest challenge as a parent."*

Do not be surprised if your child is not eager to discuss worries or problems. Some kids, particularly if they are in their mid-teens, may feel it is not cool to rap with parents about what they do with friends or see at school. But do not give up. Set aside time each week to talk about what is happening with their friends or what may be bothering them. The end of the school and work week is a good choice. It may be the best investment of time that you and your child will ever make.

Parenting to Build Self-esteem

A child's self-concept is based on messages he receives from others. The child who hears that s/he is lazy, worthless, dumb, ugly, etc., grows up to be a very different person from the child who hears that s/he is smart, dependable, handsome, etc. That is why it is vital to communicate to your child that s/he is lovable and capable (worthwhile, competent). What you do as a parent to enhance your children's self-esteem will be a key factor in their success as human beings. Making your children feel good about themselves is your single biggest challenge as a parent.

Build confidence by focusing on the positive.

- In offering praise, look for achievement, even for the smallest tasks, and make your praise specific. (*"I'm proud of the way you helped your grandmother this morning."*)
- Avoid mixing praise with criticism. Adding the word "but" at the end of any compliment negates the positive impact and hurts self-esteem. (*"You did a great job cleaning up the kitchen, but you splashed water all over the floor."*)
- Emphasize your child's special qualities and do not berate him or her for what you think is lacking.

Know the difference between praise and encouragement.

Encouragement is the most powerful motivator for change. Motivate the child to change or improve undesirable behavior through encouragement, not through rewards and punishment or intimidation. Rewards and punishments are short-lived and what is lost is a sense of control, self-confidence, and the opportunity to learn from mistakes.

Accept it when your child makes mistakes.

The best way to deal with a child's mistakes is with support, a positive discussion, and an understanding that next time it will be better. Treat mistakes as wonderful opportunities to learn.

Correct your child's actions, not your child.

Remember, experiencing a failure and being a failure do not mean the same thing. Ask yourself, "how can s/he learn or grow from the experience?'

Explain the importance of learning to improve instead of focusing on a need for perfection.

Point out that not everyone is an "A" student or can be the star of the team, and that is okay.

Example 1: If you tell your child she did great by kicking the winning goal in a soccer game, then she might understand, by implication, that if she did not perform at the same level in all future games, then she would no longer be great. Do not place conditions on what constitutes an acceptable achievement. Instead encourage the effort that led to the positive achievement. Note the difference below.

> *"All of your soccer practice this week really paid off."*
> vs.
> *"What a great game! You did great by kicking that goal."*
> or
> *"Maybe we need to practice tossing the ball around."*
> vs.
> *"I can't believe you dropped the ball. How could you be so clumsy?"*

As parents, you must show understanding. A friend told me how his grandson gets a stamp on the back of his hand every day for good behavior at his kindergarten. He earned a stamp every day during the semester except once. On that one day, his father questioned him sternly: "Why didn't you get a stamp? What did you do wrong?" To this day, the grandson only remembers the day he did not get the stamp, not the days he did. Unfortunately, the father focused on the boy's negative behavior instead of emphasizing the positive behavior. The father did not take the time to discuss the problem with his son. Instead, he responded in an authoritarian, judgmental fashion.

Teach your child how to give compliments, not just to expect to receive them.

Not only does praising another person boost the self-image of the recipient, but it also has the extra benefit of making the person giving the compliment feel good.

Remind your child that feeling good about yourself allows you to have the self-confidence to resist pressures from other kids who may want you to get involved in dangerous, illegal, or unhealthy activities like smoking, shoplifting, graffiti (tagging), vandalism, or drinking. Feeling good about yourself even helps you resist the temptation to try drugs.

The D.A.R.E. curriculum uses a "day-in-the-life" activity to illustrate self-esteem. The object is to trace everything that happens to the child in one day and then ask him to identify whether what happened was positive or negative. Events range from resisting the temptation to smoke a cigarette (good) to being criticized by the teacher for forgetting homework (bad) to being encouraged for hitting a home run (good).

Try the following activities with your children to reinforce positive self-esteem and to counter negative self-confidence.

ACTIVITY

Active Listening Role Play

Take turns telling a story.
The person listening should not interrupt.
Once the speaker has finished telling the story, the listener repeats what s/he heard.
Do this regularly to practice listening skills.

ACTIVITY

Confidence-Building Exercise

Have your child print his or her name vertically down a page. Help the child think of a word for each of the letters that describes the youngster in a positive manner.

Here is how Chris might do this exercise:

Considerate
Helpful
Reliable
Intelligent
Special

Ellen might do the same exercise this way:

Excellent
Lovable
Lively
Enjoyable
Nice

ACTIVITY

Characteristics of People With High Self-esteem

1. Ask your child to describe the characteristics of people who have high self-esteem and to write them down on paper, or key them in on a computer. Alternatively, ask your child to list things that s/he likes about him/herself.

    Examples:
    Feels good about herself
    Know the things s/he can do well
    Accepts that there are some things that s/he may not do as well as others
    Feels comfortable being part of a group
    Can solve problems as they arise
    Accepts responsibilities
    Thinks for self and usually makes own decisions
    Tries his or her best at the activities undertaken and is usually pleased with the results

2. Merely describing the characteristics of a person with high self-esteem often is not enough to illustrate the concept for a preteen. Put words into action. Before your children can accept responsibilities, you must give them some—like sweeping out the garage or making their bed daily. To feel comfortable as part of a group, encourage a child to participate in soccer, a boy's and girl's club, or supervised after-school activities. Have your child list responsibilities s/he currently has. Ask them if there are other responsibilities they would like.

4

Violence in the Home and Community

Gangs

"Mom, I'm afraid to go to school today." Parents might hear this fearful cry on any morning. Children are intimidated by gangs and the violence, weapons, and drugs that are usually associated with them. To combat these problems, some schools are resorting to such measures as searching and sealing off lockers, having students pass through metal detectors upon entry to school, or adopting school uniforms to minimize the influence of gang fashions. Yet gangs are not just confined to schools.

Gangs can range from groups as innocuous as unruly skateboarders at the mall to groups who hang out at the park and push people around to young toughs who steal your child's lunch money, sneakers, jacket, or bicycle. True, not every city or community has a local chapter of the Gangster Disciples (the nation's largest street gang, organized in 35 states), the Crips, the Bloods, or other well-known street gangs, but virtually every town has at least one bad element—a small group or clique of young people who get involved in such criminal activities as tagging, shoplifting, vandalism, bullying, or intimidating others. These ad-hoc groups are gangs, even if they do not adopt a formal gang name.

51

Lisa's Story

Recently, my friend Lisa Chong, a Los Angeles police officer, told me that her 15-year-old nephew, Gary, an honor student, was robbed of six dollars while he was shooting baskets at high school. It was a gang crime. Two older kids approached him and asked if he was a "gang banger." He told them, "No. I just play basketball." One teenage gangster said, "You're all right with me, then. Just give me your money." His aunt knew the price her nephew would pay for refusing to hand over his cash. "That gang member would have shot or stabbed my nephew. No question about it."

The youngster did not want to file a police report because he was afraid that the gang members would retaliate. "Meanwhile, with that six dollars they probably bought two forty-ounce bottles of a cheap high-octane beer and two joints [marijuana]," said Lisa.

Who Joins Gangs?

Membership in a gang can boost an insecure youngster's self-esteem. In fact, gangs sometimes offer the same emotional benefits to your child—recognition, being cared about, and a sense of belonging—as respected organizations like religious groups, Boy and Girl Scouts, and the 4-H Club. In dangerous neighborhoods, some frightened, impressionable children believe that being a member of the right gang provides them with protection. If your child shows signs of gang involvement, you need to take firm control over your child's activities, friends, dress, and finances.

Minimizing Risks

Educate Yourself About Gang-Related Behavior

Make sure that your child does not adopt the dress or clothing styles of gangs. Do not allow your child to wear clothes that promote alcohol, tobacco, or drugs. Talk to your child's teachers, D.A.R.E. officers, and playground coaches to find out what is being worn because "gangsta" fashions change and may vary by locale.

Discuss How Gangs Affect Your Community

Gang activities are a serious community problem and a great danger to your child. Gang members usually become criminals or victims of gang violence.

Discuss the importance of respect for property and the effect that graffiti and vandalism has on the victim, the vandal, and the vandal's family. (In many states, parents are liable for property damage caused by their children. Know your responsibilities.)

Ask: "What are some of the activities that gang members do to hurt our neighborhood?"

Share with your children some actual responses gathered by D.A.R.E. officers in large cities:

- More burglaries, robberies, and muggings
- Fights occur when gangs defend their turf against other gangs
- More weapons are in use
- Drive-by shootings are common
- People are killed, both gang members and innocent bystanders
- Shootings and knifings of students at school
- People are afraid and do not feel safe, either inside or outside their homes
- Drugs are used and sold

Warning Signs of Gang Involvement
Behavioral Clues

- Hanging out with known gang members or in known gang areas
- Staying out late
- Lack of interest in school—truancy, dropping out
- Personality changes
- Changes in friends
- Significant decrease or increase in personal finances
- Fights
- Flashing gang signs

Appearance Clues

- Hairstyle or clothing changes
- Lacing shoes in a "code" style, e.g., not in a typical crossover style but laced directly up the eyelets or with every other eyelet skipped
- Shaved heads or wearing headgear in a certain way
- Adopting gang jewelry (earrings, necklaces, long key chains)
- Gangster-style fashions—What you want to look for here is if your child and all his friends are dressing the same way in what is a uniform distinction from other kids and popular clothing trends. (Examples: sleeves rolled up a certain way; group wears distinctive sunglasses; everyone wears belt with the belt end pointing straight down; boxer shorts worn high with baggy, lowrider pants and long shirts not tucked in)
- Logo-emblazoned clothes favored by gangs
- Small backpacks to hide spray paint cans could indicate that the child is a graffiti tagger
- Tags on clothes or other personal items
- Tattoos—Typically gangs favor designs depicting violence, death, or a macho orientation

- Drug houses spring up and attract gangs and bad elements
- Graffiti despoils neighborhood's appearance

Know the Activities and Whereabouts of Your Children

- Make sure your children are supervised. Take advantage of community resources for supervised and structured after-school activities available through schools, churches, and local youth organizations.
- Involve your child in positive after-school activities that satisfy his or her need to belong, to feel cared about, and to be recognized.
- Never leave your kids home alone, even for a short time. Ask someone you trust to watch your children when you cannot.
- Be sure that your child attends school and knows that good grades count.
- Homework deadlines and curfews do not vary except on special occasions.
- Make sure that they maintain reasonable hours.
- Phone calls on whereabouts are standard operating procedure.
- Meet your youngster's friends and, if possible, their parents. The best way for your child to deal with peer pressure is simply to have friends who do not smoke, drink, or take drugs. Make absolutely certain that your child's friends are not gang members or unacceptable role models.
- Avoid the risks. Explain to your child the danger of going to places where gang members hang out.
- Encourage your child to use a buddy system so s/he does not go places alone. There is safety and strength in numbers.

LaWanda's Story

LaWanda R., an 11-year-old, fifth grader from New Orleans, Louisiana, witnesses fights almost daily on her way to school. So far, she hasn't been involved, but she worries she might get "caught in the middle" and this anguish keeps her mind off her schoolwork. LaWanda runs a gauntlet of gang members on her way home from school. One day she was taunted with heavy pressure to join one of the feuding groups for protection. She told her mother, who was terrified for her daughter's safety. Her mom had the presence of mind to talk to Laura's school counselor. While the counselor could not prevent the gang members from congregating off campus, he did have a suggestion: He "buddied up" LaWanda with three other boys and girls who lived near LaWanda and they walk to and from school as a group. It was the strength in numbers solution.

Involve Children in Positive Activities

If there are organizations in your area like Boy's & Girl's Clubs, YMCA or YWCA, church activities, D.A.R.E.+ P.L.U.S. (Play and Learn Under Supervision), or similar positive, structured, and supervised activities, encourage your child to join.

1. Many good ideas for parenting and children's activities are found in the family section of your local paper or in other local parenting magazines, which often contain calendars of children's and family events. These publications are usually published monthly and are available for free at libraries, groceries, and other family-oriented establishments.

2. Many cities have created Police Athletic Leagues (PAL) and other police-staffed recreation centers, especially in tough neighborhoods. Recreation that connects youth with community institutions can provide both valuable role models and an increased respect for moral behavior.

Positive Activities Keep Kids Safe

If there are none of these wholesome activities in your neighborhood, organize your own group of like-minded parents and get the kids involved in one or more of the following:

Art	Jewelry making
Baby-sitting	Jogging
Baking	Jump rope
Bike Riding	Knitting
Board Games	Model making
Card Games	Music
Checkers	Painting
Chess	Paper route
Collecting	Pets
Computers	Puzzles
Cooking	Reading
Crafts	Riding
Dancing	Rollerblading
Drawing	Sewing
Fishing	Singing
Gardening	Sports teams
Hiking	Swimming
Gymnastics	Tutoring
Horseback riding	Writing
Horseshoes	

Teach Your Child Resistance Techniques

Assertiveness Training

Teaching your child to resist uncomfortable pressures is not that difficult. Help your child learn to be assertive. Assertiveness training will serve your child throughout his or her life in a variety of situations. Developing it at an early age is critical. Assertiveness is directly connected to self-esteem, and positive self-esteem is necessary to help kids resist drugs, violence, peer and group pressures, or other uncomfortable situations.

Building assertiveness is building a foundation of strength that will command respect. Your job is to help develop a confident, assertive response style that allows a child to avoid intimidation without losing face.

For example, a child with a passive, timid, and uncertain manner is instantly recognized as weak and easily intimidated. S/he speaks in a weak voice, is afraid to speak up, has poor posture, looks nervous, and avoids eye contact with others. On the flip side, a demanding, aggressive response style provokes fights. An aggressive person speaks in a loud, angry tone of voice, has stiff posture, leans forward or gets in your face and stares.

The desired assertive response comes from a child who speaks clearly, appears confident and calm, has good posture, and maintains appropriate eye contact with others.

Instilling assertiveness takes time, so you need to role play with your child on a frequent basis. There are plenty of classes that teach assertiveness training to adults. With children, parents need to be the instructors; your home can be the classroom.

- Discuss assertiveness and explain the difference between aggressive and assertive behavior.
- Role play it. Listen and be prepared to coach your child and to answer any questions that arise. (Use the Assertiveness

Resistance Role Plays Activity at the end of this chapter or make up your own.)

♦ Emphasize that having high self-esteem (feeling good about oneself) lets you think for yourself without being pressured to do something that you believe is wrong.

♦ Stress that your child has rights—the right to be yourself, to say what you think, to say no. Review and discuss "Understanding My Rights" on the following page.

Discuss How to Deal With Stress

Assertiveness is not a cure-all for a youngster's fears. Dealing with stress in a healthy way is just as important. Talking about stress in connection with group or gang pressures or domestic violence is important, especially if using a drug to "mellow out" is an option or a temptation your child may be considering.

Youngsters, like adults, feel all kinds of stress, but usually they do not recognize it as such. Define stress to your child as a physical response or a mental feeling; any strain, pressure, or excitement s/he feels about a situation or an event. Explain to your child that stress, also called the fight-or-flight response, is the body's emergency alarm system; it prepares the body to either fight or leave. Signs of stress may include anger, excitement, increased heartbeat, rapid breathing rate, increased perspiration, tense or tight muscles. Let your kids know that everybody experiences stress and there is good stress and bad stress; it is part of daily living.

Understanding My Rights

In the D.A.R.E. curriculum, students review the following list of personal rights. Ask your child what rights s/he has, then review the following with them, asking them to interpret each boldfaced statement for you before you read the following explanation.

I have the right to be happy and to be treated with care and understanding.
This means that I am able to express my ideas and that no one should laugh at me or hurt my feelings.

I have a right to be respected as a person. I am special. I am unique.
This means that I should be treated fairly.

I have a right to be safe.
This means that no person should hurt me physically or with words or try to touch me in ways that would make me feel uncomfortable.

I have a right to say no.
This means that I am able to say no to another young person or to an adult when asked to do something that is wrong or dangerous or does not seem right to me.

I have a right to state what I feel and to hear what others have to say.
This means that I should be able to talk when it is my turn and to hear when another person is talking.

I have a right to learn.
This means that I should be proud of the things I learn and work hard to improve myself.

Speak Out and Act

- Become informed about the kinds, frequencies, and locations of crime and disorder problems in your community. Statistical information about crimes by community is often published in your local newspaper or is available at public libraries, city hall, and police facilities.
- Avail yourself of crime prevention material that is available free of charge through your local police department.
- Talk with other parents to find out what is happening in their families, the school, and the community at large.
- Find out how other parents are talking with their children about drugs and alcohol.
- Join a parent support group.
- Create drug-free environments for your children. Host drug-free and alcohol-free parties in your home or work with your child's school to sponsor similar social activities.
- Spearhead or join Neighborhood Watch or Crime Stoppers.
- Does your child's school district have a comprehensive (kindergarten through 12th grade) drug education program? Find out what it is, how it is enforced, and how it is implemented in the classroom.

Who to Call to Report Crimes or Suspicious Activities

Tell your children to seek out adults when they are concerned or threatened by anyone. As an adult, you should know who to call about specific problems in your community. Police departments usually have the following units that will take direct calls:

Gangs—to report gang activities, gang-related graffiti, threats by known gang members

Narcotics—to report suspected drug activities

Traffic—to report recurring traffic violations at specific locations, reckless driving, hit and runs, drunk driving

Vice—to report sales of alcohol to minors, pornography, prostitution, gambling, loitering

Violence

Guns

Parents must exercise complete control over any guns in their household. All guns should be kept under lock and key and should be inaccessible to children. Store guns unloaded and keep ammunition locked in a separate location.

Teach your children that

1. Guns do not and should not be used to solve problems.
2. Guns are very dangerous and should never be played with.
3. There is an enormous difference between the real life use of guns and the fantasy world of violence portrayed in movies, computer games, or television.

Domestic Violence

Seventy percent of all reported incidents of violence involve people who are acquainted with one another—that statistic includes youngsters, too. At home, in school, on the nightly news, and in films, videos, and TV shows, kids witness real acts of violence where one human being is hurting another human being. (Note: Chapter 5 includes guidelines on violence-free entertainment.)

What Is Family Violence?

Simply put, family violence is the mistreatment of one family member by another. It includes:

- Neglect—poor emotional or physical care
- Emotional Abuse—insults, threats, harassment
- Physical Abuse—slapping, hitting, burning
- Sexual Abuse—incest, rape

Family violence can cause emotional pain (depression, loss of self-esteem, anxiety), serious physical injury, work problems, legal problems, economic loss, and even death.

Violence is often triggered by drinking or drugs, which impairs judgment, quickens tempers, and makes people more likely to give in to their emotions and to react violently and physically during a dispute. Law enforcement studies have shown that virtually all domestic violence is ignited when one or both family members are drinking, abusing drugs, or both.

Violence often follows a vicious circle. Abused children may abuse siblings or, later on, their own families. Adults who abuse children often lack parenting skills and have unreasonable expectations of their children.

Actions to Prevent Family Violence and Abuse

- Get help with personal and family problems. The two problems most prevalent in society are substance abuse and domestic violence.

- — Look for risk factors in your family. If there is a history of alcoholism or drug dependency, contact a counselor at your local office of the National Council on Alcoholism or Phoenix House.
- — If you or anyone in your household is abusing your children, get help now.
- ◆ Seek family counseling.
- ◆ Recognize your tendency toward violence, overcome your shame and fear, and seek help to find alternative ways to express anger and resolve conflicts.
- ◆ Find a support network through your religious group, family, or friends.
- ◆ Look in the phone book under "Children," "Social Services Organizations, or "Crisis Intervention" to find sources of help. (Or consult the Resource Guide in the back of this book.)
- ◆ Seek protection by contacting the courts or law enforcement agencies.
- ◆ Take parent training and adult education classes. Useful offerings include such topics as child development, parenting skills, family relations, and conflict resolution.
- ◆ Change your lifestyle, if necessary.

Teach Nonviolent Conflict Resolution

The best way for children to learn that violence is wrong is through their parents. A 1993 study by the Harvard School of Public Health shows a strong connection between poor parenting and a child's subsequent predisposition to violent behavior. Another study from the American Psychological Association revealed that a history of aggressive behavior in childhood was the single strongest predictor of violent behavior in adolescence. Your goal as a parent is to prevent your child from becoming involved in violent acts.

Set a nonviolent example through:

- A peaceful home environment
- Nonviolent solutions to problems
- Violence-free entertainment
- Discipline using nonviolent punishments
- Teach your children appropriate behavior and explain the dangers of violent behavior.
- Praise your children when they solve problems constructively without resorting to violence.

Incidents involving classmates, family members, neighbors, and friends often grow out of disagreements, misunderstandings, or rumors that explode into full-scale fights.

How can your child resolve these volatile situations?

Teach him or her to just walk away if the antagonist is under the influence of drugs or alcohol. Do not even try to settle the dispute. You cannot win an argument with someone who is high because that person is not thinking rationally and could attack you physically or with a weapon.

If drugs or alcohol are not involved in the squabble, your child still needs help to resolve the problem.

- Explain to your child that disagreements are a normal part of life and it is important to respect—and understand—another person's feelings.
- Step one is to cool down and calm down.
- Then talk over the problem and have each party offer potential solutions.
- Agree on a solution that both parties can accept.

Kayla's Story

Kayla W., a 13-year-old junior high-school student from Cedar Rapids, Iowa, confronted her friend Brigit, and angrily accused: "I heard that you said I took Louisa's lipstick from her purse. If you said that, you're going to be dog meat."

Kayla grabbed Brigit's purse and dumped the contents on the ground. Brigit felt wrongly accused, insulted, and was furious. A physical fight between friends was brewing. But Brigit did not want to ruin the friendship.

First, she calmed down. Then she stated the problem, "This false rumor that I stole Louisa's lipstick is getting out of hand."

Finally, the two girls talked it over and each listened to the other one's point of view. Only then could they find a solution that they were both comfortable with.

What is a smart scenario to defuse this situation before it erupts in violence?

Kayla: "I've heard you're spreading a rumor about me. Is that true?"

Brigit: "I didn't spread a rumor. I just told a friend that you might have borrowed Louisa's lipstick. I probably shouldn't have done that. Let's go talk to Louisa."

The outcome: The two best friends cooled off, talked over the problem, listened to each other's point of view, and then found a solution they both were comfortable with. They did not resort to name calling, threats, physical violence, refuse to speak to each other, or rupture a friendship.

Suppose Kayla and Brigit could not resolve their problem?

Encourage them to seek out a trusted girlfriend or adult who could mediate the disagreement from a position of neutrality. Genuine friendships are too precious to ignore.

ACTIVITY

Assertiveness Resistance Role Plays

Q: Jena had a slumber party for her fourteenth birthday. Her parents allowed her to have it in the basement of their home. Jena's parents had lots of parties there and had a fully stocked bar and refrigerator. Her parents decided to go out for the evening, leaving Jena and her invited guests alone in the house. One of Jena's friends got into the liquor cabinet and suggested that Jena and the others drink some beer. What should Jena say and do?

A: *Jena:* "No way. My parents check the liquor cabinet all the time and I don't want to get into trouble."
Friend: "Come on, they'll never know."
Jena: "Yes, they will and they'll know who did it. I wouldn't go into your home and mess with things that would get you into trouble. We're not getting into my parents liquor cabinet. Besides I don't even like beer."

Q: Mario went to the movies with several of his friends from school. During intermission, Mario went to the restroom. While there, he saw his older brother Kevin in the corner with some of his friends taking some kind of pills. Mario asked his brother what he was doing. Kevin told him they were taking some speed and offered Mario some pills. What should Mario say and do?

A: *Mario:* "Hey man, let's get out of here, right now. This is bad news and I don't need this kind of trouble and neither do you."

Kevin: "We're just trying some of this stuff. It's safe. It isn't going to hurt you."
Mario: "How do you know? You don't know where that stuff came from. That's speed. I don't need to get high on that stuff."

If the older brother swallows some pills, Mario should call his parents imediately and tell them what happened. Kevin could overdose. He could have taken something contaminated and poisonous or damaged in some way. This is serious. Mario needs to discuss the situation with his parents and not worry about what his brother thinks. He could have saved his big brother's life and he can tell him so.

Q: Becky had been waiting to become a member of the ninth grade drill team since seventh grade. She was finally accepted after a very difficult try-out. Karen and Robin, two members of the team, were in the dressing room when Becky came in to change. Karen and Robin were smoking a cigarette and asked Becky to join them. What should Becky say and do?

A: "No, I don't smoke. I don't believe in it and I don't like the smell of it. I don't need it in my hair or in my clothes. Yeecch."
or
"No, I just made this team and I don't want to get kicked off if I get caught smoking."

Q: Carl and his cousin Roy were in Carl's room playing a video game. Carl's mom left to pick up his little sister from gymnastics class, leaving Carl and Roy alone. When the car pulled out of the driveway, Roy took out a joint [marijuana cigarette].

Carl asks, "What's that?"

Roy replies, "It's a joint, weed, dope."

"You're the dope, Roy," Carl said. You can't smoke that in here."

Roy said, "Don't be a geek Carl, one little joint can't hurt you."

What should Carl say and do?

A: *Carl:* "No way. I'm outta here. And if I were you, I'd get rid of that fast. You're going to get busted and I don't want to get involved, man."

Roy: "Hey, who's going to know?"

Carl: "I'll know. I just don't want anything to do with it. I don't need it. I don't know what's in it. I don't need the hassle."

or

Carl: "Who's being a geek, Roy? You know if my mom smells it, I'm going to get in trouble, and you know she'll tell your dad! Flush it in the toilet and let's play video games!"

Q: David and Jerome had been friends since kindergarten and did everything together. They were in the same baseball league but on different teams. Jerome made friends with some older boys on his team. The older boys asked Jerome to meet them after the game behind the bleachers and to bring David along. When everyone got there, John, one of the older boys, took out a tube of airplane glue and began sniffing it. John passed the tube to Jerome, who sniffed it as well. The glue was then passed to David. What should David say or do?

A: *Dave:* "Here, you try it" (passing it to the next kid). "I gotta go. Just remembered, I've got to pick up my sister."

John: "Come on man, try it once."
Dave: "No. That stuff smells and my parents are going to smell it on me. I just don't do that stuff. It's dangerous. It messes your head up."

Q: Michelle and Nancy went to the mall to buy some new clothes for school. They were going into the ninth grade and wanted to get clothes that would attract the attention of older boys. As they walked through the mall, they came to a booth where a major tobacco company was giving away cigarettes to adults and fanny packs, hats, and other assorted items with the tobacco company logo to the juveniles. There was a large bulletin board with an ad that said, "Don't smoke until you are an adult and can make adult decisions. Smoking is for grown-ups."

Michelle said, "I think I'm old enough to make that decision now! Smoking would be one way to make the seniors notice us. It looks adult and is cool. We don't even have to inhale."

What should Nancy say or do?

A: *Nancy:* "I'm old enough to make that decision too, and I don't think it's that cool. It's ugly, stinky. It makes your breath stinky, makes all your clothes stinky. It's stupid.
Michelle: "How do you know? You never even tried."
Nancy: "I think people who smoke look dumb. Besides, my aunt smokes and she's real sick. She's always coughing. Who needs it?"
or
Nancy: "I really don't think bad breath, smelly clothes and yellow teeth are all that attractive to senior guys! Let's go look at more clothes!"

A friend asks to borrow your new bike.

Q: "Hey, can I borrow your bike for a couple of hours? Mine's got a flat tire."

A: "No. My parents won't let me loan my stuff to anybody."
"Come on. I'll take care of it."
"Can't do it. But I can help you fix your flat."

An older brother asks to borrow your allowance.

Q: "Jack, I'm out of money. Let me borrow your allowance. I'll repay you.

A: "Hey, no, man. Ask Mom and Dad for more money. I'm saving my allowance for something I want to buy."
"I'll get it back to you. There's no problem."
"I know you will, but this is going right into my savings account where I can make interest on it. I don't even want to lose a dime on it."

A gang member pushes ahead of you in line.

Don't challenge him. Don't get in his face or space. Gang members are retaliatory. Instead, go to someone in authority and tell them you don't want your name known, but some gang guys are cutting in line and could cause a disturbance. Then go back toward the end of the line. Gang kids often carry knives, some carry guns, and they think it's cool to hurt anybody that disses (disrespects) them. Actually, it's really cool to have the guts to walk away from that kind of possible trouble.

A member of a tough group, not a formal gang, offers you a drug.

A: "I don't do that stuff. See you guys later."
Do not stand there and continue the conversation. Do not make excuses or apologies or even explain why you don't do it. They will not force the drug on you because they either want to sell it or use it themselves. Usually, by offering it to you, they want to cultivate a new customer. By giving a firm no, you show you think for yourself—and that's really cool—and that you're not interested.

Someone is teasing you about not trying a drug, calling you a "chicken."

A: "I'm not a chicken. I just choose not to use drugs. That's all."
Don't hang around for more teasing or conversation. Just walk away. You know deep down who you are and you're not a chicken.

A member asks you to join his gang or he'll make trouble for you.

Just walk away—do not run—and don't look back. Then discuss the threat with an adult authority—a policeman, teacher, parent, school counselor. Here, parents should get involved immediately. Kids should not have to handle this type of thing by themselves and worry about their physical safety.

5

How the Media Sells the Allure of Drugs and Violence

Often the messages in the media are not at all subtle: drinking, smoking cigarettes, and using drugs are cool. Violence is fine. Police are the enemy and "gangsters" are portrayed as heroes.

The Power of Advertising

On an hour-for-hour basis, kids spend more time receiving impressions from the media than from schools, parents, or churches. Advertising has been toned down over the last twenty years, thanks to industry self-regulation and harsher federal supervision, but subliminal pitches still sneak in.

♦ Joe Camel and his cartoon pals zip around in a flashy convertible, wearing sunglasses and spiffy suits. Joe Camel came under particular attack, since several studies confirmed that identity recognition of this logo among children was very high. The cigarette manufacturer was accused of purposely targeting children with this ad campaign and, as a result, an agreement was reached to ban Joe Camel-style ads.

73

- Likewise, Budweiser's animated "Bud Frogs," which croak out their names, are cute and appeal to children. After all, kids—not adults—are frog fanciers. However, a little-known fact is that Bud is also street slang for marijuana, referring to the potent buds of the female plant. Since preteens and teens love to think that they are putting something over on their parents, this Budweiser advertising campaign plays right into their need to be hip. And since Budweiser is the best-selling beer in the U.S., you have to wonder if their entire marketing strategy is not just to cultivate new customers. Clever or irresponsible? It is something you need to discuss with your children who are the targets of these promotional ploys.

- Virginia Slims sells cigarettes to young women who worry about their shape more than their health. Their slogan, "You've come a long way baby," implies that women's right to smoke is as significant an achievement as women's right to vote. Virginia Slims also sponsors tennis tournaments nationwide, but how do you reconcile tennis with smoking, which has been proven to damage lungs over the long term?

Some messages are purposely mixed to make an impact. One of the biggest spectator sports in America is auto racing. Look closely at the cars—there is not a square inch that is not plastered with sponsors' logos—usually from beer or tobacco companies. What message does this convey to a youngster who watches a car tearing around a track at lightning speed with a beer sign emblazoned on the hood or tail?

Meanwhile, the hard liquor industry broke its self-imposed ban on television advertising in 1995, so kids will be seeing more sales pitches for vodka, whiskey, and other distilled spirits. The wine industry is not far behind.

Movies and Television

Films and television are even more influential than music because audio combined with video is incredibly potent. If the theme is antisocial, the impression on youngsters can be harmful. Theaters rarely check ticket buyers' ages when screening an R-rated film, so children have easy access to films with adult content that may include sex, drugs, violence, nudity, and killing.

Big stars are who take drug roles on screen or who abuse drugs off screen are letting their fans down.

John Travolta played Mr. Cool, a murderer and heroin addict, in "Pulp Fiction," a dark, R-rated comedy.

Robert Downey, Jr., is now a waning matinee idol, mainly because of his off-screen pill-popping, heroin use, and alcohol abuse problems.

River Phoenix, the talented brooding young actor-idol heralded as the next James Dean, died of a drug overdose on the sidewalk in front of a West Hollywood nightclub.

John Belushi, one of the original "Saturday Night Live" stars and a comic genius, overdosed on drugs in a Hollywood hotel.

Drug-related triumphs and tragedies get tremendous media coverage today. The film "Gridlock'd," starring rapper Tupac Shakur, exemplifies one of the most blatant and bizarre examples of motion pictures trivializing—almost glamorizing—drugs and violence. Shakur, was affiliated with the Bloods gang in real life and, before the film was released, was murdered in a shooting in Las Vegas, Nevada. The sad thing is that he became a martyr to his many fans.

Music

How does a parent help their youngster develop the skills to resist musical messages promoting drugs, drinking, and violence? The answer: By being able to listen between the lines and understand what is driving the youth culture.

Youngsters of all backgrounds are listening to popular musical groups and watching them perform—live and on the popular music channel MTV. Some fans become true believers and are convinced that whatever their idols sing about is cool—dope, sex, guns, violence, even suicide.

Unfortunately, there are too many examples of teens who decide to emulate their rock star idols. An incident reported by The New York Times News Service shocked people because of the geographical reach of the media and the age of the victims. Two preteens in Somain, France, told their friends that they were going to take their lives just like their favorite singer, Nirvana's former band leader Kurt Cobain, from Seattle, Washington, who sang, "I'd rather be dead than cool." The preteens wore Cobain T-shirts and worshipped Nirvana's grunge rock sound. These girls were model students in the top of their class, popular, and unproblematic. They came from model families, so everyone thought that the girls were joking. After school one day they went to one of their homes, listened to Nirvana, watched a Cobain video, and played with a Beretta pistol. Later, the 12- and 13-year-old girls were found with self-inflicted gunshot wounds to the head; both were dead.

Many kids just enjoy the music's beat or a film's action. The question you have to ask yourself is how strongly is your child influenced by the media? With music videos, youngsters have gone from hearing the message to seeing the message. While MTV has sanitized its programming somewhat since its inception, you can still find music videos that extol the virtues of a pro-drug, anti-police and, in some cases, an anti-family values lifestyle.

Thirty years ago more adults were using drugs than children. Three decades ago, there were no violent video games. Gangs were not lionized by music and the movies. Nor did the fashion industry try to sell its wares by offering street-style gang fashions for everyday dress.

Kids are wired into a pop culture that is largely comprised of the "haves" and the "have-nots." The have-nots want the money and the trappings that they identify with the images of cool media stars who are making big money and getting respect. The haves come from middle- and upper middle-class homes and families. They have plentiful cash and access to a wider spectrum of entertainment sources. The haves are influenced by the media just as easily as the have-nots. There is little parental supervision because both parents are usually working, or there is only one parent, a grandparent, or another relative who serves as head of the family and frequently holds down two jobs.

Drugs, Violence, and Music: An Insider's View

Joan F., a promotion director in the music industry for twenty years, says rap and hip-hop music is often, but not always, aimed at two segments—teen listeners who fancy themselves as "gangstas" and the 8 to 12 year olds, deemed "little gangstas."

"In an economically disadvantaged teen's eye, drugs and gangs are glamorous," says Joan. "They see their parents working every day and not being able to afford any luxuries. They live in apartments and drive used cars, or their homes need remodeling. They also see kids a few years older than themselves driving fully loaded 4-wheel-drive sports-utility vehicles and wearing $150-a-pair sneakers, designer logo clothes, and gold jewelry."

The lyrics say it all. "I wanna make some 'inns' [money]. Why sling hamburgers when I can do a little drug slingin' [selling]." What's more, the kids want instant gratification. They have been without so long that they want to have what other people have and they want it now.

How a Musician's Children Said No

Drugs have been glorified for decades by musicians, movie-makers, writers, and other artists. In one case, children of a world-famous rock and roller said "no" to drugs when he suggested they sample some.

Several daughters of the late Jerry Garcia, the lionized leader of the Grateful Dead rock band, said when they were young their dad would tell them, "You kids should do drugs." Their mother, Carolyn Garcia, would also encourage them to experiment, according to press reports. But Annabelle Garcia McLean told a reporter that she replied "Mom, no. We don't want to. We learned from you guys."

Annabelle, who grew up to be a talented artist, had enough self-esteem (and common sense) as a youngster to reject her family's drug-filled lifestyle. "We saw a lot of older folks we know burn out when we were young," she said. "When we'd go to [Grateful Dead] shows, we'd see young fans—15 or 16 years old—taking way too many drugs, really being zombied. That really drove it home. You don't want to do that to yourself," she said in the interview.

Although Jerry Garcia and the Grateful Dead burst on the musical scene in the 1960s at a time when marijuana was the drug of choice, Annabelle recalled her dad as a heroin user. It caused him to nod off at times in the middle of their telephone conversations. Jerry Garcia died in 1995 of a heart attack while trying to regain his health at a drug rehabilitation center.

"Be completely open with your kids," says Chaka Khan

Recording artist Chaka Khan is a legend in the music business. During her extraordinary twenty-five year career, she has become recognized as a premier vocalist, who moves easily between rhythm and blues, jazz, pop, fusion, and funk. Ms. Khan, who prefers to be called Chaka, is exceptionally candid about how she cured a drug habit and kept her own children drug-free.

She feels "the artistic culture—not just the music industry—relies too heavily on mind-altering drugs," but it only became public in the 1960s. "Almost everyone I know has been touched by someone who has been addicted to some substance, either alcohol or drugs. I've been there and done that myself."

Chaka, who recently recorded her 25th anniversary album, "Epiphany—the Best of Chaka Khan," says she had an epiphany about her drug problem. "I just woke up one morning, had a moment of clarity and said 'whoa, this is not me.' I would have never gotten to where I am doing drugs. It was frightening. But in the end I cared for myself and quit."

At the time, the vocalist was a single mom with two young teen-aged children who she did not want to follow in her self-destructive footsteps.

"My policy was to be completely open with my kids. Don't hide it. They were curious. By discussing my drug problem with them, it took the mystery out of it. Otherwise, it's only human nature for kids to want to try something that is unknown and forbidden."

Chaka didn't mince words. "I told them the good part about it. How cocaine made me feel in the beginning and at the end, which is what they really hear and what it's really all about. The lesson I was trying to drive home to them is that cocaine is dangerous and unnecessary, and that you don't really need it."

Chaka Khan didn't stop there. "At this point you tell your children, 'If anyone offers you anything, please don't even consider taking it. You don't know what it is, where it came from, whether it's poison. If someone stopped you on the street and offered you a piece of unwrapped candy, would you take it?' Then you just have to hope that all those years of good home training kick in. You simply give it to God and pray that you've done enough."

Today, Chaka's son is 18 and her daughter is 23. "They got through unscathed," she says. Still, the singer talks to her son "all the time." She'd rather have his friends stay overnight at their home so she can keep an eye on them. "I want to see what kinds of kids he runs with. I talk to all of them, too."

But she is painfully aware she can only go so far. "When he's [her son] writing music, I try to persuade him to say something without cursing, calling people names, or without gang overtones in the lyrics. I would love to have control over what kids listen to but, realistically, there is no way I can do that. Honey, radio stations are playing it. Kids are buying it. We simply need more community involvement at all levels."

What Can You Do?

One father, Sonny T. of Kansas City, Missouri, admits he took the wrong approach. "I got so frustrated with the violent music that my son was listening to that I broke all his tapes and CDs. Later I realized that was not the answer because it only made him more defiant and more angry at me."

It is hard to single out one genre of music as promoting the wrong message. As one pop must critic states: "Like it or not, gansta rap is protected by the First Amendment's guarantee of free speech. So are such violent operas as 'Rigoletto' and 'Salome.'"

The primary answer to music that advocates violence or any other unpalatable message does not lie in censorship or suppression of ideas. Instead, the solution is, once more, parental responsibility. If the parent provides a firm foundation of morals and values, the child will be able to make the distinction between right and wrong.

A far more reasonable approach in countering media influences on your children is to take a positive approach. You cannot totally censor what children watch or listen to.

You can monitor the media.
+ Set guidelines
+ Discuss your reasons with them.

Music Guidelines

1. Examine the packaging and song titles of all music CDs and tapes purchased by your children. Some groups festoon their packages with marijuana leaves and other drugs. Titles like "Get High" are obvious references to drug use. Words like "chronic" and the number "13" also refer to marijuana.

2. Keep your own eyes and ears open. Some bands champion drug use. If you are uncertain about the musical content, ask the store manager or a clerk which groups send positive messages in their music. Or shop at major retailers that have a policy of not carrying pro-drug, pro-gang music.

3. Do not allow your children to attend live concerts if the band has a history of drug-related music or if the performers are known users. Do your homework. Investigate concerts your children want to attend. There is no concert rating system as there is for movies. Children do not need parental permission to buy tickets. Call or visit record stores and talk to the clerks to find out what they can tell you about the performers. Be aware that a concert described as "all ages" has nothing to do with the content; it merely means that no alcohol will be served.

4. Talk to your children about the damaging effects of too loud music.

5. Find radio stations with a drug-free play list, or at least one that is toned down. Call the program director of radio stations in your town to determine their format. In Los Angeles, California, singer Stevie Wonder owns KLJH-AM, and drug music is not allowed. Chicago's number-one station, WGCI, will not play rap songs that extoll drugs.

6. Initiate a petition to convince a radio station to adopt a drug-free play list.

7. Check out the Internet. There are many sites devoted to musicians and musical groups. Many include song lyrics.

8. Agree on time limits for listening to music. Encourage them to vary their activities.

9. Expose them to other types of music: classical, jazz, blues, and gospel.
10. Get them involved in a local choral group or glee club.
11. Encourage them if they express interest in learning to play an instrument.

Television Guidelines

1. Become familiar with the new rating system for television shows and use them to help establish a family standard of acceptable programs and movies. Ratings are listed in *TV Guide* and are shown on screen as the opening credits roll.
    TVY Ages 2–6.
    TVY7 Ages 7 and above.
    TVG All ages—little or no violence, strong language, and sexual dialogue or situations, but parents may wish to review first.
    TVPG May include infrequent strong language, limited violence, some suggestive sexual dialogue and situations.
    TV14 Unsuitable for children under 14. Shows can include sexual content, strong language, and intense violence.
    TVMA Designed for adults and may be unsuitable for children under 17. Shows contain mature themes, profane language, graphic violence, and explicit sexual content.
    Additional warnings include "V" for violence, "S" for sexual content, "L" for vulgar language, "D" for suggestive dialogue, and "FV" for fantasy violence.
2. Share your family's established viewing schedule with other caregivers such as baby-sitters, grandparents, and neighbors, and ask them not to deviate in your absence.
3. Control the amount of time allowed for viewing. Just as you might give a child a weekly financial allowance, provide a time allowance for television viewing.
4. Take time to discuss issues of social concern with your child. Generate two-way conversations during commercial

breaks and after viewing shows so that kids can ask questions and you can offer commentary. This is especially important when there is major media coverage of events like the O.J. Simpson trial, the Oklahoma City bombing, and other violent and frightening events that children hear about, no matter how you may try to insulate them from the real world.

5. Help a child differentiate between fantasy and reality. For instance, one person hurting another person in a school-yard fight is not the same as a television super-hero fighting a mythical monster.

6. Coordinate viewing with classroom activities. Steer your youngsters toward the History Channel, Disney Channel, Nickelodeon, or PBS when the programming is an extension of what is taught in school. In fact, the cable TV industry has a special TV guide called "Cable in the Classroom" that is available to parents with a phone call to most local cable providers.

Movie Guidelines

1. Attend films with your children.
2. Pay attention to the ratings, the movie that is playing, and the location of the theater. All should be prediscussed and agreed upon. A last-minute change in plans—different movie, different friends—should not be permitted unless your child checks with you first for approval. Often, at a multiplex, the first-choice film can be sold out, which, in the absence of family rules, gives your child a perfect excuse to see an "R"-rated movie. Once a kid has the ticket and is inside, no one checks ages.
3. Discuss the film with your child. Were there any troubling scenes? What was the message of the movie? What does your son or daughter think happened to the main characters and why? If you can stimulate conversation about

entertainment, you may well be able to short-circuit any possible media manipulation.

4. Don't just park your child at the movie to free up your time. Know when the film is over and be there to pick the kid up, or arrange to have another adult do it. Otherwise, you are setting the stage for "theater jumping"—going from one film to another inside the multiplex. This not only breaks the law, it also gives youngsters the opportunity to slip in and see a harsher film.

5. Do not rely on theaters to check ticket buyers' ages.

Part Two

Drug Information

6

Spotting the Signs and Symptoms

There is no foolproof way to know if your child is experimenting with or using cigarettes, alcohol, or drugs because there are so many jumping-off points. In fact, chances are you will not even notice substance abuse at first because your youngster will try to hide it from you. While there is no reliable barometer that will tell you if your child is involved with drugs, you should familiarize yourself with the three generally recognized stages of drug use, which apply to adults as well as adolescents.

The Three Stages of Drug Use

1. **Stage One—Experimental Use**
   Kids get acquainted with alcohol, tobacco, and other drugs to see what they feel or taste like. Your children's friends are usually the first ones to expose them to these substances. Experimentation is a classic example of submitting to peer pressure.
2. **Stage Two—Regular Use**
   There is no question that drugs can make users feel good—at least initially. The child who uses a drug regularly finds that it establishes a sense of normal well-being, not just an initial high. The user wants to recapture the feeling that a drug produces. S/he may feel a need for it just to cope with life's day-

to-day pressures. When used regularly to control moods or to blunt depression, the drug becomes habit forming.

3. **Stage Three—Dependency and Addiction**
   The third stage includes an overwhelming physical and/or psychological dependency on the drug. The user becomes addicted. A habitual user can become addicted to any drug— from tobacco to marijuana, cocaine, heroin, or inhalants.

Drug Abuser or Drug Addict—A Subtle Distinction

While addictive behavior in a young child can be hard to spot, Dr. Drew Pinsky, a Los Angeles-based addiction specialist who is seen regularly on the MTV program, "Loveline," says there are certain indicators, a preponderance of which will likely be found in a youngster who moves past drug abuse into drug addiction. These signs and symptoms of a potentially addictive personality mean that the child is more prone to experiment with alcohol and drugs for the same reasons that adults do drugs—out of curiosity, to calm anxiety, or to "mellow out."

Earmarks of the Potentially Addictive Personality

- Tremendous hyperactivity. S/he is always on the move and has difficulty just sitting still.
- Extreme sensitivity. Moods are significantly affected by his or her environment.
- Perfectionism. His or her world has to be perfect—clothes, room, grades. Often this is encouraged by their parents, who should, in fact, be stressing excellence rather than perfection, which is a frustrating goal for a youngster.
- No capacity for frustration. S/he is easily agitated at school, home, or in social situations.
- Sleep problems. The addict-prone youngster often does not sleep soundly through the night. Even though they are fatigued, their hyperactivity, anxiety, and racing mind work together to disrupt sleep patterns.

♦ Real difficulty managing anxiety. The youngster always seems to be fidgety, nervous, and jumping out of their skins.

The Los Angeles addiction specialist goes on to say that geographical location as well as culture often dictates the drugs youngsters settle down with. "In the inner city, cocaine is the most addictive compound children come in contact with. In the suburbs it's marijuana. In the middle of the country it's methamphetamines. And smeared across the face of everything is alcohol." According to Dr. Pinsky, "Alcoholism is the underpinning in 90 percent of addicts. It's the conditioning of a reward system in the brain. When the brain becomes conditioned to a chemical, it begins to demand the chemical no matter what the wishes of or influences on the individual." Addiction, he adds, is the "progressive pursuit of that chemical." For youngsters, who often do not realize that regular drinking can lead to addiction—especially if there is a family history of it—it is a short road to "getting involved with more addictive substances."

Mary Pipher, the author of the bestselling book *Reviving Ophelia,* has this to say:

> How do we know when alcohol or drug use is a problem? Heredity cannot be overemphasized. Thirty percent of the children of alcoholic parents become alcoholic.... Peers play a role. In general, kids whose friends are heavy users are more likely to use, while kids whose friends abstain are more likely to abstain.

What can parents of the potentially addictive child do?

Dr. Pinsky believes that you start by educating the child about the effects of drugs as early as kindergarten—or between the ages of six to ten.

Reading the Signs

If you suspect that your child is using drugs, raise the subject and attempt to talk about it. If your child is unwilling to talk to you, seek outside help from a counseling center or another third party. If you know that your child is using drugs, you need to provide treatment, support, and encouragement to stop.

Being aware of changes in your child's behavior, possessions, or physical appearance is a first step. When it comes to detecting substance abuse, parents who have ongoing dialogues with their children will have an advantage over parents who do not. Interaction, involvement, and communication provide an opportunity to observe early signs and symptoms of problems, if any exist. The challenge is to be alert to both overt and subtle signs and symptoms.

Behavioral Symptoms

1. **A sudden change in your child's circle of friends**
2. **A change in school grades or behavior**
   Grades may fall off gradually—straight-"A" students' grades do not necessarily suddenly nose-dive to "Ds" and "Fs."

   Check with your child's teacher to see if his or her classroom behavior has changed markedly. The National Federation of Parents of Drug-Free Youth developed the following list of school-related behavioral changes to be alert to:
   - A reduced concentration and attention span in class
   - Loss of energy, motivation, and interest in school activities
   - Sleeping in class
   - A new lack of self-control requiring more discipline
   - Socializing with a rowdier group of kids
   - A reluctance to participate in class or playground activities

- An unusual pattern of tardiness or absenteeism
- Forgetfulness
- Slow to respond to questions

3. Evasive behavior and/or lying

Even the best kids will lie or steal if they are abusing drugs. When you question them about the circumstances of suspect behavior, look for evasive eye contact or a slip in their story.

4. Look for excesses

Drugs make kids overly emotional—exceptionally happy, depressed, hostile, or angry—or overly self-centered to the point that they must have their own way and will do anything to get it, regardless of other people's feelings.

Mood-altering drugs, whether taken by children or adults, trigger sudden and extreme mood swings ranging from euphoric to depressed. A kid may switch from withdrawn and passive one minute to angry the next.

5. Overreacting to mild criticism or simple requests

A chemically dependent youngster usually gets defensive and blames others for his or her troubles while claiming to be victimized or persecuted.

6. An ability to manipulate

Instead of taking responsibility for their actions and behaviors, the child makes excuses for personal failures and finds ways to have other people solve a problem.

7. A noticeable lack of self-discipline

An inability to follow rules, to complete household chores or school assignments, or to keep appointments and commitments.

8. Anxiety

Probably the easiest drug-user symptom to spot, especially in children. Anxiety is characterized by chronic jerky or jittery movements, extreme fear, and obsessive-compulsive behavior.

9. **Monetary extremes**
   Possession of excessive amounts of money beyond what your child might legitimately earn or constant requests for money and complaints of insufficient funds might indicate that your child is selling or buying drugs.
10. **Changes in sleeping patterns**
    Getting distinctively more or less sleep is a possible indication of drug abuse.
11. **Hostile or argumentative attitude**
12. **Refusal or hostility when asked to talk about possible drug or alcohol use**
13. **Sudden loss of interest in family activities**
14. **Irregular hours or wanting to pursue activities at unusual times**

Jackson's Story

Jackson S., a dentist in Lansing, Michigan, says a switch to sudden self-centered behavior was the tip-off in making him realize that something was wrong with his daughter, Raquel. "Raquel was always the most polite, caring child in the family. When she got into junior high school, my wife and I noticed some things started to change. Raquel would come home late from school, then go into her room and play CDs. She stopped helping her mom or doing her chores. She said she was too old to do chores and that we should hire a maid to do the housework." Next, Jackson began to notice bottles of wine disappearing. When Jackson confronted his daughter, she denied the thefts at first, then confessed and admitted that she had stolen the wine to pay her dues to a club of the school's most popular girls. Drinking wine and using drugs were part of the club's initiation.

Perhaps at the top of your signs and symptoms list should be the three words "trust your gut," says Stan Vegar, Demand Reduction Coordinator for the U.S. Drug Enforcement Administration's San Francisco Division. "Most parents note changes in attitudes and actions of their preteens or teenage children, and most of them are normal and nothing to be alarmed about. A 9-year-old is going to say, 'Yeah, dad, I'll help you clean the backyard,' but a 15-year-old is going to say, 'No. I'd rather watch rock videos.'

"However, at some point, parents may notice these behaviors becoming extreme," continues Vegar. "Rather than brushing them off as quasi-normal, start putting the puzzle pieces together. If you notice a radical change in your child, it's time to get out of denial and start being somewhat suspect."

A good test? When 16-year-old Johnny wants to borrow the family car to go to the library at 7:30 p.m. to look up a fact for that really important homework assignment that is due tomorrow morning, don't just give him the keys. Get involved. Offer to drive him to the library and then see how important the trip is.

The U.S. Drug Enforcement Administration has created a laundry list of instantly noticeable physical symptoms that are often reliable indictors of drug use. If you see several of these signs and symptoms, do not procrastinate or wait for concrete proof of drug use or abuse. Intervene and address the problem immediately with your child.

Physical Symptoms

1. **Poor physical appearance**
2. **Abnormally pale complexion**
3. **Weight loss or gain**
4. **Chronic fatigue, lack of energy and vitality**
5. **Loss of appetite and excessive thirst**
6. **Short-term memory loss**

7. Continual run-down health
- Frequent colds, sore throats, and coughing*
- Chronically inflamed nostrils and runny nose*
  *When allergies are not a problem.

8. Eyes
- Bloodshot eyes
- Constantly dilated pupils
- Droopy eyelids
- Imprecise eye movements
- Wearing sunglasses at inappropriate times

9. Coordination
- Dizzy spells
- Stumbling
- Shaky hands

10. Dramatic appetite changes ranging from a sudden lack of appetite to a sudden craving for sweets

11. Changes in speech and vocabulary patterns
- Rapid speech

Environmental Indicators

Notice how your child decorates his or her room. Be observant about your child's appearance and possessions. Any of the following could be signs that your child is experimenting or involved with drugs:

- Alcohol or drug-related art or posters
- Clothing or logo gear that glorifies alcohol, tobacco, or drugs
- Magazines such as *High Times*
- Liquor and beer signs
- Possession of a fake ID or driver's license, which allows an underage child to prove s/he is of legal drinking age
- Incense or air fresheners used to mask smells
- Drug-related paraphernalia: bongs, pipes, pipe screens, cigarette rolling papers, baggies, scales, stash cans

Your child may possess some of these items and be totally innocent of any drug use, but you still can use your discovery as an opportunity to discuss such things as family rules, values, or the power of media advertising.

Other Tools for Parents

Throughout this book we have discussed the importance of being a role model, of being actively involved in your children's lives, and of knowing what they are involved in and who they are involved with. If there is one key message to take away from this book, that is it. However, there are other measures you can take to be an informed adult or parent.

1. Educate yourself

- Read all the drug-specific chapters in this book, even if the drug is not one that you think that your child would ever try or use. You might be unpleasantly surprised somewhere down the road.
- Become familiar with the appearance of illegal substances. Drug literature is available through your school, PTA, library, or local police station. Some police substations provide full-color drug identification guides free of charge as a community service. Many organizations listed in the Directory of Resources also provide valuable information free of charge. Be aware that new drugs appear on the market with regularity and the ways that drugs are packaged and sold on the street also change. Thus, it is advisable periodically to seek and review updated drug identification guides.
- Surf the Internet to check sites that provide information about drugs, alcohol, and violence. There are also a wealth of parenting sites that include chat rooms that allow parents to conduct dialogues with other parents. Many libraries now provide free access to the Internet.

2. Stay abreast of current events

- ◆ Read your local paper to stay alert to criminal and drug-related activities in your community.
- ◆ Read real-life newspaper accounts about drunk driving, drug busts, gang-related violence, and vandalism to your children or have them read the stories themselves. Afterward, discuss the articles together, making sure that your children understand the serious personal, legal, and social consequences of the person's actions.

3. Employ the eyes and ears of other adults

7

Gateway Drugs: Alcohol and Tobacco, Avoiding the First Serious Steps

What Is a Gateway Drug?

The appellation "gateway drug" is so obvious even a child can understand it. A gateway drug is a drug that opens the door to the use of other, harder drugs. Technically, gateway drugs include alcohol, tobacco, marijuana, and inhalants. This chapter focuses on alcohol and tobacco. Remember, though, when reading Chapters 8 and 9 that marijuana and inhalants are also considered gateway drugs.

"Keeping children free and clear of the gateway substances for as long as possible is your mission."

What Gateway Drugs Have in Common

- Ability to expose people to other, harder drugs
- Typically inexpensive
- Readily available

Not only are tobacco, alcohol, marijuana, and inhalants either physically or psychologically addictive, they also can be the steppingstone for a dependent personality to move on to stronger drugs. There is no guarantee that a youngster will make

97

"Cigarettes are the primary gateway drug."

the leap from gateway drugs to far more toxic and dangerous drugs such as methamphetamines, cocaine, or heroin. Research suggests that in the majority of the cases they will not. Still, who wants to roll the dice with their youngster's health and future happiness? Most addicts began their downward spiral with the gateway drugs; very few youngsters or adults jump right into hard drugs. Keeping children free and clear of the gateway substances for as long as possible is your mission.

Tobacco: Easily Available, Highly Addictive

According to a report from the U.S. Department of Education,[1] "Tobacco use is associated with alcohol and illicit drug use and is generally the first drug used by young people who enter a sequence of drug use that can include tobacco, alcohol, marijuana, and harder drugs." Tobacco use is also a gateway for other negative behaviors, not just more dangerous drug taking. "Cigarette smokers are also more likely to get into fights, carry weapons, attempt suicide, and engage in high-risk sexual behaviors," say government researchers. These behaviors can multiply into a syndrome of other troubles that carry into adulthood. In short, they set the stage for problems.

An American Lung Association official insists "tobacco teaches children Drug Use 101, which can be the foundation for other drug use." Cigarettes are the primary gateway drug because cigarettes are easy to obtain and because they do not produce the same altered-state effect on the user as alcohol or marijuana.

The age at which children will experiment with tobacco depends on their peer group, curiosity, and cultural lifestyle. In the United States, farm families and people living in Eastern urban cities generally smoke more than Westerners. But experimentation among children occurs everywhere. Japan, like much of Asia and Europe, is a smoker's haven. The Associated Press reported that "the tobacco industry may be under siege in the United States, but in Japan, aggressive advertising, a big government stake in the business, and general acceptance of smoking keep the cigarette trade thriving. "There are so many factors that encourage young people to smoke," says Bungaku Watanbe, head of Japan's Tobacco Problems Information Center, an anti-tobacco lobbying group. A survey by Japan's Health and Welfare Ministry found that 20 percent of high school and junior high school students had smoked in the past year.

The Media's Role

Chewing tobacco, pinching snuff, or smoking cigarettes, cigars, and pipes have been a part of the American landscape for centuries. Thanks to Hollywood, the rawboned cowboy who rolls a cigarette with one hand has been portrayed as an icon of individualism. Watch any circa 1940s movie and notice how often one of the stars is smoking a cigarette. In fact, cigarettes did not begin to disappear from movies and television until the late 1990s. For example, think of the James Bond movies or Don Johnson's character, Sonny, on the hit TV series *Miami Vice*. Scenes and situations subliminally linked smoking, and often drinking, with cool, grown-up behavior. The adults seemed to be having a lot of fun. And what youngster does not want to feel grown up? Fortunately, the federal government is tightening up laws regarding the sale of tobacco to minors. While many states have laws banning stores from selling cigarettes to anyone under eighteen, the Food and Drug Administration now requires retailers to ask for a photo identification from anyone who looks younger than twenty-one years old who wants to buy cigarettes or smokeless tobacco. Cigars and pipe tobacco are excluded from the new federal law.

There are pitches to start puffing everywhere a youngster turns. In 1996 the Food and Drug Administration officially labeled nicotine a drug and cracked down on advertising aimed

"The younger a child starts smoking, the more addicted s/he becomes."

at youngsters. However, the tobacco industry, which spends $5 to $6 billion a year in advertising, is battling back. In addition to sports- and event-related marketing strategies, cigarette makers have set up computer web sites as mediums for their messages.

Although tobacco companies have sued to stop them, President Clinton's administration has introduced four proposals that would put an end to strategies that have proven especially good at attracting kids:

- Ban brand-name premiums
- Restrict ads
- Ban vending machine sales
- End sports tie-ins

It is too early to tell what impact this will have on kids. Certainly, it will not make it more difficult for kids in grammar school to smoke because they usually get cigarettes from older friends or from home.

The Dangers

"Tobacco is definitely one of the fastest addicting drugs there is, so those who experiment with it are quite likely to become regular users of it," contends Scott Thomas, Ph.D., director of tobacco education for the American Lung Association of San Francisco and San Mateo counties. "I have people in my quit smoking classes who started smoking in the sixth and seventh grade. I know many smokers who started younger than that."

Dr. Thomas says that ninth graders who smoke regularly usually more than double their usage of tobacco by the twelfth grade. According to statistics from the U.S. Center for Disease Control (CDC) in Atlanta, the younger a child starts smoking, the more addicted s/he becomes. The U.S. Department of Education echoes the CDC findings. Its report, "Youth and Tobacco," says people who "begin to smoke at an early age are more likely to develop severe levels of nicotine addiction than those who start at a later age."[2]

The National Institute of Drug Abuse, which notes that a half million Americans die annually from smoking, says there are "lifelong consequences for this generation of young people because a large proportion who initiate smoking in adolescence will continue to smoke for the rest of their lives."

Solutions

How do you persuade children against taking that first puff? Chances are you, as a parent, will have difficulty convincing your child to avoid cigarettes. The enticement is very strong. Dr. Thomas says, "Young people start smoking out of curiosity and for the experience and to be part of a social group, but they quickly become addicted and get psychological benefits." For youngsters, he adds, cigarettes also "help them to form their identity"—referring to the age-old belief that you are more adult if you smoke. Unfortunately, these are real benefits of smoking. Says Dr. Thomas: "If you don't get benefits, you don't do a behavior."

Explain that there are both positive and negative results and consequences to things that we do or choose not to do.

Often it takes another authority figure, such as a D.A.R.E. officer, to counterbalance the negative peer pressure exerted on young kids. A Gallup poll found that 75 percent of the students who graduated from the D.A.R.E. program had never tried a cigarette. While drug prevention programs and educators can explain why tobacco (and the other gateway drugs) can have a long-term impact on children's lives if they start using today, you, as the parent, are the primary influence. Based on what we have learned through teaching the D.A.R.E. curriculum, focus on the positive consequences for kids who do not use tobacco and on the negative consequences for youngsters who do.

Your anti-cigarette message to your child must start early and be reinforced regularly.

As parents you need to spend as much time as possible educating your child on the dangers of tobacco—before they get hooked, especially because of the easy access to and low cost of tobacco products.

What you are likely to hear from fifth and sixth graders and older kids is that other kids are smoking cigarettes. Kids gravitate toward cigarettes because their parents and older kids smoke and that's cool. It's really all about "cool." Youngsters are looking for coolness because they are so uncool at that age. That's one reason tobacco companies are drawing a marketing bead on kids who want to feel hip.

The trick is to prevent youngsters from lighting up before graduating from high school; otherwise it is too late. By the age of eighteen, one in three persons is using tobacco.

And cigarette smoking is the first door to drug use. Kids move easily from smoking a cigarette to a joint. Once they start inhaling marijuana, it is a short leap to inhaling other easy-to-access substances or more dangerous drugs like PCP, meth, and crack cocaine.

Jordan's Story

Jordan, an eighth grader at a San Diego junior high says "if kids at school are smoking cigarettes, they're smoking pot. I don't know one person who just smokes cigarettes." Jordan, who lives in a middle-class neighborhood, says "older kids have offered pot to me a couple of times. They say 'hey, do you want to get high?' I say 'no.' They say 'that's cool.'"

Jordan, who graduated from the D.A.R.E. program in the sixth grade, says those classmates who take drugs do it "because they think it's cool." He thinks otherwise. "My brother smoked cigarettes and then pot and I don't want what happened to him to happen to me." Jordan also talks to his mother about drug use at his school. "It's pretty cool talking to my mom. She's not really judgmental. She listens. We talk." The 13-year-old has some advice for other kids tempted to try narcotics: "find a reason not to take drugs and stick to it." This, not surprisingly, is one of "eight ways to say no" taught in the D.A.R.E. curriculum.

Determine what your child thinks about tobacco. Dispel myths.

A simple true/false test at the dinner table can be fun—and revealing about your child's belief system. Some of these questions seem obvious, but ask them anyway. Try the following quiz:

1. Smoking cigarettes calms you down.	T	F
2. Cigarettes keep you thin.	T	F
3. It is easy to stop smoking.	T	F
4. Secondhand smoke is harmful.	T	F
5. A tobacco cigarette is a drug.	T	F
6. Cigarette smoking can't hurt you when you are young.	T	F
7. You look cool when you smoke.	T	F
8. Low-tar or light cigarettes are not as risky as full strength cigarettes.	T	F

The answers are surprising.

1. Nicotine is actually a stimulant. Some people say they smoke to calm their nerves, but in reality the "calming" effect they feel is their body's response to satiating its addictive need for a cigarette when too much time has elapsed between feeding its cravings and the smoker begins to suffer withdrawal symptoms.

2. Another myth to debunk is that cigarette smoking keeps you thin. This is the entire rationale behind the packaging and promotion of light cigarettes aimed at young girls and women. Every young girl is body-conscious, so the appeal is strong. These thin low-tar cigarettes are just as deadly as their competitors.

3. Nicotine in tobacco is a highly addictive stimulant that speeds up brain activity. The Surgeon General of the United

States declared, in 1988, that nicotine is as addictive as heroin, and perhaps more so.

4. Smoking reduces life expectancy, both of the smoker and the people exposed to secondhand smoke.
5. Nicotine, a major component of tobacco is a highly addictive drug.
6. The negative effects of smoking begin as soon as you start and are cumulative. Cancer and other cigarette-related illnesses can strike at any age.
7. There is nothing cool about smoking and actually people look quite ridiculous exhaling big clouds of smoke out of their nose or mouth.
8. A study released in February 1997, by the National Cancer Institute in Washington, D.C.,[3] said low-tar cigarettes can produce adenocarcinoma, a cancer named for the cells that line the narrow air tubes deep in the lungs.

Talk to your kids about advertising and media messages that promote smoking.

According to Kathryn Mulvey, executive director of INFACT, a corporate watchdog organization, "when the young start smoking, they overwhelmingly go for the most heavily advertised brands—not the generics or cheaper, lesser-known brands." Her advice: "Telling youth how they are being cynically manipulated by a greedy industry can be very effective."

The effectiveness of your message depends upon how you present the information.

Dr. Thomas says children of different ages respond to different anti-smoking appeals. "I have a multilevel rap against tobacco that begins with a discussion of the power of nicotine and explains that there are 4,000 chemicals in tobacco smoke."

One way to convince children that tobacco is something to be avoided is to explain how, over time, it hurts them.

This is likely to be more persuasive to a youngster than the gateway theory.

- Smoking kills an estimated 434,000 Americans annually and directly or indirectly causes 11 million cases of chronic illness annually.
- Cigarette smokers suffer from
  — chronic lung diseases such as bronchitis and emphysema
  — heart disease and stroke
  — cancers of the mouth, throat, lungs, esophagus, bladder, pancreas, and cervix (women)
  — osteoporosis
  — ulcers
- Pregnant women who smoke are more likely to give birth to premature or low birthweight babies.
- Smoking is a fire hazard.

Focus on short-term consequences and the effect on appearance.

Warnings about the long-term health effects often fall on deaf ears because kids are young and they feel indestructible. Youngsters often care more about their external appearance than what is happening inside their bodies. Talk about how cigarette smoke makes your hair, clothes, and breath stink. It makes your teeth and fingernails turn yellow.

To make a lasting impression about the necessity to stay smoke-free, D.A.R.E. has found that a "drug fact sheet" is very helpful. (See also Chapter 1, p. 20.) The fact sheet is simple to compile and is a good reference tool to use when discussing the dangers of drugs with your children. D.A.R.E. breaks the tobacco drug fact sheet into three categories—Using Tobacco Once, Using Tobacco for a Short Time, Using Tobacco for a While—and describes what it does to your child in each instance. Here is how we set it up:

Using Tobacco Once

- Smelly clothes, hair and breath
- Heart works harder
- Dizziness
- Cough
- Eyes sting and tear up

Using Tobacco For a Short Time

- All of the effects above plus:
- Spend more money
- Develop raspy smoker's cough
- Catch more colds
- Teeth and fingers become stained and yellow
- More difficult to breathe. Shortness of breath
- Get hooked, or dependent, on nicotine

Using Tobacco For a While

- All of the effects above plus:
- Cancer (lung, lip, tongue, mouth, etc.)
- Heart disease
- Emphysema (lung disease)
- Wrinkled skin
- Secondhand smoke affects family and friends
- Mouth sores
- Death

Couch it in terms they can relate to.

While the drug fact sheet above is certainly scary, a more dramatic fact is that cigarette smoking during adolescence appears to reduce the rate of lung growth and maximum lung function. Any child who wants to go out for sports or stay physically fit simply cannot afford to smoke. Want to letter in sports? Do not smoke or do any drugs. Take care of your body.

Find creative ways to illustrate the dangers of tobacco use.

Dr. Thomas explains the health hazards and demonstrates them. Using bubble wrap as an example of lungs, Dr. Thomas pops the bubbles to show how smoke destroys the lungs. "I also illustrate how the cilia that protect the lungs are destroyed and how that results in more colds and flu."

Dr. Thomas' message to older children covers not only their personal health but also the health of the environment. This is what he calls his multilevel prevention strategy. He stresses that tobacco companies are one of the main perpetrators of deforestation in the world. He asserts that Brazilian tobacco farmers use sixty million trees and that 12 percent of all timber cut worldwide goes into making cigarettes [wood chips are mixed with tobacco].

"You cannot just hammer a message home. "Kids could care less if you just stand there and say 'don't smoke because it could hurt your lungs,'" says Dr. Thomas, "but the fact is that it is impossible to smoke cigarettes without causing injury to the body. Disease—and mortality—is extremely high with smoking."

Kick your own smoking habit or level with your kids about yours.

We have already detailed the impact of being a role model and pointed out that, for kids especially, actions speak louder than words. Of course, if you use tobacco while you are warning your children not to, you are virtually wasting your time and being hypocritical. If adults tell children not to smoke but then turn around and do exactly the opposite, kids will determine that there really must not be anything wrong with the behavior. Children are tempted enough by friends and seductive cigarette advertising, so if you are a smoker who cannot or do not want to kick the habit, level with your child. But be aware that if you smoke, you double the chances that your children will turn out to be smokers.

Make them aware that secondhand smoke is harmful; kids should not associate with smokers.

It has been proven that exposure to secondhand smoke increases a person's risks of heart disease and cancer. Children of smokers have an increased risk of illness, particularly respiratory problems such as asthma and bronchitis. Whether you smoke around your children or someone else does, a smoker turns a nonsmoker into a passive smoker.

Chuck's Story

Chuck R. of Indianapolis discovered his daughter Teresa, age 13, was sneaking cigarettes from the house, even though he was trying hard to kick the habit. "I'd been smoking since high school, and I knew that I had to stop because I had developed a hacking cough. I'm scared witless of getting lung cancer." The family had talked about how difficult it is to kick the cigarette habit once it was started, and Teresa sat in on those conversations. She was not shielded in any way from the consequences of smoking, yet she took it up anyway.

Set antismoking rules. Make tobacco off-limits.

If you smoke, explain that you have made the choice as an adult and you fully understand the risks and consequences—that it is a physically and psychologically addictive substance. As a minor, they legally do not have that same choice and are not allowed to smoke.

Explain what withdrawal feels like.

This is perhaps your final argument for convincing your child to avoid tobacco now and forever—or at least until they are of legal age to make their own decision. If you are a current or former smoker, you are the perfect person to explain how withdrawal from any addictive substance makes the body physically sick. Does your child know a friend, a neighbor, or another youngster who started smoking and struggled to give it up?

Alcohol and Children: Why Kids Drink

Research shows that by age eighteen, when most kids graduate from high school, 90 percent of them have experimented with alcohol. Only a small percentage abstain. A smaller percentage become addicted and need help. Most grow out of heavy use, but during their school-age years alcohol can be their drug of choice.

"Alcohol is the biggest problem we have with students," insists Kathy Hill, executive director of the Sacramento, California, organization People Reaching Out. "When we look at surveys, more kids are involved with alcohol than any other mind-altering drug."

Hill contends it is the public's attitude toward alcohol that leads to such widespread use. "Parents think it's only alcohol and it's a legally approved drug for adults over twenty-one. They feel it can't be that bad when other drugs are illegal and are not seen as harmful."

Take a minute and think how often adults drink alcohol: a cold beer at a baseball game, a glass of Chardonnay with a piece of broiled fish, a gin and tonic on a warm day. Social drinking is an acceptable and pleasurable activity for millions of Americans. It relaxes you, curbs stress, and chases away inhibitions, but if it becomes a regular mechanism to escape troubles and to feel good, it can be an abuse, a dependency, and a severe problem for millions of Americans.

While experts say kids are not inclined to drink alcohol on their own, many will imitate a parent who overindulges or will go along with peers who offer it to them. In fact, once they start, children end up drinking abusively for the same reason as their parents—to cope with anxiety or stress, to manage their moods, and to release inhibitions so they can become more sociable (translation: to forget their troubles and to have fun).

Drinking at an Early Age

Children are drinking at a younger age, which is a powerful depressant on an underdeveloped central nervous system. "We are seeing kids drink alcohol at a younger and younger age—as young as elementary school," says Larry Santo, a senior probation officer assigned to the City of Tracy in California's San Joaquin County. "Clearly, if the parents drink abusively, the kids drink abusively." Santo's experience is that youngsters will start drinking beer as young as seven or eight years old, but the incidence of such youthful offenders is small. Most children do not like the taste unless their mothers and fathers or other family members have encouraged them to sip or taste alcohol around the house—considering it "cute" or a "treat" for the child. "At that age children are just small composites of what their parents are. They'll take what their parents offer or do what they see their parents doing because they [parents] are the role models," says Santo. As youngsters move from middle school into high school, they "reject their parents for their [personal] identity and begin to look toward their peers, and that can be dangerous. As a peer, I thought I was invincible, wanting to spread my wings."

Marijuana and Alcohol, A Deadly Duo

Mixing drugs has always been dangerous, but teens who smoke a lot of marijuana and who drink a lot at one sitting can die, says Ron Brogan, a former DEA official.

Here is how the combination can be lethal for kids who do not have a tolerance for alcohol.

"Marijuana anesthetizes the vomiting center in the brain...and vomiting is nature's way of purging the system of lethal toxins," explains Brogan. "Normally, when an inexperienced drinker drinks too much, they will throw up. But if they've smoked grass and are drinking heavily, they are less likely to purge, and when the blood alcohol level reaches .40, they go into a coma and die."

For the body, puffing marijuana and drinking heavily "is like taking the battery out of a smoke detector. The device is there but it doesn't sound the alarm when danger strikes."

The fact is that alcohol—and any other illegal drug—is very addictive to a child's underdeveloped central nervous system. Says Kathy Hill: "It's very, very serious for kids." Statistics bear her out:

- Junior and high school students drink 35 percent of all the wine coolers in the U.S.
- Binge drinking—consumption of five or more drinks at one sitting—is reported as early as the eighth grade.
- Alcohol-related accidents are the leading cause of death among people 15 to 24 years of age.
- Half of all youthful deaths in drowning, fires, suicide, and homicide are alcohol related.
- The U.S. Department of Health and Human Services, in a survey of high school seniors, found that 2.5 million respondents did not know they could die of alcohol poisoning.[4]

Solutions

Scary statistics can be cited from now to doomsday, but what can parents do to keep their children off alcohol until they are at least of legal drinking age?

Parents committed to keeping their children off alcohol or at least helping them make an informed decision not to drink must:

1. Be responsible drinkers themselves.
2. Keep the two-way dialogue going.
3. Discuss the negative effects.
4. Set rules.

Be an exemplary role model.

An alcohol-free home helps but does not guarantee that a child will not experiment on his or her own. Peer pressure and curiosity are strong when it comes to alcohol and tobacco.

Cynthia's Story

Cynthia M. is a fifth-grade teacher at an elementary school in Canoga Park, California. She's a single mom with two daughters—first and fourth grades—who attend the school where she teaches. Recently divorced, Cynthia was drinking daily each evening to relax. But Cynthia was not just nursing a glass of wine. By the end of the evening, she had powered down three to four glasses of vodka.

A Los Angeles police officer, Tom S., taught the D.A.R.E. curriculum in Cynthia's class every Thursday. Tom also taught at several other classrooms in the school. In one fourth grade class, he was talking about drug use vs. drug abuse. "We caution the kids that parents can make a decision to drink as long as they drink reasonably. A glass of wine, a beer, or a cocktail after work or with dinner is perfectly okay, but if a parent drinks a six-pack of beer and then goes driving, that is abusive and there is a distinction."

One student in the fourth grade class got deeply involved in the question-and-answer session at the end of the class. "She asked me how much was too much when it came to drinking alcohol," recalled Tom. His answer was general: it depends on the individual but usually any more than two drinks on a regular basis would be of concern. After class he discovered, the student was Cynthia's oldest daughter.

One day, Cynthia approached Tom and asked to talk. Over lunch, the fourth grade teacher admitted that she was struggling financially and emotionally after her divorce and began drinking quietly at home to ease her pain. She confessed, "When my daughter came home and asked me about my drinking, I started to look at myself." She realized she had to change her ways.

Among the options Cynthia and Tom discussed: private hospital alcohol rehabilitation programs, outpatient clinics, and Alcoholics Anonymous, the worldwide 12-step program that is cost-free. Cynthia joined a local chapter of AA, attends the programs, stopped drinking, and is living a happier, healthier life.

Establish a two-way dialogue with your children about drinking, whether you imbibe or not.

*"*Your message must be simple and clear cut: Drinking beer, wine, or distilled spirits is only for grownups who drink responsibly.*"*

You neither want to threaten, berate or lecture, nor do you want to be a buddy who subconsciously enables your child to drink. Neither can kids be kept on a short leash just to avoid the risk of drinking. One discussion over the dinner table will have no long-term effect. Try to draw out your children's beliefs about drinking and be prepared to counter any misunderstandings they might have using facts and without getting emotional.

In their book, *Teenagers and Alcohol: When Saying No Isn't Enough,* Roger E. Vogler, Ph.D., and Wayne R. Bartz, Ph.D., offer some common myths and facts.[5] Share them with your teens.

"Alcohol improves my mood, alters my mental state."

Though it is true that small amounts of alcohol can reduce stress in some people, heavy drinking typically leads to unpredictable and uncontrollable emotions. If someone is very angry and drinks to relax, a more likely outcome will be increased anger—and all the undesirable behaviors that typically follow.

"Alcohol makes me perform better."

As alcohol relaxes [you], heavy drinking has a detrimental effect on judgment, coordination, and reaction time...and can lead to false confidences, which can have deadly consequences.

"Alcohol feels great."

The short-term effects are usually pleasurable, the long-term effects negative. They include: hangovers, interference with restorative sleep, foolish and or dangerous behavior, legal trouble, potentially deadly outcomes if driving occurs, impulsive sexual behavior, long-term health problems.

"If I drink coffee or eat something, it will sober me up."

Once alcohol is in your bloodstream, there is nothing you can eat or drink to hasten metabolism. Certain other chemicals, like caffeine, can "open your eyes," but you are still mentally and physically impaired.

Offer loving but firm advice with clear boundaries and consequences by setting down firm guidelines.

Your message must be simple and clear-cut: Drinking beer, wine, or distilled spirits is only for grownups who drink responsibly. Underage drinking is not only breaking the law, but also can seriously injure your health, your future success, your friendships, and possibly even kill you. According to the National Highway Transportation Institute, seven young people a day are killed in automobile accidents due to alcohol. An arrest on a teenager's driving record can be devastating to the entire family. Unexpected, costly legal fees, and possible loss of insurance or sky-high premiums are just two of the lesser consequences.

Set a rule that your child must never drink and drive.

Set a rule that they are never to get in a car with someone who is drinking or who drinks while driving. Instead, either drop off and pick up your child at a parties and social events or work with a friend or neighbor to coordinate transportation if you suspect there will be drinking at some point during the night. Or tell your child to call for a taxi cab. The point is to have rules about drinking and driving and a transportation plan, and to make sure everyone abides by it.

Calculating Blood Alcohol Content

BAC measures how much alcohol is in the bloodstream. Even many adults are not aware of how BAC is computed. For example, a BAC of .10 means that one tenth of 1% of your total blood content is alcohol. In many cities and states, this is considered legally drunk. Anyone operating a motor vehicle in this condition is deemed "driving under the influence" and is subject to arrest.

BAC readings depend on two factors: body size and how much you drink at any one time. A youngster with a small build or a teen who has two cans of beer quickly can have a higher blood alcohol content than an adult who had four glasses of wine.

Be prepared for other families having different standards of acceptable behavior.

Beware of the trap sprung by kids who say "Johnny's mom and dad let him have a drink of beer so why can't you?" If that is true, then your child should not be hanging around with Johnny or visiting Johnny's home when his parents are drinking. Other cultures often have different attitudes about drinking.

Do not joke about alcoholism or drunken behavior.

There is nothing funny about either being drunk or parodying someone else who acts silly when they are intoxicated. Injecting humor into such a serious subject trivializes and encourages it.

Know the facts about alcohol use and abuse and discuss them with your children.

Most parents who drink responsibly feel confident that they know the pitfalls and signs of alcohol abuse. Yet, there are some surprising facts that many adults may not realize. For instance, the alcohol in a can of beer is equivalent to the potency of a six-ounce glass of wine, which is equal to an ounce of 80-proof whiskey. This is important for an adult to understand and to explain to kids. Children automatically assume that beer is not as strong as a so-called "drink," but it is. Even 12-ounce wine coolers, which kids think of as soda pop, can pack a wallop.

Pregnant woman should not drink at all. Fetal alcohol syndrome is responsible for an estimated 400,000 babies literally born drunk annually—addicted to alcohol at birth. Infants who come into the world this way face the double threat of having to detoxify immediately and the very real possibility of not receiving proper postnatal care. And kids born to alcoholics tend to grow up to be alcoholics, a combination of genetics and learned behavior.

While alcohol is a gateway drug that can lead to other, stronger chemical dependencies, it has its own addiction: alcoholism. Both the American Medical Association and the American Psychiatric Association classify alcoholism and drug addictions as diseases. This is a point to make with your child in your discussions and to reinforce over and over. Alcoholism is a progressive disease that only gets worse by drinking irresponsibly.

Just as kids should know the facts on tobacco, here is the fact sheet D.A.R.E. uses on alcohol. Go over it with your child.

Using Alcohol Once

- Illegal for minors to use
- Drunkenness
- Slurred speech
- Loss of coordination
- Increase in violence and crime
- Death (overdose)
- Reduces inhibitions
- Increase in accidents
- Loss of judgment
- Impairment

Using Alcohol for a Short Time

- All of the effects above plus:
- Slows thinking (become forgetful)
- Changes in personality (moody, aggressive behavior)
- School work suffers
- Get hooked, or dependent, on alcohol

Using Alcohol for a While

- All of the effects above plus:
- Weight gain, alcohol has a lot of calories and is fattening, which can increase the risks of heart disease
- Cirrhosis (disease) of the liver
- Hurts relationships with family and friends
- D.T.'s or delirium tremors (mental confusion and shakes)

Confronting Personal Behavior

Younger children are more curious than teens, who are more headstrong. So you have to be honest in your response to their questions. Here is a suggested dialogue.

◆ ◆ ◆ ◆ ◆

Child: "Dad, when did you have your first drink?"
Parent: "I was about your age but I didn't really like it. I had a beer because a neighbor boy gave me one and I didn't want to look like a sissy. But it gave me a headache and made me woozy."
Child: "So if you drank a beer at my age, why can't I have one?"
Parent: "Because I made a mistake, and I don't want you to make one. My parents didn't discuss all the problems of drinking when I was a child so that's why we're talking about it. Drinking is for grownups who want to drink, but plenty of them do not. I happen to drink a glass of wine at dinner sometimes because I enjoy it. But now I know that I don't have to drink to impress anyone."
Child: "Have you ever been drunk?"
Parent: "Yes, and it was a terrible experience. I drank too much and I had a horrible headache and really could have hurt myself in lots of different ways. I was a teenager and didn't know what I was doing or just how powerful alcohol was. It taught me a lesson though. Thank goodness I wasn't driving. However, I knew a kid in school who was drinking and driving and got into an auto accident that killed himself and two passengers."

◆ ◆ ◆ ◆ ◆

Drinking at a young age could lead to the point where "drink" takes control of your life—and possibly destroys it. That's the extreme. With your love, candid communications, and continual caring, your child will wait until the legal age to decide to drink—and then only socially.

8

Marijuana: Pot Today Is More Dangerous Than You Think

Every parent should be aware of two alarming points: More kids are smoking marijuana than at any other time in history, and the drug is ten times more powerful than the marijuana that was smoked in the last three decades. Ten times!

Ten years ago, the primary psychoactive ingredient in marijuana, THC (tetrahydrocannabinol), averaged 3 to 5 percent. Today's skilled marijuana growers crossbreed different seeds and strains and use hydroponics (growing plants in nutrient-rich solutions without soil) to produce pot containing up to 30 percent THC. The potency has skyrocketed.

Growing and selling marijuana is no longer a sideline for hippies who want to get high with their friends. Growing and selling powerhouse pot is big business. Today's drug culture is dominated by criminals who see your child—any child—as a customer to be cultivated and exploited. In fact, it is fairly common for marijuana dealers to sprinkle methamphetamine dust or hallucinogens like PCP (phencyclidine hydrochloride, a.k.a. "angel dust") or even LSD (lysergic acid diethylamide) on low-grade grass to boost its kick, its price, and a user's dependency. Drug dealers, like business people everywhere, want to build up a regular clientele. One puff of this more powerful marijuana can get an adult "stoned" (intoxicated, high) instantly. Imagine what it can do to your child's brain and body! It is vital that you educate yourself and your child about the power and perils of marijuana.

What Doctors and Scientists Say

Although marijuana has been around for centuries, no one really knows how destructive it can be. No long-range studies on the effects of using marijuana have been completed. In addition to THC, marijuana contains over 60 other cannabinoids (the psychoactive ingredients of marijuana), plus around 400 other chemicals, many with long-term effects that are unknown to medical science.

"Marijuana makes our brightest kids average, our average kids dull, and our dull kids almost incapable of learning."

Regardless of the research that remains to be done, the truth is that today's current crop of marijuana is more physically and psychologically addictive, and potentially even more destructive. Yet some permissive parents, who may have smoked in their youth, see marijuana smoking as a passing fancy—a "stage" their child is going through. This is a tragedy.

According to Professor David H. Farb, Ph.D., chair of Boston University School of Medicine's Department of Pharmacology, THC alters the functioning of certain nerve cells and neurotransmitter systems in the brain. As a result, marijuana literally alters the mind—slowing it down—and affects sounds, sights, and balance. Marijuana distorts the ability to process information and affects short-term memory and, therefore, the ability to learn. Dr. Bill Beachum, executive director of the Center for Drug-Free Communities, likes to share a startling statistic with parents. "We have over 6,000 studies on marijuana since 1968 and not one of them shows that marijuana increases learning. It does nothing positive for their cognitive or intellectual development and retards their emotional development by creating a false sense of well-being, which shuts them off from reality. Marijuana makes our brightest kids average, our average kids dull, and our dull kids almost incapable of learning."

The Basics

Marijuana has more slang names than any other drug. Pot is the most common; however, it also is known as grass, weed, mary-jane, tea, hay, and by other names. Hand-rolled marijuana cigarettes are called "joints," "reefers," or "doobies."

Cultivation, Appearance, and Methods of Use

Marijuana is derived from the plant Cannabis Sativa, a member of the hemp family, which grows in warm climates in many regions of the world. Although average growth is about three feet high, a plant can grow up to fifteen feet high with a stalk up to four inches thick. In appearance, cannabis sativa closely resembles a tomato plant. Most plants have green leaves with seven to nine leaflets per leaf. Marijuana is made from the plant's flowers and seed heads, which are picked, then dried. The color of dried marijuana ranges from grayish-green to greenish brown. Dried leaves can look like tobacco or parsley.

People use marijuana by smoking or eating it. It is easily baked into foodstuffs, although smoking is by far the most popular and traditional method, either through hand-rolled cigarettes or pipes. Cigarette papers for rolling joints are readily available and easily obtained, or the pot can be put into a pipe or bong (water-filled pipe) and smoked or inhaled. Dope is easily stored in film cans and baggies.

Hashish or "hash," a derivative of marijuana, is not as prevalent among youngsters. Resin is squeezed from marijuana flowers and seeds, compressed into "bricks," and allowed to harden. To use it, a person breaks off a chunk of hash and smokes it in a pipe.

Finding any of these items in your child's possession is a pretty reliable indictor that s/he is using, so be alert to them regardless of the child's age.

What Happens to the User?

As with any drug, the effects of marijuana vary depending upon the personality of the user and the amount and frequency of use. Fifteen to thirty minutes after using marijuana, a person begins to relax and experience a feeling of euphoria or a sense of well-being. If the person is alone, s/he may become drowsy and fall asleep. In a group, the user's inhibitions often drop and s/he may become cheerful and talkative. Senses are stimulated—colors may appear more vibrant, music may sound clearer, and the feel of textures may be enhanced. At this stage the person is high or intoxicated, and coordination, concentration, reasoning, and judgment all are impaired.

Documented side effects of marijuana include:

- Increased heart rate
- Increased pulse rate
- Loss of short-term memory
- Damage to infection-fighting white blood cells
- Impaired sexual development and fertility
- Lung cancer
- Feelings of "burn out," isolation, depression
- Anxiety and, in acute cases, panic reaction
- Preexisting emotional problems may worsen
- Frightening hallucinations, although rare, may occur among those who use large or "doctored" quantities

If marijuana can have these effects on adults, imagine the toll it can take on children and adolescents, who have not fully developed physically, psychologically, and emotionally. Another serious ramification is that today's more powerful pot can serve as a dangerous gateway to stronger, harder substances.

Signs of Use

♦ Distinctive odor
♦ Dry mouth and throat
♦ Increased appetite, often with cravings for something sweet
♦ Bloodshot eyes
♦ Dilated pupils
♦ Euphoria
♦ Difficulty concentrating
♦ Muddled thinking
♦ Disorientation
♦ Lack of motivation
♦ Productivity drops
♦ Paranoia
♦ Paraphernalia such as cigarette papers, roach clips, pipes, bongs (water pipes), pipe screens

What Can You Tell Your Children?

Parents must explain to kids that smoking either cigarettes or marijuana is unhealthy.

♦ Both are drugs.
♦ Both are addictive.
♦ Both are illegal with one key difference—use marijuana and you can go to jail.

Explaining the immediate consequences of using marijuana is essential, but "when you tell a 12-year-old kid they can get lung cancer or addicted, they see that as a long-term consequence that happens to someone else," says Ed Arambula, a sergeant assigned to the Los Angeles Police Department's D.A.R.E. Division. "So discuss it from their point of view."

Some instant consequences:

♦ You can get caught.
♦ You can get in trouble.

- You can get a police record.
- You can hurt your health.
- You can get poor grades.
- You can get kicked off sports teams.
- You can lose your friends.
- You can lose your parents' trust.
- It can hurt your self-esteem.
- It can cost you money.
- You can hurt your reputation at school and in your community.
- It can hurt your family and relatives.
- You can injure someone if you drive or work while under the influence.

In explaining consequences, be prepared to answer some tough questions from your child. The current furor over the medical use of marijuana sends a mixed message to kids and gives some the impression that marijuana is more of a medicine than a drug. While it has been proven to be effective in reducing nausea from cancer chemotherapy and in the treatment of glaucoma, these facts might tend to decriminalize it in the impressionable minds of young people. What is not stated or emphasized is the fact that the marijuana grown by the government is produced under very strictly controlled circumstances and the potency of the THC is regulated. The federal government is not buying pure, powerhouse marijuana from illegal growers.

Health Risks

First, explain that anything you smoke is harmful to your health and, for years, tobacco companies have labeled cigarettes as such in compliance with federal laws. While tobacco companies have admitted for some time that cigarettes cause lung cancer as well as other health problems, kids need to know that marijuana also has health risks and can cause lung cancer.

It's Illegal

Not only is marijuana unhealthy, its use is illegal and exposes users to a criminal culture. Alcohol is a legal drug for people over the age of 18 or 21 (depending on state law). Marijuana is not legal at any age. Furnishing, whether selling it or giving it away, violates the law in all states, and possession and use is illegal. A youngster caught with less than an ounce of marijuana could be considered a drug dealer if the pot is prerolled in cigarette form and packaged in a baggie or plastic envelope.

It Is Not an Appropriate Response to Stress

Explain to your kids that while marijuana may seem to offer a quick escape from stressful and emotionally painful feelings, it provides only a temporary reprieve.

A child who is rebellious, bored, subject to teasing and peer pressure and who is feeling stress, is also open to ways to escape. Parents must introduce them to the real world of facts, costs, and consequences.

By the sixth grade, children should know that there is no magic formula for avoiding pain and stress. They have to face life on life's terms, and when difficulties arise, deal with them and not try to avoid or escape problems.

Indeed, if a youngster turns to drugs, or explores them beyond being curious, Dr. Beachum says parents must bear a major responsibility, and not always because they are neglectful or tuned out to their child's problems. "We tell them life is wonderful and to have a good time. Where we as parents and educators miss the boat is that we fail to tell them that life is also difficult, tough, and disillusioning. We have to give them the skills to cope with life." Problem solving, conflict resolution, and assertiveness skills are effective techniques for dealing with stress. (Note: These are covered in Chapters 1 and 3.)

There Are Serious Long-term Consequences

Drug Testing

Many employers routinely test new employees for drug use. Drug testing is prevalent in athletics, from high school to professional teams.

Any youngster who uses and drives a car or plays sports should consider how a drug test can change their lives. Positive drug tests and/or a criminal record can limit your choice of colleges or jobs.

Most parents—and virtually no youngsters—do not realize that the biological half-life of the drug's potency-measuring cannabinoid, THC, is five to seven days. "If a child, or anyone, smoked a joint on Tuesday, a week later they would have 50 percent of the drug in their system. Testing can pick up marijuana in your blood or urine 25 days after you stop using it," says Dr. Beachum.

Sexual Risks

Sometimes marijuana is used in a conscious attempt to lower a person's inhibitions and resistance to sexual acts. This opens the door to the possibilities of becoming pregnant or of contracting sexually transmitted diseases (STDs) or AIDS/HIV.

Regular marijuana use also impairs sexual development and fertility, produces menstrual irregularities, and contributes to the production of an abnormally low sperm count, which could well come back to haunt people when they try to start a family.

A Major Factor in Accidents

Half of the traffic fatalities each year occur because someone was driving under the influence of alcohol or drugs. Drunk driving can cost youngsters their driving privileges, boost their insurance rates, and kill them and innocent victims involved in an accident. Marijuana has many of the same effects as alcohol in reducing a user's perception, reflexes, and alertness. Marijuana when combined with alcohol impairs a user's abilities to an even greater degree.

The pharmaceutical company Smith Kline Beechum, in a study of accidents among transportation workers responsible for the public's safety—airplane pilots, bus and truck drivers, and railroad engineers—found that marijuana, when present, was often used in combination with alcohol and/or other illegal substances. The state of Alaska decriminalized marijuana but had to recriminalize it when traffic accidents and industrial mishaps soared. Additionally, productivity plunged and substance addiction climbed sharply, but these trends were also reversed when drugs were once again outlawed.

My Child Is Smoking Marijuana

If parents find their child smoking or selling marijuana, do not accept an apology, ignore it, or overreact with threats. A kid who is dealing generally is also using. First, try to find out why the child has been using drugs and for how long.

"Do not use the threat of going to the police to scare a child," warns Arambula. "If you take them and the marijuana to a law enforcement official, they will be booked as a juvenile and released back to you, the parents. Hopefully, the child will see the seriousness of what they did, see the consequences of their actions, and realize the parents mean business and will hold them accountable. Let the child know he or she is going to be monitored closely." (Even though a youngster has a record as a juvenile offender, it can be sealed or expunged when s/he turns twenty-one.)

Suppose you as a parent choose to put your own head in the sand—out of shame, ignorance, or because you are using marijuana as well. In virtually every city, you can be prosecuted for violating a law—contributing to the delinquency of a minor.

Even if you are only using, Arambula says, "The court could determine, in an extreme case, that you are an unfit couple and the child could be taken away from you." If you are going through a divorce—or wind up in a future child custody battle—you could lose custody of your child to your spouse.

In Summary

FACT: Children are beginning to smoke marijuana at a younger and younger age.

FACT: The number of children who use marijuana before ninth grade has doubled.

FACT: Marijuana today is ten times more powerful than in the past.

FACT: Use of marijuana during a child's formative years can have serious detrimental effects on the development of the immature body.

FACT: Possession of or use of marijuana is illegal.

FACT: Marijuana is carcinogenic and causes lung cancer, even more so than cigarettes.

9

Inhalants: Danger Right Under Your Nose

Q: What is the third most widely abused drug that is also virtually free, easily accessible to kids of all ages, and often used right under their parents'nose?

A: Most people would not correctly identify the broad category of drugs known as "inhalants," and they would be equally surprised to learn that only tobacco and alcohol are more popular among drug-using youngsters.

Q: Is sniffing glue, paint thinner, gasoline, nail polish remover, marking pens, air fresheners, and other vaporous substances actually that harmful to a youngster?

A: Absolutely, and more damaging than you can imagine! Chronic inhaling can injure the brain, lungs, and central nervous system, often instantly, sometimes permanently. In some cases, the first whiff of a toxic inhalant can be fatal. This is known as Sudden Sniffing Death Syndrome (SSD). Every time kids use inhalants, they are playing Russian roulette because habitual sniffing erodes brain cells and other vital organs—and any one "hit" can be the final one.

Q: Are inhalants a bigger threat than other gateway drugs?"

A: On an immediate basis, yes. These chemicals enter the body quickly—either sniffed through the nasal passages or huffed through the mouth—and can linger in the brain, lungs, and circulatory system longer than alcohol, tobacco, and marijuana.

Inhalants include gases, propellants, and other solvent-based products:

- Aerosols, such as hair spray
- Amyl nitrite
- Anesthetic gases: chloroform, ether, nitrous oxide
- Benzene
- Butyl nitrite
- Cleaning fluids
- Cooking gases (Sterno)
- Correction fluids (white out)
- Cosmetic products, such as nail polish remover
- Gasoline
- Glue
- Lighter fluid
- Marking pens
- Paints
- Paint strippers or thinners

Q: If inhalants are so dangerous, why would any youngster sniff or huff?

A: With inhalants, youngsters have a smorgasbord of easily available choices, plenty of places to take quick whiffs, and most inhalants do not cost them a dime. Kids use inhalants for all the same reasons that kids use any drug—boredom, ignorance, peer pressure, low self-esteem, lack of parental awareness and supervision. Still, the primary reason kids huff and sniff is to get high, to escape, and to "float" for a few minutes.

For most parents this question-and-answer session will be a shocking wake-up call. When you think of drugs that trigger an immediate high, you might typically imagine a child using marijuana, cocaine, or methamphetamine. And you figure that they have to obtain these drugs from an acquaintance or a dealer. But with inhalants, kids never have to find a dealer or even pay for them, in fact, they do not even have to leave their house to get high.

Categories of Inhalants

Inhalants are right there in your garage, under your kitchen sink, in your laundry room, sitting around in your family or hobby room, or hidden away in the child's own bedroom. According to the National Inhalant Prevention Coalition (NIPC), some 1,400 separate products are identified as toxic inhalants with the potential for abuse. There are three primary categories of inhalants: nitrous oxides, volatile nitrites, and petroleum distillates. You do not need a Ph.D. in chemistry to recognize them. In fact, every parent should have a basic understanding of what they are and how they can injure a child.

Nitrous Oxides

Nitrous oxide, invented in the 1770s, is mixed with other gases as an anesthetic in medical procedures and is also an aerosol propellant for something as seemingly harmless as canned whipping cream. Most people have had an experience with inhalants. For years dentists used nitrous oxide as an anesthetic to deaden the pain for a tooth extraction, and some dentists still do; you may know it as "laughing gas." It puts people in a floating, dreamy, pleasurable state, gives you the giggles and an intense, momentary high.

Yet laughing gas is nothing to laugh about when it gets into the wrong hands and is used for the wrong reasons. Thieves steal canisters of nitrous oxide from dental offices and hospitals and often sell it to hip and naïve kids. Self-styled entrepreneurs, often wearing T-shirts that read "Just Say NO [nitrous oxide]," peddle balloons of nitrous oxide at drug-infested, frequently deadly rave parties where other, more toxic inhalants are passed around or sold as well. Parents buy tanks of helium to inflate party balloons.

Hitting the Helium Is a Risky Party Trick

Giving your child a "hit" of helium gas while you are blowing up balloons at a party is no different than offering your youngster a sip of beer at a backyard barbecue or a puff off your cigarette. "Inhaling this gas [helium] changes the way vibrations come through the voice box," says Dr. Earl Siegel, associate professor of emergency medicine at the University of Cincinnati Medical Center. "Sometimes people, as a party game or in jest, deliberately inhale helium into their lungs, and it has an activity on the voice box that makes them sound like Donald Duck."

Dr. Siegel notes that inhaling helium is not instantly injurious. "Serious cases are rare and mostly related to the mechanical damage of introducing a highly compressed gas into your lungs." But it is the parental behavior that bothers him. "Promoting any practice that encourages the unnecessary introduction of chemicals into our bodies is unwise. I think we can quack like a duck without helium."

Using helium, a low-toxicity version of nitrous oxide, is no laughing matter. While taking a whiff of helium is not as toxic as sniffing a rag soaked in paint thinner, it is still risky and can lead to lung damage, seizures, or worse. The September 1996 *Annals of Emergency Medicine* reported on a 13-year-old boy who inhaled helium from a pressurized tank, lapsed into unconsciousness, and suffered a seizure that lasted ten minutes. Doctors discovered that the teen had a cerebral gas embolism plus lung damage caused by involuntary lung expansion. He recovered after being placed in a hyperbaric chamber for several sessions.

Volatile Nitrites

Amyl nitrite, one of the volatile nitrites, is rarely used by youngsters unless they steal it from the medicine cabinet. This is a powerful prescription drug for people suffering from heart problems or respiratory ailments like asthma. Sometimes it is administered as an antidote for cyanide poisoning. It is like a combination chemical relaxant and jump start.

Thrill-seeking older teens and adults, who have access to the drug, may use it during sex to provide a jolting high that first relaxes the muscles then heightens the intensity of a climax. It is also known to be used by some skydivers, who use it for an extra rush of excitement when they bail out of a plane.

Amyl nitrite's slang names are tip-offs to possible effects. On the street, small glass vials of amyl nitrite, a clear, yellowish liquid, are known as "poppers," "snappers," "amyl," "jack hammer," "bullet," or "rush." Users open the vials by crushing them with their fingers and inhaling the vapors. "This causes the blood vessels to dilate and the heart to beat faster," says William Bailey of the Prevention Resource Center at Indiana University. "Simultaneously, the amyl nitrite reduces the oxygen supply to the inner part of the brain and creates a sudden and intense weakness and dizziness that can last 30 to 60 seconds."

Butyl Nitrite, or "poppers" are an unregulated clone of amyl nitrite, often disguised for marketing purposes as incense or as room deodorizers. Packaged in tiny amber bottles, butyl nitrite is sold as "rush," "jolt," or "locker room" in bars, liquor stores, or adult bookstores. Poppers are addictive psychologically but not physically. High-school boys looking for sexual conquests will occasionally entice girls with "poppers," hoping that the drugs will reduce inhibitions and resistance. Adults will often buy and resell butyl nitrite to teens and even preteens.

Butyl nitrite has the same euphoric effects as its prescription-only sibling, amyl nitrite, which last for a few seconds to a couple of minutes. "Poppers" trigger a brief tidal wave of highly oxygenated blood to the brain. William Bailey describes it with clinical accuracy: "Individuals experience low blood pressure, followed by an increase in blood pressure, flushed face, dizziness, and headache. The rush occurs quickly and dissipates quickly, so experienced users are inclined to maintain a high by using increasing amounts of the inhalant."

There has been a widespread clamp-down on butyl nitrite sales, but manufacturers are trying to evade it with products consisting of the chemical form "cyclohexylnitrite." This inhalant is being pushed as an instant sensory cyclone. Beware.

Petroleum Distillates

Petroleum distillates are the third broad category of inhalants—and the most dangerous. Essentially, they are vapors or gases from a variety of petroleum products. Huffed, sniffed, whiffed—call it what you want—these inhalants are extremely powerful drugs that depress the central nervous system and intoxicate the mind. And not just for a few minutes either, the effects can last for hours.

The most potent fumes come from pure petroleum products—gasoline, kerosene, gasoline additives, lighter fluid, certain glues, as well as a little-known petrochemical called "toluene." Petroleum distillates are also found in typewriter correction fluids and in the aerosol gases in spray paints, hair sprays, and canned cooking sprays. They are all popular and easy to obtain.

How Prevalent Are Inhalants?

It is hard to track and tally youthful sniffers and huffers. The most recent figures indicate that 476,000 youngsters, aged 12 to 17, were using or experimenting with inhalants in any given month in 1995, according to the U.S. Substance Abuse and Mental Health Administration. The same study found 676,000 people used inhalants for the first time that year.[1] Moreover, the trend is growing. The "Monitoring the Future Survey" conducted by the National Institute of Drug Abuse found that, by the end of 1995, 22 percent of eighth graders nationwide used inhalants.[2] However, according to Harvey Weiss, executive director of the National Inhalant Prevention Coalition, inhalant use and abuse generally starts before the teen years, and sniffing and huffing often lead to using harder, illegal drugs. "Inhalants should be considered a gateway drug because, for many youngsters, it's their first experience with getting high."

"All it takes is a nose or a mouth."

Kids Pay a High Price for Inhaling

According to Dr. Weiss, "Most kids understand it as 'huffing,' 'sniffing' or 'bagging' because they'll put their head in a bag filled with, say, gasoline-soaked rags, shake it, and huff a huge amount of the concentrated fumes in one breath." They do not have to cook them, mix them, roll them, or inject them. Drug paraphernalia is not needed. All it takes is a nose or a mouth.

Many adults—and most kids, simply do not realize how dangerous, damaging, and deadly inhalants really are. Over a thousand people die every year from sniffing or huffing. Because the chemicals in inhalants flood into the lungs in such high concentration, they can have a more toxic impact than any other abused drug. It is difficult to make a child understand that. The harmful effects of crack cocaine and heroin are well publicized and children know that they are illegal and costly, so they may think twice about using them. On the other hand, common household products like nail polish remover, hair spray, or model airplane glue are found in the home or are easily and inexpensively purchased at stores. Hence, the child who wants a quick high often does not think about—or know about—the health risks. S/he wants the thrill, the rush. In many cases, inhalants deliver a fast buzz, but that is often immediately followed by a headache and nausea. The pleasure is fleeting and the pain remains, but kids can develop a dependency—an addiction—to the momentary pleasure.

The Effects

Kids often feel that they are indestructible. They live in the moment and do not think long term. They do not worry about their personal safety unless a parent or a concerned adult takes the time to sit down and explain what sniffing and huffing can do to their body.

Inhaling familiar household products can hurt any child, teen, or adult. When inhaled through the mouth or nose, inhalants depress the central nervous system and displace the oxygen in the lungs. Initially users may lose self-control and feel giddy or drowsy. They can lapse into unconsciousness. Death can occur from suffocation: the nervous system is depressed to the point that breathing stops or the user is unable to remove the plastic bag from their face or they suffocate from inhaling their own vomit.

Chronic inhalant abusers may permanently lose the ability to walk, talk, and think. The adverse effects on the body and mind are a mile long.

Physical and psychological ravages include:

◆ Damage to the brain, lungs, heart (arrhythmia), liver (hepatitis), kidneys
◆ Damage to the central nervous system
◆ Temporary blindness
◆ Bone marrow damage
◆ Loss of bladder and bowel control
◆ Coma or unconsciousness
◆ Glaucoma
◆ Permanent damage to the throat and nasal passages
◆ Injury to teeth and gums
◆ Severe depression
◆ Psychotic behavior

Dr. DeBlois of the Child Psychiatry Division of the Stanford University Medical Center works with kids in the Adolescent Substance Abuse Program. Before that he worked with adult felons at California's maximum security Corcoran State Prison and at North Kern State Prison. He has seen first-hand the long-term effects of chronic huffing and sniffing, and he is not reluctant to share them. Inhalant abuse is a "cheap high" with tragic and costly consequences, he reports. "It doesn't happen overnight, but chronic abuse creates psychological problems. I see adults who have problems with memory, who cannot concentrate, have very poor judgment, who cannot think. It's like a kind of Alzheimer's disease. It's irreversible."

Huffing and sniffing toxic inhalants repeatedly has "permanent effects that do not go away," explains Dr. DeBlois. Each time you inhale, there is an acute trauma to the brain and it compounds the damage. Inhalants are not like nicotine or alcohol, where you develop a tolerance....Every time you do inhalants, you experience an intense high, which adds more acute damaging effects over the long haul."

How to Spot a Sniffer of Huffer

Of the 1,400 products that are harmful when inhaled, huffers and sniffers prefer a handful. Dr. Ashok Jain, assistant professor of emergency medicine at the University of Southern California and associate director of the Los Angeles County Drug and Poison Information Center, says two thirds of the kids who sniff or huff use spray paint or gasoline. Older teens inhale nitrous oxide or laughing gas. Rubber cement, model airplane glue, paint remover, paint thinner, and rubbing alcohol are abused by younger kids, primarily because they are available and inexpensive. Since the late 1990s, freon, a gaseous substance, has emerged as a favorite of preteen kids of all races.

There is no one tip-off to parents that a child is sniffing or huffing. "At the first alarming sign, move quickly," says Dr. Jain.

"If your kid has a reddish line around his (or her) mouth, is not 'acting right,' and you smell chemicals on the breath, you know there is trouble, and other kids—friends, siblings—are probably doing it, too. Yet none of them know the long-term effects—the permanent damage to their brain, their nervous systems. . . ."

Signs and Symptoms of Inhalant Use

Environmental Indicators

+ Discovery of inhalant paraphernalia (empty aerosol cans, soaked rags, stained plastic bags)
+ Stockpiles of magic markers, glue, propellants, solvents

Physical Indicators

+ Sores, rashes around the nose and mouth
+ Paint marks around nose and mouth
+ Chemical, gasoline, or sweet odor on breath, body, clothes
+ Red, watery eyes
+ Pupils can appear either constricted or dilated
+ Decreased respiration
+ Lowered heart rate
+ Impaired vision
+ Fast, deep, or labored breathing
+ Headache, nausea
+ Nosebleeds, nose drips
+ Sneezing
+ Coughing
+ Slurring words, slow "thick" speech
+ Loss of motor coordination—stumbling, poor balance
+ Involuntary voiding
+ Weight loss (long-term use)

Behavioral Indicators

+ Euphoric, boisterous, giddy, intoxicated behavior
+ Slow reactions, responses to questions
+ Disorientation, confusion

+ Depression
+ Apathetic behavior
+ Fatigue (long-term)
+ Memory loss
+ Easily irritable, moody
+ Loss of appetite
+ Falloff in grades or classroom alertness
+ Sudden lack of interest in sports or social activities
+ Withdrawal from family and friends
+ Neglect of personal appearance, hygiene
+ Violent behavior

Preventative Measures

When you talk to your kids about huffing and sniffing, your main mission is prevention.

Talk in terms of avoiding putting poisons and chemicals in their body.

As an icebreaker, remind them how you discussed that "you never stick your finger in a light socket because it could hurt you very badly." Explain how sniffing these poisonous fumes—and call them poisonous fumes—can do the same thing. "By the age of four, children have heard about poisons," says Weiss of NIPC. "They know not to drink a glass of gasoline because it will make them die." Explain that sniffing substances that give off fumes, vapors, or gases is another way to poison yourself.

Hold a personal safety session.

Round up a cross-section of household products that can be inhaled and, without terrifying the youngster, read the warnings on the labels and explain the dangers. Although a product may not have a frightening skull and crossbones on its label, any product with toxic ingredients includes a printed warning similar to the following: "Intentional misuse by deliberately concentrating or inhaling the contents can be harmful or fatal."

Set boundaries on products used in your own home.

This does not mean putting all your paint, paint thinners, antifreeze, or hair spray under lock and key. Simply identify the kinds of products that are a source of serious trouble if they are huffed or sniffed and explain that you will not tolerate any experimentation. Encourage them to ask you questions.

Several chemicals found in products that may be abused as inhalants are extremely dangerous. Avoid household storage of any products containing toluene and trichloroethylene listed as an ingredient.

- ◆ The chemical trichloroethylene attacks the heart muscles and causes ventricular arrhythmia, which is a fluttering of the heart. Though removed from many products, it is still available in dry cleaning fluid and can cause sudden death.
- ◆ Toluene, found in certain glues, is a highly toxic chemical that concentrates in the cerebellum of the brain, warns Dr. Jain. Youngsters who sniff it suffer an immediate weakness throughout their body, slurred speech, hallucinations, and a disruption of the blood's electrolytes, which can cause "significant" sickness. Inhaling toluene alters sodium and potassium levels, making a youngster lightheaded and faint.

Remain vigilant

Many parents of inhalant abusers do not even realize that their kids are using. From his vantage point at the University of Southern California and through his association with poison information centers nationwide, Dr. Jain says, "Most (inhalant) abuse occurs after dinner, between 6 PM and 8 PM, when children are in their rooms and their parents are watching television and not supervising." The effects of various inhalants, he adds, "only last about two hours, so it is hard to catch kids who are doing it. And, because the effect doesn't last long, children have to abuse these inhalants more often."

Ask if they are aware of any kids who huff.

If their answer is "yes," try to find out exactly what these kids are doing. If someone is using glue or gasoline, explain how that can affect a person's body and health and stress how you do not want to see your son or daughter suffer that same fate.

What to Do If Your Child Is Using

Parents who discover their kids are huffing and sniffing "should take the problem seriously from the get-go," insists Dr. DeBlois. Parents who find a child experimenting with inhalants should immediately talk with a school counselor. "The counselor can help parents understand the developmental level of their child and whether they can and will listen." If you feel your warnings and explanations are falling on deaf ears, take the child to an adult drug and alcohol rehabilitation program and let him or her sit in on several meetings. S/he will see real addicts and will hear their problems and life stories. Attending meetings of Alcoholics Anonymous or Narcotics Anonymous can have the same impact. "Remember, adolescents live in the 'here and now' and they feel quite invincible, so they do not easily see the long-term effects of drugs that parents see."

Because inhalant abuse can have a variety of strange effects on a child's body, parents should contact their local poison control center for information and guidance. Dr. Jain says 10 percent of kids who use inhalants—both first-time and chronic huffers and sniffers—wind up in a hospital emergency room. Most do not require medical treatment, only parental supervision, discipline and, if addicted, professional intervention and counseling.

Until a child can build self-esteem, resist peer pressure, and assert their beliefs about right and wrong, even the most chilling consequences of huffing and sniffing may not prevent them from taking that first, and possibly fatal, whiff. By paying close and caring attention, sharing your concerns, and listening to theirs before they reach the rebellious years of middle adolescence, you and your kids have an excellent chance of sidestepping the minefield of inhalants.

10

Raiding the Medicine Cabinet

It is important to make distinctions among using, misusing, and abusing drugs and medicines. *Using* medicine is following the directions on the label or from the physician who prescribed it. *Misusing* the drug is when a person disregards the directions and decides "if one pill is good, then two pills will make me feel better twice as quickly." *Abusing a drug is using it recklessly to get high, escape, be accepted, or for any inappropriate reason.*

Most youngsters who take legal drugs for purposes other than medical reasons usually use the nonprescription kind, with the most popular ones being diet aids, stimulants to stay awake, allergy and sinus medicines, pain relievers, and cough preparations. Other drugs that are frequently abused by children and teens include over-the-counter sleeping aids and prescription tranquilizers and pain medications.

Over-the-Counter Drugs

Diet Aids

Teens take diet pills to curb their appetite and to lose weight. When they discover that diet pills are also a source of energy, some keep on taking them. Continued use of diet pills is unhealthy, and users risk becoming psychologically addicted. Mark Hobbs, a Florida pharmacy owner and a member of the American Pharmaceutical Association, advises parents to pay particular attention to over-the-counter diet pills that include the ingredient phenylpropanolamine, a substance related to ephedrine and amphetamine and available in various popular nonprescription diet aids as an appetite suppressant.

Stimulants for Staying Awake

Many of the so-called "appetite appeasement" pills sold in drugstores and supermarkets contain caffeine. While they curb hunger, they are also a stimulant. Teens often use nonprescription drugs to stay awake to study for tests or to write last-minute reports or term papers. But popping these pills, however harmless (unless gobbled in massive amounts), tends to become a crutch behavior and could lead to a reliance on or abuse of prescription stimulants like Dexedrine or other amphetamine-based drugs that are found in certain medicine cabinets or bartered, swapped, or sold at schools.

Pain Relievers

The mass media bombards us with ads and commercials for over-the-counter pain killers, and the message seems to be "take two and feel better for any ill." It is no wonder that kids who cannot get—or have not yet been exposed to—the addictive prescription downers in the benzodiazepine family (Valium, Xanax, Ativan, Librium) will try Advil, Tylenol, Motrin, Aleve, or plain old aspirin to try to mellow out from stress and pressure. Reaching for a pill for every pain or every time you feel under pressure is a habit-forming reflex that kids should understand is not good for their health or their bodies.

Nonprescription Cough Preparations

Over-the-counter cough preparations are among the most commonly abused drugs because one of the primary ingredients is alcohol, and in certain brands it can be as high as 14 percent or 28 proof! Cough syrups used to be medicinal-tasting. Now, they are often fruit-flavored and somewhat tasty, which makes the promise of a pain-free high all that more appetizing to kids who may abuse them. A kid who uses these products can get a buzz or an alcoholic high. Usually its popularity spreads by word of mouth and it becomes the "drug of choice" in a community for six months or so. Kids who want cough medicine's alcoholic buzz usually get it from liquor—if they can obtain it. Teens who abuse cough medicines generally stop after a while because they feel it is a "kiddie" drug and, therefore, not cool.

However, cough medicine is abused by youngsters for another reason: Many brands contain Dextromethorphan hydrobromide (DM), which has an hallucinogenic effect when consumed in large quantities. DM is an effective cough suppressant that is found in about 150 over-the-counter drugs. While manufacturers claim that the ingredient DM is not physically or psychologically addictive, cough medicines with high alcoholic contents can certainly be addictive.

Prescription Drugs

Although prescriptions are given under a doctor's supervision and are prepared by a pharmacist, they can be dangerous when:

◆ Taken incorrectly

◆ Used by someone other than for whom they were prescribed

◆ Taken for other than the prescribed medical condition

◆ Combined with other drugs or alcohol

Depressants and stimulants are the prescription drugs most likely to be abused by adults and, thus, pose a risk to children who raid their parents' medicine cabinets. Many prescription drugs are acquired illegally, either obtained through bogus or pilfered prescriptions or stolen from drug manufacturers. Inform kids that it is illegal to fill or use another person's prescription.

Depressants

Depressants, which decrease brain activity, are designed to help a person relax.

Barbiturates

Commonly prescribed for high blood pressure, tension, and insomnia, barbiturates or "downers" are depressants that slow down the central nervous system and produce a relaxed state in the user. Muscles relax, resulting in slurred speech and an unsteady gait. Because they make the user groggy, s/he can forget how many pills were taken and accidentally take more, resulting in a drug overdose. Barbiturates can be addictive if taken for a long enough time, or fatal if taken in large amounts. Overly large doses can put the part of the brain that controls breathing to sleep, resulting in death. Barbiturates also can be deadly when combined with alcohol. Common barbiturates often have an "al" suffix (Seconal or Nembutal) or are given nicknames according to their colors ("black beauties," "blue angels").

Tranquilizers

Tranquilizers, which are prescribed to help people deal with anxiety and to treat some forms of mental illness, are the most widely abused depressant prescription drugs. Ativan, Librium, Miltown, Valium, and Xanax are some well-known tranquilizers. People can become dependent on tranquilizers because, with withdrawal, unpleasant feelings return.

Stimulants

Stimulants, which increase brain activity, are designed to make a person more alert.

Amphetamines

Amphetamines, also known as "uppers" or "pep pills," are stimulants that make the user feel alert and energetic. Amphetamines are prescribed for short-term weight control, lethargy, attention-deficit disorder with hyperactivity, and to keep a person alert. Common uppers include such brand-name drugs as Dexedrine and Methedrine. Methedrine, nicknamed "speed," is considered the most dangerous. Crank, an illegal form of speed that appeared in the 1980s, is covered in Chapter 12.

Stimulants have a high abuse potential because their stimulant effect is followed by a letdown period characterized by fatigue and depression. To relieve this letdown, users take another dose, which can become a vicious cycle. When abused, stimulants can also cause violence and mental illness. Additionally, there is some concern that use stunts a child's growth.

Prescription Cough Medicine

While not as freely accessible as over-the-counter cough medicines, prescription cough medicines are far more dangerous to the youngster who abuses them. Most contain not only alcohol but also codeine, a strong narcotic that alleviates pain and suppresses coughs. Codeine is habit forming because, even though the prescribed amounts are small the doses are concentrated.

Ritalin—A New Drug of Abuse?

Ritalin has been around for a long time, but only recently has become widely prescribed for youngsters diagnosed with

Attention Deficit Disorder (ADD) or Attention Deficit Hyperactivity Disorder (ADHD). Symptoms of these disorders include a short attention span, inability to focus attention, hyperactivity, and impulsive behavior. Ritalin, the brand name for Methylphenidate hydrochloride, is a central nervous system stimulant. While the prescription of a stimulant to treat hyperactive children may seem counterproductive, in fact the effect is just the opposite: The stimulant generally calms the child.

The use of Ritalin is controversial because of a growing concern about whether it is being properly prescribed to treat actual medical problems or if it is overprescribed simply to control undesirable behavior that has its roots in other, nonmedical causes. According to the Drug Enforcement Administration, there has been a huge increase in the U.S. production and consumption of Methylphenidate hydrochloride. An estimated 1.5 million American children are on the drug—2.8 percent of all Americans under the age of 19—double the number since 1990. Whether or not your youngster is a candidate for Ritalin is something you should discuss with a pediatrician or physician. However, the DEA points out that methylphenidate can lead to "severe psychological dependence."

According to Drug Enforcement Administration reports, kids are crushing their Ritalin and snorting it. Or, they are not taking the pill at all and, instead, selling it to other youngsters for $5 to $10 apiece. Ritalin abuse is becoming so prevalent that the federal government is conducting conferences that are coordinated by the DEA for parents, prevention specialists, pharmacists, physicians, and educators. If Ritalin is prescribed for your child, you should closely supervise how your child takes the medicine. Usually, one pill is taken in the morning and a second in the afternoon, often at school. Ideally, the medication should be taken under the watchful eye of the school nurse who administers medicines to youngsters who are under a doctor's care. The reality is that budget cuts have eliminated the school nurse at many schools. Teachers cannot be responsible for monitoring how medicines are taken.

Antidepressants

The new antidepressants Prozac, Zoloft, and Paxil, are exceptionally popular among adults who report that they correct a
chemical imbalance in the brain that causes depression. The
treatment of adolescents and young adults with antidepressant
drugs is another alarming trend in medicine. Advocates claim
that clinical depression often begins in the formative years and
goes undetected until a person reaches their twenties and thirties
or suffers some psychological trauma. While there may be valid
medical reasons to administer antidepressants to a youngster, a
second and even third medical opinion might be warranted with
powerful drugs such as these.

If your child does require one of these new generation of
antidepressants to cope, make sure that you personally dispense
the drug and that it is not taken to school. If you or someone in
your family other than your child is under a doctor's care and
taking these pills, be aware that youngsters are now starting to
abuse them. So far there have been few reported incidents of kids
abusing these powerful psychotropic medicines in the same way
that Ritalin is reportedly being snorted or sold, but drug abuse is
faddish, and one substance is fashionable for a while until
another emerges to take its place.

Dr. Ann Dietrich, a Columbus, Ohio, pediatrician who spe-
cializes in emergency medicine, has seen some cases of "kids
doing combo drugs like Effexor, which is an antidepressant, a
treatment for attention-deficit disorder, and an amphetamine for
getting high. Teenage girls abuse them because the amphetamine ingredient helps them lose weight.

Solutions

What can you do to avert accidental ingestion or abuse of over-
the-counter and prescription drugs by your children?

Find a secure place to store medicines.

If your children are very young, the hazards are obvious. Medicines of all kinds should be kept out of reach and out of sight. "The most common victims of poisoning [and accidental drug ingestions] are young children," says Sven Normann, director of the Florida Poison Information Center at Tampa General Hospital. He reports that 60 percent of the poison patients are less than five years of age, with the majority being 12 to 36 months old. "These are kids getting into purses or into medicines either left out on the counter or found in the medicine cabinet."

"It's not a frequent problem," says pharmacist Mark Hobbs, "but very young kids see their parents take a handful of colorful pills in the morning and they think it's candy." Depending on their age, a kid's thought processes do not separate use from abuse. Even when the child takes his or her own daily vitamin, a youngster does not understand the differences among pills, which can lead to some grave, even fatal mistakes—depending on the drug and the amount consumed.

Sweep your home clean of outdated and unused drugs and medicines.

Avoid risks and temptations by disposing of any out-of-date drugs or prescription medicines along with those that are no longer being taken for a specific illness. Do not stockpile prescription medicines because you feel a previous condition may return some day. Most likely, your doctor will prescribe a newer, more effective medicine, a different dosage or frequency.

The best solution can be summed up in one word: education.

It starts with you and your attitudes and behaviors toward drugs. "If parents are teaching their children to solve their problems with pills, then it's really the parents behavior we need to change," says Joye Ann Billow, professor of pharmaceutical sciences at South Dakota State University. When parents consistently resort to pill popping or drug taking to cure a variety of ills or symptoms, youngsters begin to think that this is an accept-able and normal behavior. Unwittingly you are communicating to your kids that drugs are a quick solution for making you feel better. Worse yet are instances when, in an effort to persuade children to take some medicine, parents tell them that chewable aspirin or some other pediatric drug is "candy." This sends a powerful—and wrong—message that drugs are candy.

As reiterated throughout this book, kids are impressionable and mom and dad are role models. Children think they are doing the right thing or acting grown-up when they emulate their parents.

Rosemary's Story

Rosemary K. of Baton Rouge, Louisiana, is a divorced mom and dental hygienist who is on her feet all day. She suffers chronic pain in her hip from an old injury. "My hip hurts every morning, and some days I can barely get out of bed." Rosemary got in the habit of asking Leanne, her seven-year-old daughter, to bring her Vicodin, a prescription pain killer, every morning along with a glass of water.

"I never thought anything about it until the day I got a call from the school nurse," recalls Rosemary. Leanne was caught with two Vicodins and was going to share one with another second grader. "She told her teacher that her mother took one every morning and it always made her feel good for the rest of the day. She didn't see anything wrong with taking the pill. Thank God, she didn't [take it]."

At first Rosemary was angry that Leanne stole her pills and took them to school. Then she felt guilty. "It never dawned on me to explain why I was taking the pills and why she should never touch them."

Educating your child about medicines is an ongoing process, not a single conversation. The Non-Prescription Drug Manufacturers Association, whose members make an estimated 150,000 to 300,000 different sizes and strengths of over-the-counter drugs, promotes full-disclosure labeling and urges consumers to read labels, to study ingredients, and to heed any warnings. But how many preteens or teens, let alone adults, actually do?

Explain to your young child that medicine is not a treat but a treatment to cure an illness.

With preschool and young children, explain that the proper use of medicine is a key to good health, just like brushing your teeth. Use the word "medicine" to refer to legitimate treatment products. The word "drug" should only be used when referring to illicit drugs, stresses the National Council on Patient Information and Education.

Explain to children that medicines should never be taken without mom or dad's supervision.

The only exceptions to this rule should be a trusted relative or adult who may care for your child when you are away. If a child is being treated for a medical condition and you are not at home when the medicine should be given, make sure that a responsible adult has the proper instructions. Also, be sure to tell your child never to take any medicines (or anything, for that matter) offered to them by strangers.

The following are some other key points that should be explained to children.

♦ To be effective, medicines must be taken in precise doses at specific times for certain periods of time. Anyone who takes a medicine without knowing and following these directions or instructions can hurt themselves.

♦ Taking medicine when you are healthy and not ill can make you sick. Explain that prescription medicines are prescribed by a doctor and prepared by a pharmacist to treat a specific illness for one person; people do not take other people's medicine because it can hurt them, and it is against the law. Adolescents and young teens who may deliberately abuse a medicine should understand that medicines have powerful side-effects that can produce a range of different results— from a mildly unpleasant feeling to serious physical and mental reactions.

+ When your youngster is old enough to understand, read labels with them and discuss ingredients.

+ Explain that some medicines are not individually prepared by pharmacists but are manufactured and sold in drug stores because they can be used by more than one person—pain relievers and cold medicines are good examples. Emphasize that these are medicines, too, and they are only to be taken when symptoms warrant their use, and only when mom or dad determines that they should have them.

Differentiate between curative and preventative substances.

Although both may be in pill form, they are designed for very different purposes. Medicines are designed as curative substances and should not be taken unless you are sick. Vitamins, on the other hand, are preventative substances designed to promote good health.

If you take medicines regularly, explain why to your children. David Nevins, executive vice president of the American Ambulance Association, says parents on medication should candidly say, "We're taking this for a reason. You don't have to take this because you don't have the same reason." Just don't make it a mystery.

Educate yourself about the potential problems of prescription and over-the-counter drugs.

Parents who plan to talk to their kids about medicines should do some homework. As mentioned previously, there are fads in drug use. Your neighborhood pharmacist can be a strong ally and resource. Pharmacists are aware of commonly abused drugs and can assist you in identifying pills and other substances that you may find in your youngster's possession.

Few people know that Syrup of Ipecac is a new drug of abuse. It is a craze among teenage girls, who abuse it to keep off weight. A teenage girl will eat a pizza, ingest the syrup to regurgitate, vomit, then take a laxative. Continually repeating this process can injure the heart, stomach, and other organs.

Explain about medicines calmly. Do not lecture, threaten, or use scare tactics.

Out of sight and out of reach may prevent accidental ingestions, but it is not going to deter the child or teen who wants to try drugs. "Young teens get medicines from medicine cabinets or from mail-order pharmacies or from their friends in school," says Sven Normann, a Florida Poison Information Center Director. Parents must take the time to explain the facts of life about medicines and other legal drugs to their children. Kids want facts. Teens who may be tempted to abuse medicines should get a straightforward, unemotional warning about the potential dangers. When a child reaches the teen years, s/he typically becomes more rebellious. As a result, your message has to be stronger because they will be making informed choices. One fact they probably do not know is that prescription medicines may have the same narcotics in them that are also sold illegally on the street, but these narcotics are used as ingredients, in conjunction with other ingredients, to treat a specific condition. Perhaps the strongest way to get the message across is to point out that medicines and other legal drugs are safe—when taken as directed and in the proper dose. Two Advils are perfectly safe to alleviate a headache, but fifty Advils may potentially be lethal.

Adolescents will often abuse more than one drug at a time and should know the worst-case scenarios. Dr. Robert Moore, professor of pharmaceutical science at Samford University in Birmingham, Alabama, does not mince words: "A tranquilizer or anti-anxiety medicine is a depressant to the central nervous system. It's like alcohol in a tablet form. If you take them and also start drinking, you have two central nervous system depressants going at the same time and it could lead to death."

Concluding Thoughts

This may sound like the ABC's of parenting, but the fact is that most of us learn about medicines by trial and error. According to Dr. Patricia Bush, a professor emeritus of pharmacological sociology at Georgetown University Medical School, "This is a common, everyday activity for parents—teaching kids about medicines, but there is nothing in health education that teaches people about responsible use of everyday medicines." Typically, the only children who know about medicines are kids with certain medical conditions like asthma, diabetes, or some other chronic ailment that requires daily treatment.

When used as directed, either administered under a doctor's care or give by a parent who follows the doctor's advice or the directions on the label, drugs are usually safe and helpful. But drugs, whether prescription or nonprescription, are only safe when they are used as directed.

11

Steroids and "Sports" Drugs: A No-Win, Fast Way to Lose

One way to keep kids off drugs, many parents believe, is to get them involved in sports. Build their bodies, their competitive spirit, their will to win, and they will avoid anything that harms their health. Plus, kids who play sports associate with other athletically inclined kids and steer clear of the "druggies and stoners."

Unfortunately, this is pure fantasy sometimes. Driven, compulsive young athletes who want to pump up their strength, size, and speed virtually overnight can be the most desperate users. In their obsessive quest for fame, victory, physical conditioning, and, often, parental attention and recognition at any cost, some kids are habitually swallowing or injecting anabolic steroids, and their parents are none the wiser.

Athletes are supposed to embody excellence, sportsmanship, and fair play. And many do. But some youngsters, eager to be the best they can be as quickly as possible, will take shortcuts with drugs like anabolic steroids and human growth hormones that promote rapid muscle development.

Unless you were a competitive athlete, chances are you do not know about anabolic steroids. Why? Because traditionally, the media focused on the more visible and more dangerous drugs—marijuana, angel dust, heroin, cocaine, and methamphetamine. In the 1960s, when pop cultural figures were singing the praises of getting high, you never heard an athlete talk about using drugs to enhance performance—shooting steroids in his leg muscle to help him bench press an extra 50 pounds of iron or to stop a fullback. Future All-Americans do not cheat, or fool with Mother Nature. Wrong. Today with sports commanding huge audiences and sports figures receiving adulation and huge salaries, the pressure on a kid with potential is enormous.

And that pressure starts long before college superstars are wooed by professional teams. High-school freshmen who want to make their football team may to experiment with steroids to accelerate growth. "They may not want to be bodybuilders per se," says Marcel Pappalardo, a Gold's Gym manager in Arlington, Virginia, and former high-school wrestler, "but you find them in the gym at 14 or 15 where they are exposed to the culture."

The time to watch your child, he advises, is over the summer. "They're [users] getting younger and younger these days. They think they're too small and they want to be a big high-school jock and make the team. They've heard [about steroids] from other guys who have gained 20 pounds over the summer and 15 pounds of it is muscle."

Only recently has the general public become aware of the issue, due largely to media coverage about the use of steroids and growth hormones by Olympic athletes in their continuing quest to set new athletic records. One of the first major publicized incidents of steroid use in athletic competition occurred in the 1988 Olympics when Ben Johnson beat Carl Lewis and set a new Olympic record in the 100-meter dash. A few days after the event, traces of an anabolic steroid were found in Ben Johnson's urine. He admitted that he resorted to the use of drugs because of the pressure to win.

You may be surprised to learn that it is not just competitive athletes who use steroids. "The Drug Enforcement Administration estimates that there are 3 million steroid users in the United States alone. The majority of those are believed to be bodybuilders or adolescents trying to impress girls with bulging biceps (an estimated 600,000 users are teenagers)."[1] An ongoing study conducted by the University of Michigan and funded by The National Institute of Drug Abuse reveals that:[2]

- Almost 2 percent of eighth-graders (12- to-14-year-old kids) are taking steroids to pump up their developing bodies.
- 5 to 12 percent of male high school students and 1 percent of female students have used steroids by the time they are seniors. [The DEA does not track how many high school students keep using steroids after they graduate, but since the "benefits" disappear when users stop taking the drugs, there are powerful incentives to keep abusing.]
- The American Heart Association estimates that at least half of Division 1 college football players have used steroids over substantial periods of time, which means they probably started using in high school.

The New Users

Steroids are dangerous drugs because they do not initially space out a youngster or get them high. What is more, the teenage boys and the smaller percentage of teenage girls who take them are usually high achievers. Frederick C. Hatfield, Ph.D., of the International Sports Science Association, reports that youngsters' oft-quoted reasons for using steroids include:

- Fear of not making the team or getting noticed by pro scouts
- Peer pressure
- Need for acceptance
- Dares and/or challenges to use
- Competition for girls
- Concern about inability to compete if other guys are using
- To improve personal appearance or performance, resulting in increased self-esteem
- Athletes' historical use of performance-enhancing aids to gain the elusive competitive edge (Many highly paid, highly

publicized, and highly talented athletes have admitted to or been caught using anabolic steroids.)

- Feeling invincible or immune to the harmful effects of anabolic steroids and other sports drugs
- Lack of belief in the medical community's risk warnings

Anabolic steroids are sold in gym locker rooms or around the facilities. Richard Aubrey, president of Body Factor, personal training and injury rehabilitation consultants in San Francisco, says it is virtually impossible to find a steroid-free gym, adding that older bodybuilders are often "dealers" to younger members.

"Anyone seriously playing a competitive sport in high school or college can be exposed to or offered anabolic steroids."

Arnold Schwarznegger freely admits he used steroids to get huge, but the five-time winner of the Mr. Universe title is now adamantly opposed to them. In the *Encyclopedia of Modern Body Building*, Schwarznegger writes, "teenagers should never take anabolic steroids in an attempt to build up the size and strength of their muscle structure. During the teenage years, young males are already in their most anabolic [growth] state, with testosterone flooding the system. Adding synthetic anabolic at this point is totally unnecessary." Unfortunately, Schwarznegger's message to stay drug-free and to build your body the old-fashioned way—by wise nutrition and muscle-straining workouts—is often overshadowed by the fact that he is an internationally renowned film star commanding big money, and many equate his achievements and success with the use of steroids.

Steroid dealers do not just ply their trade at gyms and health clubs. They often sell in and around schools, out of cars, and even their own bedrooms when their parents are not at home. Adults sell to college and high-school kids and some parents even supply their own kids and their pals. Just because your child is not an aspiring Mr. or Ms. America, All-American gridiron star, or a body-beautiful fanatic, do not think anabolic steroids are not a potential problem. Virtually anyone seriously playing a competitive sport in high school or college can be exposed to or offered anabolic steroids, claiming it is an "edge," not really a drug.

The Appearance Factor

Twenty years ago, only jocks were "juiced" or "sauced," using anabolic steroids to be bigger and stronger. Today there is a new and growing group of steroid users and abusers: teenagers who will never play competitive sports or work out with weights. Their sole concern is personal appearance and wanting to impress and attract the opposite sex. These drug abusers are seeking physical perfection and the self-confidence that comes with knowing they are strong, hard-bodied, and lean—muscular with less fat. As a result, they do not consider themselves hard-core drug users. It is this rationalization you must address.

What Is An Anabolic Steroid?

Few people even know *what* an anabolic steroid is. "Anabolic" means tissue building, and anabolic steroids are synthetic male hormones or synthetic testosterone, a chemical replication of the natural male sex hormone. The human body produces many natural steroids. Among these are the male and female hormones that determine gender and control growth from puberty through adulthood. The body may not function properly if it produces too much or too little of any hormone. Nature's testosterone affects the body in two different ways:

1. *anabolically,* which stimulates growth, and
2. *androgenically,* which increases the male sexual characteristics (facial and body hair, deeper voice, sexual drive).

Steroids are constructed to maximize the anabolic or growth effects and to minimize the androgenic effect.

Steve's Story

The Sinister Side of Steroids— An Ex-Abuser's Personal View

Steve is 28, an environmental health specialist, and healthy. He is also lucky. When he was in the eleventh grade, he was hooked on anabolic steroids. Although not physically addicted where his body craved the drug daily, he was psychologically dependent. It gave him the self-confidence and strength he needed to play first-string varsity football at Cleveland High School in Reseda, California—and win.

Steve was 17-years-old and 165 pounds when he started taking steroids. He was switching positions from quarterback to outside linebacker and he needed to build muscle mass fast. A teammate's father—"a football fanatic and sort of a seedy guy"—got him the drugs. Called Dianabol or "D-Ball," a bottle of one hundred "orals" [pills] cost fifty dollars in 1988.

Did Steve know the risks of taking anabolic steroids? No. His mother and father had divorced when he was eight and his dad did not keep in touch, so he had no male figure in his life. He hid his abuse from his mother and his coach. "Only a few other players, close friends, knew I was taking steroids, and they were using too." Before long, Steve was injecting the drug into his body.

"No one told me about the risks." He was not scared. "I loved them at first because they worked. I gained thirty pounds of muscle over the summer and weighed 200 pounds by the time football season started. I never felt in better shape. Before (steroids), I was bench pressing 225 pounds and went to 310 pounds. I was quicker, too. Did the 40-yard dash in 4.9 seconds, down from 5.4 seconds."

Steve insists he did not take enough steroids to suffer the serious side effects—shrunken testicles, hair loss, liver damage and puffy "chipmunk" cheeks. He stopped when his mother discovered the drugs in his bedroom; he kept them between his mattress and box springs. "She found them but thought they belonged to someone else. I think she was in denial—couldn't believe that I would take illegal drugs. She was really mad and flushed them down the toilet." After that, Steve switched to amphetamines because they were cheap.

Older and wiser today, Steve regrets using anabolic steroids and considers himself "incredibly fortunate" that he did not suffer any permanent damage. A bachelor, he claims he would never let his son take the drugs and would explain the risks "before he started competing in sports and heard about them from other players. I'd want him to give his best possible performance—drug free. Still, with all the emphasis on sports and winning today, I can tell you, steroids are the sinister, silent epidemic."

Human Growth Hormone

"The most popular substances among elite athletes these days are Human Growth Hormone (hGH), erythropoietin (EPO), and designer steroids."[3] Human Growth Hormone is a favorite among male weight lifters and athletes. According to Dr. Bob Goldman, president of the American College of Sports Medicine and coauthor of *Death In The Locker Room II*, "Athletes are always looking for new alternatives, and the quick way to pack on muscle, and unfortunately they are looking toward growth hormone as this new panacea, even though it probably is ineffective for that purpose."

hGH is produced by the pituitary gland. At present, the only legal use of hGH is to treat dwarfism, which is caused by a disorder of the pituitary gland that results in a deficiency of this hormone. hGH suppliers, who obtain the natural hormone from cadavers or a synthetic version from labs, have little trouble dealing it to athletes because there currently are no tests that can detect hGH or EPO.

Chances are your child will not be exposed to hGH, but s/he might be persuaded to try it if young, impressionable, and a hero worshipper, especially since the name of the hormone does not sound risky to a youngster who is small in stature, naive, and who wants to speed up the growth process for any one of a variety of reasons.

It is extremely unlikely that teens will abuse hGH flagrantly, but, if they do, it could lead to grotesque physical distortions such as acromegaly, also known as "Frankenstein Syndrome," in which facial features are enlarged, the head and jaw becomes elongated, hands and feet grow, and the abuser's height can shoot up. Large doses of the hormone can interrupt the body's metabolism, attack the heart, and cause death.

A huge stumbling block for teens is the price of hGH, which traditionally runs $500 to $1,500 for a six- to 10-week cycle. Experts say the availability of synthetic hGH is a real threat to youngsters because demand for it will likely drive down the price and, thus, make it more accessible.

Alternatives to Anabolic Steroids

Other known alternatives to anabolic steroids include Clenbuterol (a drug used by veterinarians to promote muscle growth in livestock), Winstrol-V (the "V" denotes veterinary use), gonadotropyl-c (extracted from the urine of pregnant women), Sostenon 250, Spiropent, Proviron, Maxigan 50%, and Gamma Hydroxybutric Acid (GHB). The latter is legal and sold over the counter in drug and health food stores as a sleeping aid, but GHB, though touted by athletes as a stimulant for muscle growth, can send a kid into a coma if s/he overdoses on what is perceived to be a harmless tablet. Far from harmless, GHB can cause vomiting, dizziness, tremors, seizure-like body movements, difficult breathing, reduced heartbeat, and low blood pressure levels.

The Dangerous Effects of Steroids

When people use synthetic hormones they are upsetting the body's natural balance and there can be serious consequences. Synthetic anabolic steroids produce the same physical changes in a body as the male sex hormone testosterone, the key difference being that the flow is not controlled by the brain. Synthetic testosterone produces physical changes in a way that is out of control. Also, use of synthetic testosterone may cause the body to stop producing its natural supply of the male hormone testosterone while it is still producing its supply of female hormones.

Some effects are the same for males and females:

- Rapid weight gain—adding muscle mass, not fat
- Excess body and facial hair
- Flushed, yellowish, oily skin
- Face breaks out in acne, which may also appear on chest, back and shoulders. Severe acne breakouts can result in permanent scarring.
- Voice deepens
- Changes in genital size
- Changes in blood pressure and cholesterol levels
- Joint stiffness, pain, swelling
- Depression and psychological withdrawal
- Insomnia, irritability
- Feelings of frustration and anxiety
- Psychotic symptoms (paranoia, delusions, hallucinations)

Other effects are gender-specific. Male steroid users lose physical signs of maleness and female steroid users lose physical signs of femaleness.

Repeated use has the following effects in males:

- Shrinkage of sex organs
- Breast enlargement, males begin developing breasts
- Thinning of scalp hair
- Sterility

Even though they produce natural testosterone in their ovaries, synthetic testosterone affects girls in the opposite way it affects boys. Regular or short, intensive use gives girls an "irreversible masculinity," says Fredrick C. Hatfield of the International Sports Science Association.

Repeated use has the following effects in females:

- Diminishes breasts, females lose breast size.
- Produces excess facial and body hair
- Enlarges sex organs
- Irregular (or zero) menstrual cycle (Girls abusing anabolic steroids have fewer menstrual cycles and may skip a period for several months.)

"Anabolic steroids can actually stunt their growth because they were never intended to be used by 14- to 16-year-olds whose growth plates are still developing," says Richard Aubrey, of Body Factor. Steroid abuse throws the body chemistry out of whack during puberty and early adolescence, a time when "their own natural hormones are on the rampage."

Steroid abuse can cause liver damage, cancer, and heart disease. Heart disease is the leading cause of death among steroid users, followed by cancer of the liver. Synthetic steroids can cause blood vessels to clog, resulting in high blood pressure, strokes, and death. Anabolic steroids in pill form can be lethal to your liver because a normal 200 milligram dose must be absorbed by the liver in one day. Injectable steroids are formulated to have longer life spans, usually up to 17 days. They bypass the liver and go directly into the bloodstream.

"Heart disease is the leading cause of death among steroid users."

Yet for this *benefit,* a youngster often has to plunge a needle 1 to 2 inches into a muscle, usually the gluteus maximus—the rump.

However, let's be honest. Certain synthetic steroids, when prescribed by a doctor and supplied by a pharmacist, can be beneficial when used to treat asthma, arthritis, breast cancer, the chronic blood disease called Lupus, and AIDS patients who are suffering from "wasting syndrome." Synthetic anabolic steroids, on the other hand, are flat out illegal.

Telltale Signs of Steroid Use

A signal of anabolic steroid abuse is uncharacteristically aggressive, on-edge behavior—anger, hostility, user may adopt a new swaggering gait.

While anabolic steroids are supposed to work on the body, they can upset brain chemistry. Steroids, for instance, boost cortisol, the body's principal stress hormone. Youngsters can suddenly become aggressive, even violent, sometimes psychotic. Usually, this accompanies heavy steroid use, but depending on the child's physical and psychological makeup, even low-level users can fly off into "roid rages," a term coined to describe the violent outbursts that steroid users can fly into for no apparent reason.

Excessive amount of time spent at the gym, lifting weights.

Needle marks and punctures in legs, buttocks.

New words and phrases in their vocabulary.

Some examples include "on the juice," "on the sauce," "on the roids," "popping," "oils," "waters," "cycling, "stacking," "pyramiding." "Cycling" is a practice in which a kid uses steroids from six to fourteen weeks, then either stops or cuts back the dosage for the same length of time. "Stacking" involves using different anabolic steroids at the same time, figuring it speeds up muscle growth. "Pyramiding" involves using different steroids in varying dose size and is exceptionally dangerous. Bodybuilders, weight lifters, and football lineman can be the worst abusers because size and strength are personal assets they desire and they often take the highest doses as well as "stack" and "pyramid."

Overly preoccupied with appearance, flexing in front of mirrors, friends, family.

Excessive sexual activity.

Heavy doses of synthetic testosterone supercharges an already increased libido and can trigger sexual activity that might otherwise be constrained.

Preventive Measures

In the face of skepticism, peer pressures, and the competitive demands on children, what should a parent do? How should a parent explain the risks of steroid abuse to a kid who plans to use the drugs for three months and hears from locker-room scuttlebutt that they are not physically addictive?

Explain that a user must keep using steroids to get their benefits.

Gold Gym's manager Pappalardo says inexperienced users think they are quick, permanent fixes that can be easily started and stopped. "But parents should tell them that the truth is unless you are taking steroids all the time, you will deflate. It is better to get into a fitness program early, stick with it and not take any shortcuts."

It is up to parents to stress how anabolic steroids can upset the internal chemistry of young, developing bodies, especially the endocrine or hormonal system— sometimes permanently.

Dr. Linn Goldberg, professor of medicine at Oregon Health Sciences University, heads a program called ATLAS (Adolescents

Training and Learning to Avoid Steroids). Dr. Goldberg and his ATLAS speakers tell kids to "look at all the great things that can happen to you when you take anabolic steroids. They can directly affect your heart, elevate your so-called bad LDL (low-density lipoprotein) cholesterol level, lower your good HDL (high-density lipoprotein) cholesterol level, make your blood clot easier, produce cysts on your liver, cause jaundice, uncontrolled aggression and even psychosis (like going crazy), stunt your height and close off the growth plates in your long bones." To emphasize the risk, his organization uses the following analogy: "Steroids may be the quickest way to build muscle mass, but then jumping is the fastest way to get down a ten-story building." Dr. Goldberg says the most persuasive messenger is another athlete because peer to would-be peer communication works, and he encourages concerned parents to seek one out if they feel their child is susceptible.

If your teenage son or daughter is spending an excessive amount of time at the gym working out, doing weight training or serious body building, get to know the manager and staff.

Find out if the gym or health club tolerates the use of steroids. Do they have a policy against using, and, if so, is it enforced? "There is always someone doing steroids in a club, but if we find out about it here, they're ejected," says Marcel Pappalardo of Gold's Gym.

Reinforce that it takes time and commitment to be your personal best.

A good message for the competitive youngster says Pappalardo is the following: "People who take drugs including steroids are cheaters and they will be cheating in everything they do. They're lazy—they are not pure competitors in the gym or on the field—and eventually it will catch up with them." Aubrey echoes this sentiment: "The number one job with kids who are concerned with strength and appearance is to help them get in the habit of regular exercise, aerobic and supervised physical training, and healthy, balanced eating. Kids who believe and practice this philosophy for living will almost always avoid steroids and other drugs. It's a matter of pride."

Parents of kids who are athletically minded or obsessively concerned about their appearance, weight, and physique should sit down with them and explain the risk/benefit ratio of steroid use.

Ask if the benefit of taking steroids is worth the risk. Is it worth the potential shame of testing positive on a random, surprise urine test at school, work, or in sports competition? Are they willing to risk numerous physical side-effects of serious steroid use that often cannot be masked? Are they aware of the very real risk that they could be ingesting a contaminated chemical bootlegged in from halfway around the world?

Anabolic steroids have been a controlled substance in the United States since 1988. Anabolic steroids are usually manufactured and smuggled in from Germany or Mexico. Mexico accounts for 85 to 90 percent of all illicit steroids on the U.S. market according to an agent with the California Department of Justice's Bureau of Narcotics Enforcement. Since synthetic steroids cannot be legally produced in the U.S., no government agency monitors laboratory conditions or the purity of the drugs produced. Thus, the steroids available in this country can be contaminated or even fake—bogus pills and potions sold to the naive. "Half the anabolic steroids sold today are fake," contends Dr. Goldberg. "They're manufactured in unsupervised labs and could have bacteria in them. You don't know what you're ingesting or injecting."

Make them aware of the penalties for use or possession.

As a result of the Anabolic Steroids Control Act of 1990, anyone caught selling or possessing these substances can be arrested, jailed, and/or fined. The Drug Enforcement Administration treats anabolic steroids and anyone who abuses or deals in them the same way as it does cocaine addicts and traffickers: severely. Penalties are extremely harsh. Under recently stiffened federal laws, the maximum sentence for a first offense for trafficking in anabolic steroids is five years in prison and a $250,000 fine. The second offense can send the dealer to prison for up to 10 years plus a $500,000 fine. Simple possession of illegally obtained steroids carries a maximum penalty of one year in federal prison and a minimum $1,000 fine. This is not a wrist-slapping offense for any youngster.

Monitor your kids' sources of income.

This is just as important as keeping tabs on their whereabouts, friends, grades, and sports performances. Based on his research and experience in the field, Dr. Goldberg says youngsters who abuse steroids are always chronically short of cash. "Habits" range from $35 to $200 a month and up. That is a substantial sum for a high school student who is training, practicing, scrimmaging, or working out while other youngsters may have part-time, after-school jobs. How does a youthful steroid abuser get the cash to pay for these drugs? The same way any adolescent drug user does—stealing money from you or others, borrowing from friends, getting in debt with their dealers, and selling, trading, and bartering anything of value.

In Conclusion

Steroid abusers observe a code of silence. Only teammates, close friends, and their suppliers know for sure that they are using. Ironically, all know it is illegal, but somehow they rationalize it as "whatever it takes to win" or "it's my choice." Even former adult users are convinced that their use of steroids was not as bad as hard-core addicts' use of cocaine, heroin, or methamphetamine because they did not get physically addicted. Their self-image was of the strong athlete, the perfect body, the glamorous figure—not a druggie.

Kids usually don't try steroids until their teen years—around 14 or 15 at the earliest. Teens who abuse steroids usually go undetected in the beginning because their parents simply cannot imagine that their presumably healthy, athletic children would knowingly put something dangerous in their bodies. Give them the facts of life—and the risks—of pumping artificial, illegal drugs into their bodies. Then keep an eye peeled for telltale signs of possible use. It may sound melodramatic, but Saturday afternoon's football hero can be Sunday morning's jail inmate if it is discovered that his game-winning performance was powered by illegal anabolic steroids. *Avoid steroids* is the message that parents, teachers, coaches, and gym instructors must get through to impressionable youngsters bent on hurrying up their growth.

In today's fast-paced, technologically oriented world, youngsters are bombarded with a sense of instant gratification. Many have a hard time understanding the "no pain, no gain" concept of physical and emotional development. With superstar athletes leaping off the sports pages to the front pages, from weekend TV to prime time and all the way to Hollywood fame and fortune, today, more than ever, it is important for you to edit for your youngsters legendary Green Bay Packer coach Vince Lombardi's anthem: "Winning isn't the only thing. Winning (fairly and legally) is everything."

12

Illegal Stimulants: Cocaine, Crack, Meth

A lthough many adults may have experimented with marijuana during their youth, chances are that only a small percentage of today's parents have encountered the strongest of the illegal stimulants—cocaine, crack, and meth. Ten to twenty years ago, the use of powdered cocaine was confined largely to those who had the cash to afford it. During the 1980s, cocaine's offspring—"crack" cocaine appeared on the scene as a cheap high that anyone could afford. What started as a big city ghetto drug soon became a nationwide problem as drug rings fanned out across America and set up sales organizations to bring coke, crack, and the new designer or "club" drugs to smaller cities, towns, communities, and the suburbs. Among their prime customers: kids looking for a thrill and without the will or the skills to say "no." Now, hard-core stimulant drugs are available everywhere.

What Are Stimulants?

Stimulants are drugs that act on the central nervous system and temporarily quicken the functional activity of an organ or some vital process. Not all stimulants are unlawful. There are natural, legal, and illegal stimulants. Adrenaline is a natural stimulant produced by the body and triggered by stress. Legal stimulants include nicotine and caffeine. Nicotine is the primary stimulant in cigarettes, cigars, chewing tobacco, and pipe tobacco. Caffeine, another legal stimulant, is found in chocolate, coffee, tea, and some soft drinks. It boosts alertness and reduces fatigue, at least temporarily, and lots of people rely on caffeine for a morning or afternoon energy lift. Judging from the proliferation of gourmet coffee shops nationwide, caffeine seems to be the fuel-du-jour for today's fast-track world. Caffeine is also an ingredient in many nonprescription drugs, such as appetite suppressants.

Alcohol, in its initial effect, can also act as a stimulant. Other stronger stimulants, federally regulated under the Controlled Substances Act, are lawfully prescribed to treat attention deficit disorders, narcolepsy, obesity, and other medical problems.

Illegal stimulants, classified by the federal government as drugs of abuse, include bootleg or nonprescription amphetamines, cocaine, crank, and designer drugs. They are far stronger and more addictive than legal stimulants, and much more harmful to kids. Users who experiment with them experience a sudden euphoria—that exhilarating rush or flash that addicts find irresistible. Those who want to duplicate this euphoric sensation will try it again and again or, in an attempt to feel twice as good, double or triple the doses. In a relatively short period of time this behavior can become physically and psychologically addictive. As part of the addiction process, the body develops a tolerance to the drug and the cravings force the abuser to use it more frequently and in increasing amounts to recapture the original euphoria. Once the user is hooked, s/he needs to feed their addiction to stave off a physical or psychological crash, which can bring about a combination of depression, anxiety, and total exhaustion. Here are the outlawed stimulants that your children are exposed to today.

Cocaine (Powdered)

According to the DEA, cocaine is the most potent stimulant of natural origin. Through a chemical process, it is extracted from the leaves of South American cocoa plants to produce a white crystalline powder. Cocaine can be snorted, injected, or smoked. Typically it is snorted up the nose from thin lines of powder arranged on a small mirror. It goes directly into the brain, delivering a rush in three to five minutes. Hard core addicts who want a quicker high will dissolve the powdered cocaine in water and inject it by needle into the bloodstream. Powdered cocaine cannot be smoked, but processed cocaine or "crack" can. Crack is chipped into small pieces and heated in a special pipe that vaporizes it so it can be inhaled, a technique known as freebasing.

If marijuana was the popular drug of the 1960s, powdered cocaine was the party drug of the late 70s and early 80s. In 1985, according to the National Household Survey on Drug Abuse, 8.5 million Americans were using it least once a month. Ten years later, by 1995, the same survey found that only 1.45 million people were regular users. The demand for powdered cocaine is still dropping. Typically, powdered cocaine is not a drug that is abused by children or young teens, unless they are from affluent families. Normally, if a kid starts to snort powdered coke, experimentation begins in the senior year of high school, first years of college, or on the lower rungs of a high-stress professional job.

Pure cocaine is a fantasy; criminals cut (dilute) it with powdered sugar, baking powder, talcum powder, scouring powder, and other ingredients. With any adulterated drug, there is always the risk of contamination and not knowing the potency of what you are getting. You have no idea what you are putting in your brain and body, regardless of the assurances you receive.

Drug popularity runs in cycles, and while powdered cocaine consumption is leveling off at the moment, there is no telling when it might stage a comeback. Because it is viewed as the drug of choice for the affluent and influential, it carries a certain cachet.

Crack Cocaine

If powdered cocaine is out of reach for your child because of the cost, crack cocaine is not. Crack or rock cocaine is cheaper to produce and thus cheaper to buy than powdered cocaine. The name crack comes from the cracking or popping sound that it makes when it is burned. "Crack first appeared in the mid 1980s and it made cocaine available to the masses," says a cocaine analyst for the Drug Enforcement Administration in Washington, D.C. "Crack is like fast food—cheap, plentiful and it made this [cocaine] elite, expensive drug available to anyone who had ten dollars."

> "Crack is like fast food— cheap, plentiful and it made this [cocaine] elite, expensive drug available to anyone who had ten dollars."

Crack looks like pink, white, or tan pebbles or crystalline rocks and can be manufactured anyplace in the United States, usually in abandoned apartments, trailers, houses (hence the term "crack houses"), or anywhere there is a stove. Adult criminals and older members of youth gangs take powdered cocaine, mix it with baking soda and water, and cook it at a high temperature until it turns into a base that sits and solidifies into a crystallized rock of cocaine. Small pieces are chipped off the rock and sold for as little as $10.

"Crack really grabbed hold in the inner city," says a DEA analyst, "and it ravaged people who abused it. The temporary rush is faster than powdered cocaine—instantaneous—but the high doesn't last as long. The "feel good" energy jolt of powdered coke lasts about 20 minutes versus 12 minutes for crack. The euphoria of crack quickly fades, so people binge to stay high, smoke crack over and over again and become almost immediately addicted."

Knowing the Risks

Kids initially get sucked into crack in one of several ways—as customers they are turned on to it by other kids who promise them the rush of pleasure and energy of cocaine for as little as $10. Dealers recruit kids to sell it but do not want their junior dealers to take the drug themselves, knowing that anyone who uses will steal and cheat to feed their addiction. Some kids work a couple hours in the afternoon for $10 to $15 an hour wearing a surgical mask and shaving crack off rocks of cocaine. As part of their job, they package crack in vials for adults and other kids to sell on the street. This arrangement is a little more difficult for parents to detect because kids won't exhibit the physical symptoms of abuse. But any alert parent who monitors their child's whereabouts should be suspicious when the youngster is several hours late from school or comes home with money in his pockets from a new job that he has never discussed with you. Even if they are not selling or using, as middlemen, they are committing a felony.

In what should be ongoing conversations with your children about the dangers of drugs, do not neglect to discuss the risks associated with cocaine use, even if you think your children would never use it. The following are the pertinent points to make.

Cocaine addiction is one of the toughest to break.

Cocaine is one of the hardest drug habits to kick. When addicts stop, "they often suffer from depression and anxiety, and the inability to experience pleasure from normally pleasurable activities," reports a spokesperson for the Partnership For a Drug-Free America. "This makes it extremely difficult for the recovering addict to stay clean. Cocaine takes over your life and causes you to lose interest in everything else. Research on monkeys has shown that animals will press a bar over 10,000 times for a single injection of cocaine and even choose cocaine over food and water.

Adult crack abusers almost always ruin their lives. "They burn up their life savings, prostitute themselves, forget about their jobs and families. Some addicts smoke crack nonstop over an entire weekend until their bodies give out."

Cocaine, particularly crack, is disastrous to the health of those who abuse it.

As a harsh, immediate stimulant to the central nervous system that acts on the "pleasure centers" of the brain, it triggers a quick-to-instant euphoria and a heightened sense of self-confidence. It also dilates the pupils, elevates blood pressure, heart rate, respiratory rate, and body temperature. Crack cocaine, because it is smoked and inhaled, is also damaging to the lungs.

The list of health risks and acute physical effects for cocaine abusers is long. Problems range from the nuisance of a runny or stuffy nose experienced by occasional users to the ulcerated mucous membranes and permanently damaged nasal passages suffered by chronic users who snort it. Anyone who shoots cocaine by injection is exposed to AIDS, hepatitis, or other diseases caused by contaminated needles.

Abusers also experience insomnia, loss of appetite, anxiety, irritability, restlessness, hallucinations, paranoia, seizures, even heart attacks, cerebral hemorrhage, and respiratory failure. Abusers who die from the drug often overdose on it, but there is no specific antidote to counteract an accidental or deliberately large dose. Crack users who smoke at home can affect the lungs of small children living in the same home. Women who smoke crack while pregnant can deliver infants who are addicted at birth ("crack babies") or who will start life with health problems and a possible genetic predisposition to drug addiction.

The violence created in a community by the abuse of an incredibly powerful drug like crack is startling and often deadly and anyone is a potential victim.

When the inner cities became saturated with crack cocaine and prices started to drop, the drug rings moved from urban centers to smaller cities and towns where they could get higher prices. Criminals set up illegal money laundering and manufacturing operations and distribution infrastructures for selling other drugs to local residents. In moving their drug industry to these smaller cities they also brought violence with them.

It is illegal.

Possession or sale is a felony. Laws regarding the sale of cocaine typically stipulate jail time coupled with heavy fines.

Amphetamines

Among the most widely abused stimulants, amphetamines come in pill, capsule, or powder form. They are inexpensive and easily obtained through prescriptions. Amphetamines is a catch-all term for a class of stimulants or "uppers" that can be considered an artificial adrenaline. Their effects include alertness, energy, increased confidence, and loss of appetite. Side effects include hyperactivity, irritability, insomnia, cardiac irregularities, elevated blood pressure, and gastric disturbances. The drugs are easily abused and addiction can result in psychosis or death.

The first amphetamine was sold as an over-the-counter drug called Benzedrine to treat nasal congestion. Amphetamines were dispensed to American troops during World War II to keep them awake and energized in battle. Not long ago, "speed" was a catch-all slang term for pep pills. Some were illicit drugs, others legal diet pills popped by students to power them through the night as they crammed for final exams or churned out term papers. Soon, long-haul truck drivers, athletes, and students were taking amphetamines in pill form ("speed," "black beauties," "white bennies," "dexies," "beans") to keep them pumped, alert, and theoretically, at maximum performance levels. In the sixties, amphetamines were reclassified as a federally restricted drug sold only by prescription. The older class of amphetamines are still abused by students, but the current threat to youngsters is the more treacherous mutation—methamphetamine (meth).

Methamphetamine

On the street methamphetamine is called "synthetic cocaine" because it is manufactured, not developed from living plants. Some drug enforcement officials call it the "poor man's cocaine." The El Paso Intelligence Center, a national agency that sends narcotics information to law enforcement agencies worldwide says that it is popular because it is cheap and lasts longer than cocaine or crack cocaine. General Barry R. McCaffrey, director of the Office of National Drug Control Policy warns parents that "methamphetamine is a drug with particular appeal to students using it for recreation, to increase school performance, or to simply stay energized for long periods of time." High school adolescents see meth as an acceptable alternative to crack and a way to curb their appetites, control their weight, and energize themselves on demand.

It enters the brain faster than other amphetamines, producing a quicker, stronger high, and, thus, is more addictive. It cranks up your energy and self-confidence to superhuman heights. The jolt or the kick is so strong, so instantaneous and so fleeting, abusers desperate to repeat the pleasurable effects quickly become addicts. Meth addicts have been known to go without sleep for a week or longer. Some develop "methamphetamine psychosis": suffering from hallucinations or paranoia and becoming hostile and physically attacking anyone at the slightest provocation.

Meth comes in different forms, including as pills or a powder, and can be swallowed, injected or snorted. Many users prefer a smokable form of meth that contains hydrochloride and looks like clear chunky crystals of ice, hence the nicknames "crystal meth" or "ice."

Meth abuse is widening and is a huge problem for law enforcement. Around since the 1960s when it was popular with motorcycle gangs and thus earned its nickname "crank," meth is making a strong reemergence on the street owing to inexpensive manufacturing processes. After gaining a foothold in the West, sales of methamphetamines have been exploding and moving eastward. "Other drugs like marijuana, cocaine, or heroin come from plants and are usually smuggled in," says the methamphetamine coordinator for the Drug Enforcement Administration. "All it takes to make $10,000 worth of meth is $500 worth of chemicals and a trailer or some other clandestine lab. Drug traffickers realize they do not have to spend millions in overhead for pilots, boat handlers, paying thousands of peasants in Bolivia to pick leaves, or worry about customs officials."

How big is the problem? Immense. In 1994, the DEA seized 263 meth labs nationwide. In 1995, they busted 362 labs. In 1996, federal drug agents shut down 879 meth labs. In 1997, the DEA expects to close 1,300 labs and that does not include meth lab busts by state and local law enforcement. One federal drug official estimates that in 1997, the California Bureau of Narcotics alone will seize 1,000 clandestine methamphetamine labs located in trailers, RVs, garages, hotel and motel rooms, and vacant apartments. As one lawman puts it, "this isn't just an increase in labs. It's a dramatic explosion."

Not only is methamphetamine a health hazard for users, it is a safety hazard for dealers and for any innocent victims who may be nearby because of the highly volatile nature of the ingredients. Labs have blown up while meth is brewing on the stove and lives have been lost.

Addressing the Dangers

Make sure your children know these drugs are illegal.

Possession or sale is a felony. Laws regarding the sale of methamphetamine typically stipulate jail time coupled with heavy fines.

In talking with your kids, try to find out what they know about speed, crank, ice, or crystal meth and use those street terms.

These drugs are usually encountered in the teen years and high school seniors are not going to relate to a discussion peppered with scientific or pharmacological terms.

Spell out how these drugs affect their mind and body.
Those who take meth or any form of "speed" can suffer from:

- Schizophrenia or hallucinations, where you feel like you are losing your mind
- Convulsions
- Paranoia
- Sudden rise in body temperature to as high as 107-108 degrees, which can result in irreversible brain damage,
- Impaired speech
- Jerking and twitching
- Nausea and cramps
- Dry and itchy skin plus acne and other skin sores

Those are just the immediate possible side effects of doing meth. It can also cause panic, anxiousness, severe depression, lack of interest in food and friends, and aggressive behavior. Chronic usage causes fatal kidney and lung disorders, stroke, permanent psychological problems and even death.

Parents can also emphasize that meth is a drug youngsters should never, ever consider starting because the withdrawal process is agonizing. Going through a meth withdrawal includes severe craving, stomach cramps, vomiting, fatigue, anxiety, depression, insomnia, confusion, and memory loss that can last for a year or longer.

13

Designer Drugs, Heroin, and Hallucinogens

Criminals have no shortage of dangerous drugs to sell or cravings to satisfy. In fact, foreign drug suppliers are competing with outlaw chemists in the U.S. for market share. And with new drugs and old "favorites" flooding the streets and driving down prices, dealers are forced to cultivate new, loyal users in order to keep their cash flowing.

The following paragraphs will give you snapshots of other classes of drugs that are within the reach of kids today. They are harsh, often habit forming, and take a tremendous toll on young minds and bodies. Youngsters have no idea how these substances can damage their health and disrupt their lives. And, in most cases, neither do their parents. Once you are aware of the very real dangers posed by these drugs, make sure you share this information with your children.

Designer Drugs

Despite their alluring names, designer drugs are not pretty, nor are the effects they produce. They are called designer drugs or analogs because they are analogous to controlled substances. Concocted in illegal laboratories, designer drugs can be any class of drug that can be chemically replicated, which is why they are so hard to regulate. They are designed for abuse and have had their chemical structures altered specifically to get around existing laws.

Many designer drugs are bought and consumed at rave parties, underground clubs, rock concerts, dances, and other musical venues. Designer drugs are favored by adventurous teens and college students who fancy themselves on the cutting-edge of music and fashion. As mentioned previously, drugs go in and out of fashion. The following designer drugs are some popular ones that have been around for a while.

MDMA

MDMA is an abbreviation of a long chemical name for a drug also known on the street as Ecstasy, XTC, Essence, Adam, E, or Clarity. Ecstasy is the best known of the designer drugs, mainly because of its name and low price. Basically, it is a cross between an amphetamine and a hallucinogen and is taken in pill form. As a stimulant, it unleashes energy and is commonly used to help kids stay awake at a rave. Users also experience surreal, visual distortions. The typical reasons for using it are for its stimulant effect and for the cachet of taking the drug of choice at that night's party. Often kids at these drug fests get so revved up, they unwittingly mix different drugs. Youngsters who take Ecstasy or any illicit drug given away or peddled at giant gatherings take a whopping risk. "You never know what's going to be in it," says the Drug Enforcement Administration's expert on designer drugs. "We've seen Ecstasy pills that are only Excedrin and others that are pure amphetamine."

Ecstasy has a long list of known and suspected negative effects on abusers. It is fast acting and produces sensations of emotional warmth and alertness. It pumps up the heart rate and blood pressure, so users may become hyperactive. It can produce blurred vision, fainting, chills, sweating, muscle tension, and disorientation due to such effects as panic, anxiety, depression, and paranoid thinking. Research on rats and monkeys have shown that Ecstasy reduces the level of serotonin (a neurotransmitter that affects sleep, memory, depression, and other neurological processes) by 90 percent for at least two weeks.

Date Rape Drugs

One of the most appalling drug-related threats today is date rape. Although it can happen to anyone, females, teenagers, and college freshmen ages fifteen to twenty-five are the most vulnerable group. In some cases the assailant manipulates a victim by slipping a drug into a drink in order to knock the person unconscious and sexually assault him or her. "It isn't a widespread practice nationwide and we don't know how long it has been occurring, but we definitely know it's a serious problem for teenagers and young people," says the D.E.A. expert.

Rohypnol ("Roofies")

A rohypnol tablet, also called "the forget pill" or "rochas," is a sedative in the benzodiazepine family of depressants that is ten times more powerful than the well-known prescription tranquilizer Valium. While sold legally in more than sixty countries to treat insomnia and to relieve anxiety, it is outlawed in the U.S. Rohypnol is touted by dealers as a fast way to mellow out for two to eight hours without drinking alcohol. When "roofies" are combined with alcohol, the effects and dangers multiply. One or two tablets dissolved in an alcoholic drink can produce almost immediate drunkenness and amnesia. Victims have reported taking a drink at a party or a bar, passing out and being raped while they were unconscious. Afterward, they are unable to remember any details of the assault. Worse yet, a person does not know when they are being victimized, since "roofies" have no odor, taste, or color. Assailants can crush a tablet in their hand, slip it into a drink, stir it—all undetected. Five to ten minutes after the "roofie" is ingested, the victim becomes dizzy, nauseated, feels chilly and feverish, and stumbles as if intoxicated. Then s/he blacks out. As one drug agent puts it, "this is not new. They used to call it 'slipping them a Mickey Finn.'"

Ironically, students as young as 13 or 14 are popping "roofies" out of curiosity borne of its date-rape notoriety. Those who experiment with it want to be accepted, to be cool. Even smart, high-achieving teenage girls are abusing the drug because it has a sexy, forbidden aura about it and, consequently, some think it makes them more attractive to boys. Plus, the pill seems more like a prescription medicine than a drug like marijuana and is easier to conceal from their parents.

But it's not just the so-called "date rape drug." It's also called the "Quaalude of the 90s," and law enforcement officials are finding it on school campuses and at parties. "It's in the schools, kids are taking it, and it has nothing to do with sex," says San Diego County Sheriff's Detective Connie Johnson. "It has everything to do with ease of availability. The price is low, it's easy to take, and it's easy to hide." In spring 1997, over 30 youngsters in the San Diego area were caught using the drug at school, and several wound up in hospitals. One 15-year-old boy stopped breathing after he and some classmates mixed Rohypnol with alcohol and chugged the drink. He eventually recovered, but school officials were terrified. Tom Pence, an assistant principal at Eastlake High School in Chula Vista, California, told reporters, "It was frightening...the student was lethargic and limp. It basically looked like he was unconscious."

Few teens chronically abuse "roofies" because they are so powerful, but they can be addictive. And abusers quitting "roofies" usually suffer a painful withdrawal. Warns one drug treatment expert, "Think of roofies as alcohol concentrated in pill form. One tablet is like drinking a six-pack or two of beer." For teens with low or zero tolerance to alcohol, the effects are much more toxic. The real risk is in unintentionally overdosing because your drink was spiked, which can lead to a coma and possible death.

Gamma-Hydroxy Butyrate (GHB)

GHB is another designer depressant with many similarities to Rohypnol but with one major difference. GHB is a natural substance found in the human central nervous system. Chemists cloned it and it was sold in pill form as a natural diet and sleep aid in the 1980s. Suddenly, abusers were overdosing on it and the U.S. Food and Drug Administration and many states banned the sale and manufacture of GHB. Now the drug is manufactured illegally. GHB (also known on the street as "Georgia Home Boy," "Salt Water," and "Grievous Bodily Harm") affects people differently. Some abusers hallucinate. Others experience a feeling of drunkenness. Some feel nauseated, dizzy, drowsy, or have epileptic-type seizures. Still others feel hypnotized. As with any depressant, users can become physically and psychologically addicted to GHB. A dose of three grams or more can cause seizures, attack the heart and lungs, and result in coma or death.

Parents of teens who regularly attend mass musical gatherings should definitely warn them about the perils of GHB. Even supposedly well-supervised events are not immune from becoming drug fests. On New Year's Eve 1996, 31 teens were rushed by ambulances to hospitals—four in critical condition—after swallowing a combination of GHB, Ecstasy, roofies, and FX, described by police as "an orange mystery liquid" passed out in bottles. The drugs were "floating around," police said, among 10,000 young people attending a rave event in Los Angeles, where dozens of deejays were playing techno-music from different stages. One teenager told *The Los Angeles Times* he saw other kids "wheeled out in wheelchairs and in gurneys. People were really [messed] up. There's mass drugs going on in there. People are going crazy."

Law enforcement agencies report that GHB is also used as a date-rape drug because a two-gram dose slipped into a drink can render a victim unconscious.

Cat

Methcathinone or "cat" is an illegal stimulant that caught on in 1993, largely because of its catchy street name. Distributed as a powder, it is typically mixed with marijuana and smoked or injected. Cat is similar to a methamphetamine, delivering a burst of energy, speeding the mind, and turning off the appetite. It can cause convulsions, paranoia, nose bleeds, body aches, pounding heart, tremors, anxiety, and a "crash" followed by depression after a binge.

Fentanyl

Chances are kids will never knowingly buy or use this drug, but they may encounter it if they get involved in heroin. Fentanyl, first synthesized in Europe in the 1950s, was introduced to the U.S. in the 1960s as a surgical anesthetic, particularly for heart operations. In the 1970s, criminal chemists began cloning the compound as "synthetic heroin" and dealers established a market for it. Street Fentanyl also can be the real thing stolen from hospitals. Virtually all fentanyl is sold to hardened addicts who inject, snort, or smoke it. "The problem with Fentanyl," says a Drug Enforcement Administration analyst, "is that no one even on the street is really familiar with it and that a dealer could sell it to a kid looking for real heroin." The negative effects of Fentanyl are indistinguishable from heroin except that it is a lot more potent, so even small doses can be fatal.

Hallucinogenics

A hallucinogenic drug, popularly known as a psychedelic or mind-expanding drug, is a substance that alters consciousness. The most common hallucinogenic drugs include mescaline or peyote, psilocin and psilocybin, and LSD. Historically, hallucinogenics have been used in primitive societies to cure illness, facilitate meditation, placate evil spirits, and enhance mystical and magical powers. Their effects can be quite varied and depend on the personality and environment of the user as well as the dosage and potency of the hallucinogen. Among the effects, which can range from pleasant to very disturbing, are altered perception of time, space, and objects and imaginary sensations. While not habit forming, a chronic abuser may need to take increasing quantities to replicate an original effect.

Phencyclidine (PCP)

PCP was developed in 1959 as an anesthetic for hospital surgeries on humans. Later, it was used by veterinarians to sedate large animals during surgery, thus acquiring the street name "elephant tranquilizer." PCP was banned as an anesthetic for human use in 1965 when the medical community discovered surgical patients were experiencing side effects of delirium and confusion. Today, PCP is concocted in makeshift labs. Dealers sell it as a white crystalline powder or as tablets or capsules and it can be eaten, snorted, injected, or smoked. Sometimes abusers sprinkle it on marijuana joints or mix it with tobacco or leafy spices and smoke it.

"PCP is still a problem today but not on the same scale that crack and heroin is," reports a Drug Enforcement Administration analyst. He says PCP's heyday was in the late 1970s when it was the low-cost urban drug. Southern California street gangs first manufactured it, then criminal organizations set up dealer networks in large cities to push it. In the 1980s, crack flooded the cities and largely replaced PCP as the cheap inner-city street drug of choice.

Known as "angel dust," "rocket fuel," "zombie," "whack" or "embalming fluid," the last street name is probably the most appropriate; it is a reality-distorting hallucinogenic that can kill by paralyzing the respiratory system—depending on the size and purity of the dose and the health of the abuser. PCP can act as a stimulant or depressant or double as both simultaneously. Some users claim the drug gives them an eerie out-of-body experience. Others exhibit a drunkenness as if they have powered down too many drinks. PCP users can become violent, threateningly aggressive, and even temporarily psychotic. They may suddenly develop superhuman strength and often do not feel pain. In some cities, police have had to use taser guns that fire an electrical charge to subdue someone high on PCP.

A high can last two to four hours, but the after-effects can last for several days, even months. Before or after they crash, abusers can suffer anxiety, depression, paranoia, fear, or panic. Because PCP is not always eliminated by the body and can remain stored in fat cells, the drug can be reactivated by exercise or stress; users can suffer a full-blown convulsive flashback or lesser psychological reactions months or longer after taking their last dose. Mixing PCP with alcohol or other central nervous system depressant drugs can put the user into a coma or a coffin.

Chronic PCP abusers are rarely scrupulous about the dosage and ingest large amounts that can blur their vision, affect their speech, and cause nausea, vomiting, short-term memory loss, severe hallucinations, and delusions. To someone high on PCP, a tame house cat can appear to be a snarling lion.

Before cheaper crack cocaine appeared, street dealers would sell regular cigarettes or "Shermans" (an unfiltered skinny brown cigarette) dipped in liquid PCP. The prime customers were mostly out-of-work adult males. In those days, says a federal drug agent, "even the most depraved dealer would try to keep this stuff away from kids. A watch commander in the narcotics division of the Philadelphia Police Department says today "drug dealers will sell anything to anyone including selling PCP to kids."

Lysergic Acid Diethylamide (LSD)

Many illicit drugs had at least some clinical medical benefits before they were widely abused and outlawed. Not LSD. From the day it was discovered in 1938 by Dr. Albert Hoffman as a mood-changing chemical, LSD has never been prescribed to treat or cure a physical or mental illness, although it was once used as a research tool for studying brain disorders. LSD (a..k.a. "acid," "blotter," "windowpane," or "white lightning") is the most commonly used and most potent pure hallucinogenic or psychedelic drug sold on the street today. "Dropping" (swallowing) a microscopic amount of acid—equal to a few grains of salt—can send an LSD user on a so-called psychedelic trip where s/he hears colors, sees sounds and puts the mind into sensory overload.

Synthesized from lysergic acid diethylamide, a fungus that grows on grains, LSD is a powerful mind-altering drug, but no one realized it until Hoffman himself accidentally swallowed some in 1943 and reportedly hallucinated. LSD gained worldwide notoriety in the 1960s when the self-annointed drug guru, Dr. Timothy Leary, grabbed media attention by extolling the virtues of "tripping" on LSD. Leary, then a university professor, hyped the drug as powering a journey of self-discovery. San Francisco musicians hopped on the bandwagon and created an entirely new genre of music—acid rock. The fashion industry kept the movement going by creating psychedelic fashions. LSD use took a hiatus in the early 70s, when cocaine stole the spotlight, but then staged a comeback.

In the 1990s, a new generation of kids and young adults are discovering LSD. In the August 1996 Drug Abuse Warning Network (DAWN) report from the U.S. Substance Abuse and Mental Health Services Administration, emergency room admissions from LSD episodes rose 91 percent between 1993 to 1995. The DAWN report does not identify the cases by age, but drug agents report growing LSD abuse among teenagers, mainly middle-class high-school students. The American Council of Drug Education says that one out of five high-school students who have admitted to experimentation with a drug have tried LSD. On the other hand, the potency of today's LSD is down—from 100 to 200 micrograms per dose in the 1960s to 20 to 80 micrograms, according to the DEA. However, as little as 25 micrograms of acid can trigger hallucinations.

LSD is sold in many formats: impregnated on small pieces of paper (many sporting printed, psychedelic designs) and sold as "blotter acid," as thin squares of gelatin called "windowpanes," or as small tablets known as microdots. It is odorless, colorless, has a bitter taste, and is easy to stash or transmit. Some dealers even put it on the backs of postage stamps. Abusers lick it off the blotter, swallow pills, even—unbelievably enough—put liquid or gelatinous LSD directly on the eyes. The acid trip can last from two to twelve hours.

Like PCP, anyone who abuses LSD does not have the foggiest notion of what they are about to experience. If a teen is troubled, abusing other drugs, in a sour mood, or dropping a strong or contaminated dose, s/he can go on a bad trip. Hallucinating trippers have reported seeing monsters, spiders, and all kinds of bizarre things. Emergency room physicians who have treated LSD abusers say they come in panicky, confused, anxiety ridden, and scared silly. Users can fear they are going insane or about to die. Others are delusionary and suffering tremors. Although not physically addictive like heroin or cocaine, using LSD puts a strain on the body and mind. It dilates the pupils, elevates body temperature, blood pressure, and heart rate, causes sweats and sleeplessness and kills the appetite. LSD also parks itself in the body, so abusers can suffer flashbacks and unexpectedly resume the trip.

Ketamine Hydrochloride ("Special K")

Veterinarians know this drug as an animal tranquilizer used in pet surgeries. It was introduced in the 1960s by a pharmaceutical company who sold it to anesthesiologists for surgical procedures on humans, principally for treating battle wounds during the Vietnam War. By the 1970s, it was being abused as a recreational drug, and in the 1980s it was bandied about in the underground club scene as "Vitamin K." When the rave craze in Europe crossed the Atlantic to the U.S., the drug resurfaced as "Special K," a very powerful hallucinogen similar to PCP and LSD. It causes bizarre hallucinations where time stands still. Some abusers call it "psychedelic heroin" or "new Ecstasy."

Ketamine is a white powder that resembles cocaine and it is snorted or smoked. Normally, Ketamine is not found on school campuses. If teens do experiment with it, generally their sources are fast-lane friends who try to stay on the cutting-edge of fads and trends. But if your kid is impressionable, a status seeker, easily influenced or anxious to be cool, you could have potential problems. Often youngsters are introduced to Ketamine in ways that seem harmless to them—sprinkled on tobacco or marijuana and smoked. Heavy, older abusers combine it with harder drugs like heroin, cocaine, and Ecstasy.

Abusers have reported amnesia, delirious episodes, stumbling, and an inability to control their motor functions. Snorting or smoking Ketamine can attack the respiratory system and fatally paralyze it.

Psilocybin/Psilocin (Mushrooms)

For thousands of years, natives of Mexico and Central America have dried and chewed mushrooms or brewed them into a tea during religious rituals that produced vivid, visual hallucinations. Certain varieties of these mushrooms contain tiny amounts of two hallucinogenic chemicals—psilocybin and psilocin. Mushrooms hit it big in the 1960s among hippies, artists, writers, and anyone looking for a mild high. Two grams of natural "shrooms" or a 3- to 8-milligram dose of lab-manufactured synthetic psilocybin or psilocin produces a five- to six-hour high where time stands still, moods and mental states change, and colors, shapes, and sounds visually ricochet around in the mind.

Mushrooms are not a guaranteed tranquil trip. Depending on their potency, the abuser's experience, personality, and emotional sensitivity, the reaction can vary from mild to wild to frightening. Hallucinogenic mushrooms can be bought by mail or from dealers and peers. But, again, buyers and users never know what they are getting. Dried mushrooms look alike and the young and inexperienced could be ingesting poisonous mushrooms that cause permanent liver damage or death within hours. Some drug dealers have no compunction about sprinkling supermarket mushrooms with LSD or PCP and passing them off as a harmless hallucinogenic.

Mushroom abuse largely disappeared at the end of the so-called "flower power" generation. But they reemerged in the mid-1990s and caught on with teen heavy metal music concert-goers in major cities and with suburban, middle-class junior high and high-school students in the Sunbelt states who view them as "cool and mystical."

Mescaline

In northern Mexico and the southwestern United States, natives and Indians use a small, spineless cactus called peyote, which contains the hallucinogen mescaline, in their spiritual rites. Mescaline is a mind-altering drug extracted from the dried, button-like tops of dried peyote plants. For the moment, its popularity has waned.

Heroin

Heroin is produced from opium, which is obtained from seed pods of the oriental poppy. In its pure form it is a white to dark brown powder, but it comes in many shades and colors since it is often cut with other substances. Traditionally, the drug was injected with a syringe into a vein, although it may also be snorted. Regardless of how it is taken, heroin is a painkiller and is highly addictive. New users and addicts alike feel an immediate, intense pleasurable rush or high that turns into a calm, peaceful, relaxed, dreamlike trance where problems seemingly disappear. Heroin acts fast, reaching the reward and pleasure centers of the brain in fifteen to thirty seconds when it is injected or "mainlined" and in a scant seven seconds when smoked.

Heroin, a narcotic, is perhaps the most widely feared drug. The worst possible news is that heroin is back in vogue today with a vengeance. There is more of it, the price has fallen, the purity is higher, and you do not need to jam a needle in your body to experience the high. And the image of the traditional user—a down and outer or a junkie laying in the gutter or on a tenement floor with a hypodermic in his vein—is changing as well.

Heroin sales dried up from the 1970s to the mid 1980s after the DEA choked off the supply channels, first from Mexico, then from Southeast Asia. But in the 1990s, South American traffickers hooked up with U.S. organized crime families to import heroin that is up to 85 percent pure and even more addictive and dangerous. Researchers at the Public Statistics Institute in Irvine, California, say worldwide production of heroin leaped 85 percent between 1987 and 1995, while prices for a gram of pure heroin dropped 50 percent. In California, heroin-related hospital admissions surged 70 percent between 1991 and 1995 to a record high, according to study released by the Public Statistics Institute in July 1997. The 1996 National Household Survey on Drug Abuse found that the number of serious heroin users has jumped from just over 68,000 in 1993 to 216,000 in 1996. It also found that more people were sniffing, snorting, and smoking heroin.

Pushers have a tantalizing new sales pitch: Today's "smack," "horse," " black tar," "tootsie roll," or "junk" is purer, so it can be snorted or smoked. Worse yet, potential abusers are being told that smoking heroin in cigarettes or pipes and snorting it through a straw is not addictive like "shooting" or injecting it. And, since you don't need a needle, you can forget about AIDS/HIV, hepatitis, or other infections associated with intravenous use. In March 1996, ABC's news magazine show *Turning Point* aired a program called "Heroin: The New High School Drug." Meredith Vieira reported one of the lures of heroin as follows: "You no longer have to prepare it, or cook it, or inject it. In a society with a fast-food mentality, heroin has become a drug of convenience." Add to this the starring role heroin was given in hot cult films of the mid-1990s, like *Trainspotting* and *Pulp Fiction,* and the dangerous derivative of the harmless poppy plant is back in fashion, flowering and focusing on kids. In fact, some youth-oriented apparel makers were blatantly hawking a "heroin chic" look in their ads—using emaciated, grimy, hollow-faced models—until public uproar caused them to pull the campaign.

"In a society with a fast-food mentality, heroin has become a drug of convenience."

"Certainly, most of the users are older, but now, with snorting, heroin is creeping into the younger age brackets," says a DEA analyst specializing in heroin. "Young kids are going to parties and being told heroin is like alcohol, only a little stronger. You don't have to inject it, you can snort it without getting addicted." It removes the old stigma of the mainlining hype and replaces it with images of trendies taking powdered cocaine up their nose in stylish settings.

With access to a larger supply, some cocaine dealers are now selling heroin as well to their customers who may combine the two drugs. The practice is known as "speedballing." This lethal combination killed the talented actor John Belushi, one of the original stars of *Saturday Night Live.* Heroin also is taken by drug abusers who want to come down from a cocaine or methamphetamine high.

Symptoms

- Pinpoint pupils
- Droopy eyelids or a sleepy look
- Slow reflexes
- Poor coordination
- Dry mouth
- Slurred speech
- Scratching
- Needle marks or tracks

Preventative Measures

Explain the devastating toll heroin takes on the user's mind and body.

Among the effects: irregular or slower heartbeat, impaired night vision, constipation, skin infections, vomiting, slurred speech, fluctuating blood pressure, respiratory problems. Heroin interferes with the body's ability to fight off infection, so users are more prone to malnutrition, tuberculosis, circulatory problems, and sexual infections. Injuries or medical conditions may go unnoticed because of heroin's painkilling effect. Abusers who inject heroin leave themselves open to AIDS/HIV or hepatitis. Children who are born to a heroin-addicted mother are often premature, are addicted at birth, and must suffer through agonizing withdrawal at birth—if they are not stillborn.

Make sure that kids understand the powerfully addictive nature of heroin.

Regular abusers build a tolerance to it and need larger or more frequent doses or "fixes" to get the same initial effect. Once an abuser develops a physical dependency, s/he has to feed the habit or get violently sick and start a painful, nauseating physical withdrawal.

Heroin withdrawal can be a painful or a torturous experience. Kicking a low-dose heroin habit is like suffering through two to three days of the flu. Trying to stop a heavier habit can take 36 to 72 hours of relentless fevers, chills, vomiting, convulsions, diarrhea, cramping, and shaking. Officials at the Partnership for a Drug-Free America contend it can take months or even years to recover from the physical addiction to heroin: "Fighting the psychological addiction is a lifetime battle" dealing with cravings and depression.

Discuss criminal implications.

Heroin addicts who do not have the financial means to stop the cravings often resort to crime to feed their habit. While not as potentially violent as crackheads who may brandish a gun in a robbery, heroin addicts will shoplift, snatch a purse, steal a car, or rob a home or business for cash or property that they can convert to drug money.

The penalty for trafficking in less than a kilogram of heroin is a minimum of five years for a first offense; a second offense brings a penalty of ten years to life.

Part Three

Problem Solving

14

"My Kid Is on Drugs.
What Should I Do?"

Philip's Story
Are You Wearing a Blindfold?

When Philip was nine years old, he was the classic golden kid—blonde, blue-eyed, tanned by the Hawaiian sun, and with a smile that literally gleamed. His mother, Tammy, was busy and involved with Honolulu social circles. His dad, Steve, was a Navy fighter pilot who was away from home for months at a stretch. "Tammy and Steve probably told their kids not to do drugs, but they weren't paying attention to what their kids were doing."

Apparently not. When he was young, Philip's 15-year-old brother and 14-year-old sister introduced him to marijuana and "magic mushrooms." Recalls Ellen, who became Philip's stepmother after his parents' divorce, "all three kids were on drugs, acting out their frustration at being ignored by what looked like the perfect family. Steve was in serious denial about his kids involvement with drugs. It was like he was wearing a blindfold when he wasn't wearing his flight helmet."

Philip was twelve when Ellen and Steve married. Ellen found her stepson to be manipulative and desperate for attention." After marijuana, Philip wanted a faster, higher high. "I caught Philip sniffing spray paint from a sock one day and immediately took him to a Navy counseling and advice center." There, the family learned about toluene, an ingredient in spray paint that creates a high but also cripples the brain.

Ellen says she tried to jolt her husband into reality by telling him just how deeply his son had sunk into drug abuse. "It was hard for him to admit it to himself. In the military you have this code of silence—never show any weakness—and this carries over to the family, where anything negative is a secret from the outside world."

Ellen began investigating rehab centers, but her husband couldn't believe the problem was critical and he was resisting all help. "We finally got Philip into counseling, but it didn't help because we could never get to the core issue of why he was using. Nobody in the family was talking about the problem except me. For the next several years, Philip was on the run—from home, from hospitals, from rehab programs. At thirteen, he disappeared for six weeks from a residential drug rehabilitation center in Honolulu and was found living with an adult man. "I'm convinced that he was molested and that only made things worse," said Ellen.

When Steve was transferred to San Diego, Philip's life went downhill. He dropped out of high school, started using psychosis-inducing crystal methamphetamine, and was stealing to support his drug habit. By this time, his father was frustrated and frantic. "Philip never talked about it but just kept running—from the California Youth Authority and from hospitals," said Steve. "We were at our wits end and tried several community outreach programs including one that involved setting limits and boundaries and required kids to sign a contract that they will not break these barriers. If they do not comply or if they run, the door is closed to them and they have to go to another home—not their own—or fend for themselves. These kids weren't just druggies, but they were dysfunctional kids, and it takes a network of parents to make it work. This strategy is extremely difficult for a lot of parents, but it works in many cases."

But not for Philip. He ran again. Ellen has never seen him since he left the program, although she spoke to him on the day his father died of cancer. "All I know is that he lives in San Francisco, he is HIV-positive, and a heroin addict," she says sadly. "I don't know if the HIV is from a bad needle or from prostitution. All I keep remembering is him saying, 'I'm going to change. I'm going to change.' It all started with marijuana and, yes, he changed. It kept getting worse."

An angry Ellen has some "real-life advice" for parents who want to spare their kids—and themselves—the pain that drug use inflicts on a family.

"Stay absolutely on top of who your kids are hanging out with and what they're doing after school," she insists. "After you meet the youngsters, meet their parents and build a network so everyone can talk about potential problems, like when a new kid enters their circle of friends and introduces drugs or a drug dealer to the entire group. Keep in contact with teachers and school officials and be alert to danger signals such as your child skipping school or spending long hours in their bedroom," says Ellen. She says Philip began cutting classes with another young girl and hiding out in her bedroom. "I went over and had lunch with her mother who told me, 'My daughter doesn't want to leave her bedroom. There is also a terrible smell in the room and I can't get it out of the curtains.'" Ellen says she went into the bedroom, took one sniff and told the woman, "That's marijuana, that's grass. Turns out she was in denial and frightened of what her husband might say or do."

Bottom line: Blindfolds are comfortable, but when it comes to kids and drugs, they can be heartbreaking.

Matt's Story

"I Blew a Potential Career As a Pro Athlete, But I'm Alive"

Meet Matt P. today and you might think "Here's an all-American kid, confident, bright, with real promise." Matt is twenty-three, husky, handsome, well-dressed, polite, poised, and smart. He is currently the marketing director for a publishing company focusing on high-technology industries. Yet just six years ago, Matt was in a drug and alcohol rehabilitation facility. He landed there after a horrific childhood that would have psychologically demolished many youngsters.

Matt's story vividly illustrates how preteen experimentation with gateway drugs, if unchecked, can escalate into impulsive sampling from a smorgasbord of illegal and potentially deadly substances. It also proves that a parent battling personal problems can still guide a troubled child through the precarious adolescent years.

Matt started off life with two huge strikes against him. His father was sent to prison for life plus thirty years when Matt was just six months old. His distraught mother sought emotional refuge in drugs and alcohol. It was Philadelphia in the late 1970s and Matt's earliest memories are frightening. "I remember wandering around a really small one-room apartment that only had a kitchenette and a bathroom, and there were always different men there with my mother. There was drinking and the men were usually violent. I remember people getting drunk and fighting."

At the age of five, Matt began to escape from the apartment to find friends to play with, sometimes breaking other kids' toys or getting into fights. "I now know I was trying to get my mother's attention. She was the only person I could trust, but she was always preoccupied with men." Another early memory was when two men wanted to marry his mother and she asked him to help her choose. "I remember at the time thinking it was kind of weird to ask me 'which man would you like to have as your father.' She married the one I chose, but he turned out to be an alcoholic who was physically and emotionally abusive to me and my mother." His new stepfather would flare into a drunken rage then take off and abandon Matt and his mother for days. His mom provided the only stability in Matt's life, but she was usually intoxicated or strung out on drugs.

As he got a little older, Matt could not stand being at home, so he sought out any friends he could find to play any game he could. He was good at sports, but he quickly developed another skill. He started stealing when most kids were starting school. At six, Matt stole ten dollars from a baby-sitter and took three buddies to a Dairy Queen for ice cream and hamburgers. When he was eight, his mother enrolled him in a nearby summer day camp, but she was usually passed out in the morning and couldn't drive him. So Matt stole "two or three dollars every morning from my mom or whoever's pants happened to be in the house so I could buy things for other kids just to make them my friends." Several times he was caught stealing, but he never got more than a lecture.

His first brush with drugs was at age nine, when a friend stole five cases of Marlboros off a delivery truck. "We all thought it was a cool thing to smoke cigarettes." Before long, he was lighting up marijuana cigarettes. "I was hanging out and smoking cigarettes with older kids when one of them said 'here, try a joint.' I crawled underneath a car to smoke it. I was maybe nine or ten, and I don't really remember the effects. My first experience was quick." But he liked feeling accepted by the older boys.

Matt says he did not use alcohol as a preteen because he was "turned off by what it did to my mom and her friends." He first got drunk as a high-school sophomore when he realized "everyone drinks." The occasion was an unsupervised party at the home of a high-school friend. "Someone had brought 180 proof pure grain alcohol and mixed it with fruit juice. I was the drunkest kid at the party," he admits. "I was stumbling around, got into fights, and ended up passing out in the bathroom. My mom took me to church the next day, and I remember being hung over and how bad I felt—physically and emotionally."

Matt and his mother moved from Philadelphia to Cleveland, where they stopped drinking and drugging with the help of Alcoholics Anonymous. But a few years later, when they moved back to Philadelphia, Matt, now a high-school junior, sought out his old "running buddies." They were all sixteen and abusing marijuana. One friend was a dealer and Matt, headstrong and out of control, got caught up in the action. "These were upper middle-class kids, and they were mobile. They all had cars and we'd drive to New York and buy marijuana."

These weren't joyrides. Matt and his other 16-year-old friends would collect anywhere from $400 to $2,000, drive to the tough Bedford Stuyvesant district of Brooklyn, connect with dealers in their late twenties, and buy a pound or more of marijuana. Matt says the pound of pot would be repackaged in Philadelphia and sold at a substantial profit. He claims he did not deal the drugs, but he never had to pay for any marijuana that he smoked, either. "They were my buddies."

By the time he was a high-school senior, Matt was playing football and baseball and was on the wrestling team. He was also smoking marijuana every day—usually after school, so it didn't affect him in class. "Luckily I did relatively well in sports and I'm smart, so I got good grades. But I noticed the grass affected my drive. I had a lack of ambition, a lack of determination. I didn't apply myself. Nobody in the crowd I was running with wanted to do their homework. We were all rebellious."

Pretty soon the drugs started grabbing the reins of Matt's life. Smoking marijuana fired up his curiosity to try even harder drugs, like PCP, usually at parties. Matt contends he was "never a big [angel] dust head." The risk was just too great, but he abused it nonetheless and considers himself fortunate that he wasn't left with any mental scars. PCP, he says, put him in a time warp and spaced him out. He lost control and lost touch with reality. For a bigger thrill, he began dropping acid. "LSD is scary because it really distorts your reality, but I was curious. Acid trips can last twelve hours. You can go to sleep, wake up and still be tripping [hallucinating]. I've also seen people who just never came back from acid trips. Today, they're completely dumbed. They're drifters, wanderers."

From the hallucinogenics, it was a short hop to snorting cocaine. "It all happens so quickly. You start experimenting with one drug and, soon, whatever is around, you find yourself doing it. And this was the late 80s when it seemed that everybody was abusing cocaine." He swears he did not smoke crack, but only because there was so much negative publicity about crackheads and the dangers of the drug that even he and his friends were terrified of it. "I've heard the effects of crack are like cocaine multiplied times ten. It's like being yanked to the top of a skyscraper on a rope real fast and then being dropped."

Matt lost control right about the time he was graduating from high school. His mother, now clean and sober, knew her son was using even though he contends he "never really got addicted." He said he only smoked pot and drank on a regular basis on Friday and Saturday nights, which he denies, oddly enough, as being an addiction. However, his mother, in drug and alcohol recovery, knew otherwise. She had caught him drunk twice and warned him if it ever happened again, he would not just lose his car and driver's license, she would sign him into an alcohol and drug rehabilitation program. "She sat me down and said, 'look, you have all the classic signs and behaviors that can ruin your life.'" Among them: alcohol and drug abuse in the family, a possible genetic predisposition to abusing both substances, both an absent parent and a dysfunctional parent during childhood, the scars of being physically abused as a child, plus a lifetime of bottled-up anger that he never dealt with.

Matt says he listened hard and thought about what she said, but it didn't sink in. Reality hit when he went to yet another party as a high-school senior and the police, acting on a tip, raided it. But not before Matt had gotten high again on marijuana and alcohol. His mother carried out her promise. She immediately placed her son into a drug and alcohol treatment facility. She also told him that she was the person who told the police that minors were at a party where liquor was being served. And she told Matt she would do it again and if he wound up in jail, he would have no one to blame except himself for his bad judgment and poor choices. Sure, his childhood was hardly idyllic, but his mother knew that only the abuser/addict could battle the addiction.

Matt says the rehab program forced him to take a hard look at himself for the first time. He had earned a full academic-athletic scholarship to a local private college that was in jeopardy because of his drug taking, and he did eventually lose it. During his rehab, Matt says he was evaluated as being a "chemical abuser" but not physically addicted to drugs; that insight gave him hope for the future. It also made him face some truths. "I had blown a good potential college and possible pro athletic career because I really hadn't worked hard enough—hadn't concentrated," says Matt. Part of it, he thinks, was simply not having a father to talk to, to guide him, to encourage him, to say "you're good at this, let's get to work, let's practice." But he's not blaming his problem on his father; in the end it was Matt's choice to drink, use drugs, and run with a crowd that did the same.

After rehab, Matt got out of the drug culture, realizing he

had the gifts of intelligence and health, a supportive mother who knew from experience the dangers he faced, and a second chance to make something out of his life. He enrolled in a community college, lapsed briefly when he "smoked some weed" but then gave it up and hasn't touched any drug since, except for alcohol, which he drinks "only socially now and then."

Matt feels blessed he was able to escape the drug world. "Most of the people I was with got caught up in the culture and dropped out of life, even though they weren't dummies." One friend bound for Penn State University, planned to give up his hidden life as a high-school dealer but was going to make "one last run." On his way back from the buy he was pulled over by Pennsylvania state troopers who found a half pound of marijuana stuffed in his trousers. "They pulled him out of the car, threw him down on concrete, pointed guns at his head, handcuffed and arrested him." The felony bust instantly changed his life.

When he starts his own family, what does Matt plan to tell his children about drugs? He paused and thought for a minute. "I'm too young to even think about it now, but I don't want to be the person who says never, ever touch a drink or a drug or deny that I did it. I'll tell them this stuff is not good for you and explain, in detail, how I came to get involved. I'll also spend a lot of time on my family history—our family history—and explain that addiction is a fact of life for us and that anyone in our family could get involved with drugs—even you, my own child."

Davey's Story
Sidestepping the Quicksand

Glenda R. has always prided herself on leading a charmed life. She grew up in a loving middle-class family in Columbus, Ohio. Mom worked part-time at a real estate office. Dad was a Protestant minister with a large congregation until he retired. Her older sister went to college for two years, joined the Peace Corps, settled down, and is happily married with three children. "Mine is a storybook family," says Glenda.

Glenda graduated from Ohio State University in 1975, worked as a computer engineer, and spent most of her twenties on the management fast track at local consulting company. There she met and married Richard, the marketing vice president. At twenty-nine, Glenda and Richard had a son, Davey, and, two years later, a daughter. They bought a comfortable home on a tree-lined street in an nice, safe neighborhood in Columbus.

Fast-forward to 1994. Glenda is developing computer software programs out of her home and raising her kids. Richard is working around the clock to launch his own business. Davey is ten years old and entering the fifth grade. "He is a good boy, a good student, respectful to his parents, and unfailingly polite to adults," she says proudly. He is also a whiz at soccer. Richard and Glenda alternate taking him to practice and attending all his games.

One day Glenda was late in picking Davey up from soccer practice because of a traffic jam. "I saw him over in a corner of the soccer field with a couple of his teammates. I hated to just honk, so I walked over to the group and I noticed something strange," she says. "A cheap plastic lighter and a half-smoked cigarette were lying on the ground and all the kids were looking guilty—not exactly ashamed—but as if they had something to hide." She didn't say anything and did not cause a ruckus, although her first reaction was to get an explanation on the spot. Glenda knew something was up but decided to discuss it at the family dinner table that night. "It took a lot of self-discipline to say nothing. I wanted to say 'wait until your daddy comes home, young man.' But I kept cool." So did Richard, even after he was briefed by Glenda on what she saw.

When the family sat down to eat, Glenda addressed her son. "I'm sorry I was late to pick you up from soccer practice. Traffic was terrible. How did it go?"

"Fine," said Davey, not looking her in the eye.

"Who were those boys?" Glenda inquired. "I don't think I've met them before."

Davey nervously replied, "Just some of the kids on the team."

Glenda, still calm, said, "It looked like one of the boys was smoking."

Davey, picking at his food, responded, "Well, he was just playing a game."

"What kind of game?" asked Richard.

Davey, smiling, replied, "Roger thought of it. He calls it 'watch what I do and the coach will never know it.'"

"How do you play that game?" asked Glenda.

"We started with cigarettes. We each sneaked a puff. The coach was so busy he didn't even notice. Another time, Roger brought some vodka from home and we all drank it. Roger said since it was clear and odorless the coach would never know and would think it was water."

"How do you feel about that game?" asked Richard, "and why were you playing it? You know cigarettes and liquor are for adults."

"I really think they are being stupid," says Davey, "but they're on my team and I don't want to look geeky."

"Davey," says his dad. "It's not cool to do things to your

body that can hurt it. It's not cool to break the law, which is what you're doing. And it's really not cool if you're caught by the coach and kicked off the team. You want to play sports in junior high, high school and maybe some day in college. Start messing up now and you're going to mess up later."

Glenda and Richard didn't just drop it there. And they didn't sweep it under the rug. "We met with the coach, who is also a parent with a son on the team," Glenda said. "His son wasn't involved but two other kids were, and we talked to their parents, too. They were shocked." Roger's dad started to blame the coach for not keeping a closer watch on the kids. Richard cut him off by stating that it is the parents' responsibility to instill good values in their own children.

After the coach got the lowdown on what was happening at soccer practice, he asked Roger to either quit "playing your game" or quit the team. Roger quit the team. "Davey quit seeing Roger and has been hanging with other kids who know that getting good grades is cool," says Glenda.

Postscript. Davey is in junior high school today. It's a bigger school and there are drugs on campus, but Davey is clean and his circle of friends are clean. He's playing basketball and is on the student council. Says Glenda: "We were lucky. But we also didn't flip out. I can't imagine what would have happened had we really lost it over a half-smoked cigarette."

What Should a Parent Do?

The first reaction is fury, says Dr. Herb Kleber, professor of psychiatry at Columbia University and medical director for The National Center on Addiction and Substance Abuse in New York City. "Most parents are furious. 'How could you do that in our house? How long have you been lying to me?' They are not just angry. They're outraged."

Stay calm. This is the first thing parents should do when they discover their kid is using drugs. Whether your youngster is swiping your cigarettes, stealing beers out of your refrigerator, or getting high on marijuana after school—don't panic.

The fact is your kid has probably been sneaking around for some time but you just haven't noticed. Chances are, you didn't want to notice. Other youngsters do drugs. Not yours. This kind of denial is understandable. In fact, it's normal. "If my kid is smoking and drinking underage or using an illegal drug and breaking the law, it's my fault. I've blown it. I'm a bad parent and the world is going to know about it." That's a typical second reaction. These parental rationalizations are normal, but if you catch your kid using drugs, you need to take swift action—without blaming yourself or your child. What you need is an immediate intervention. This is not a stage your kid is going through. This is not a phase. This is not a fad.

If Your Child Is Experimenting

You do not need to call in a drug treatment professional right away. First you must find out exactly what you are really dealing with and how severe the problem is. A teenager who smokes pot every so often is not the same as someone who is getting stoned after school every day with a couple of buddies. The first kid is an experimenter who is now an occasional user and may be among the 80 percent who will never have a long-term problem with drugs. The second kid is a frequent user, perhaps psychologically addicted, who is prone to try stronger illegal substances. Both situations are serious and should not be tolerated. Both kids are breaking state and federal laws. While treatment tactics vary, a parent's initial reaction should be the same.

In a cool, noncombative, nonconfrontational manner, get to the heart of the problem quickly.

Dr. Kleber advises that you do not go on the attack. Instead ask straightforward, logical questions such as the following:

♦ "What seems to be going on here?" *not* "What the hell are you doing?"

♦ "How long has this been a problem? *not* "Have you been lying to us all this time?"

♦ "Why don't you tell us how this all got started? *not* "Where are you getting drugs?" "Who is selling you this stuff?" "Where are you getting the money? Are you stealing it?"

♦ "How do you feel about yourself when you try it?" *not* "How do you think your mother and I are going to feel if you get arrested and this winds up in the papers?"

Home Drug Test Kits: Save Your Money

Testing your kid with a home drug test kit from the pharmacy sounds like a smart idea to make sure s/he's drug free. In truth, it's a bad idea.

Kids who are experimenting with drugs usually feel guilty about it, and you are probably going to have a tough time talking with them about drug use and earning their trust. If you threaten or surprise them with a drug test at home, it will only widen the wedge of mistrust.

The only advantage of a home drug test kit, in my opinion, is to help your child cope with peer pressure. If pushed to experiment, he can always say "I can't because I'm being drug tested." But even that sends the wrong message. It's far better for him to say "No, I don't do that stuff because it messes you up"—as long as he genuinely believes it. And that truth is something you need to impart.

If you, as a parent, cannot talk calmly about the problem with your youngster, find an objective third party s/he trusts and will talk to. Some likely candidates are the child's doctor, a religious professional, a social worker or a psychologist experienced in adolescent substance abuse. Another relative? "The kid isn't going to trust an aunt or an uncle because they're family and it's just like talking to their parents." Nor does Dr. Kleber suggest getting the kid's teacher or coach involved at this stage. "The youngster will be very reluctant to be honest because he is afraid his problem will somehow be leaked to his friends, schoolmates, and teammates." Dr. Kleber, a psychiatrist himself, would avoid a psychiatrist at this point. "It's overreacting."

Get at the truth—right now.

Getting an honest answer at this point will be challenging. Kids caught drinking or using drugs will almost always deny it or try to minimize the problem. "Kids using on a regular basis, who are stoned just to get through the day, will say they're only using once a week, and once-a-week users will say it's once a month," says Dr. Kleber. "Pot users will swear they've never used anything stronger and never will. It's one thing to cop to marijuana use and a very different thing to cop to using acid or other, stronger drugs." Kids will offer all kinds of excuses, he adds. Typical alibis include that they found it and didn't know what it was or that they were just holding it for a friend but don't use it themselves. Even when youngsters are caught red-handed, parents often believe their lies.

Establish immediate consequences that will have an impact and that you can realistically enforce.

There is a natural tendency to try scare tactics—the scared-straight approach. It rarely works. Instead, take something away that the kid values and explain a reason for each punitive action. For instance, a teen with a driver's license cannot drive for two weeks. If s/he is caught again, driving privileges are revoked for a month and you may call the police. You are taking the keys to his or her car because alcohol or marijuana affects reaction time

Roxanne's Story

"I accidentally knocked a shoebox off an end table when I was cleaning his room," recalls Roxanne M. an insurance adjuster from Fort Worth, Texas. "A bunch of little round tin foil packages shaped like small bullets spilled all over the floor. I flushed them down the toilet." Her 16-year-old son, Joe, came home and hit the roof. He explained his friend was selling hashish but was allergic to it and couldn't have it in his own home. He asked Joe to watch it but not try any. Joe said, "I was just about to give it back and get it out of my room and now I'm going to have to pay for it."

Roxanne says she bought the story because she was afraid her son would be beat up. Only after Joe was caught selling LSD to an undercover officer at a hamburger stand did she realize she had been conned by her own son. "Deep down I assumed he might have been using," admits Roxanne, "but I just didn't want to face it. I never thought he would sell it."

and depth perception and anyone driving with these or other substances in their body is a hazard on the road—to themselves and to others.

Spell out consequences.

Using illegal drugs or drinking under age is breaking the law. You can get a police record. Another reason you're punishing your youngster for using is because drugs can damage their health, even at their young age. Telling youngsters that they may get lung cancer from smoking isn't enough to make them stop because kids feel immortal. Instead try messages such as: "Smoking can aggravate bronchitis, cause a recurrent smoker's cough, and make you smell bad. With alcohol, you lose control, you can seriously injure or kill yourself and others, plus it inter-

Want to Work? Don't Do Drugs

Kids who want to work may be asked to take a drug test when they apply for a job. If their drug test is positive, they won't be hired. "The courts have upheld the right of the employer to do drug testing," says Daryl Grecich, communications director of The Institute for a Drug-Free Workplace.

"Kids, whether or not they're in the workplace, are the workers of tomorrow. Most employees do not do drugs and they absolutely do not want to work with drug abusers. Drug abuse increases accidents, injuries, and possible death for users and those around them. Drug abuse hurts productivity, which raises the price of the things you buy—and hurts morale. And the nondrug-abusing employee has to pick up the slack of the drug abuser."

feres with your memory and kills brain cells, so it will hurt your grades. Both are also addictive, and once you start using on a regular basis, it's very, very hard to stop." These are all things that can happen now.

Lay down laws and enforce them.

Your kid used but you are giving him or her a chance to change behaviors on their own. There are rules. When there is a party, the youngster knows mom or dad will call and make sure there is responsible adult supervision. Don't be swayed by pleas such as, "Come on, Mom, you're making me look like a sissy." Either the party is supervised, drug and alcohol free, or the kid is not allowed to attend.

If Your Child Is a Regular User

There are several schools of thought regarding intervention and treatment. One approach, says Dr. Kleber, is to strike a bargain:

The deal: "I'm not forcing you into treatment. You're forcing yourself into treatment by your behavior. I'll give you three weeks to see if you can stop using on your own. You agree to a drug test at a doctor's office every week. At the end of three weeks, if you haven't stopped, you agree to see a treatment professional without being dragged in kicking and screaming."

Understand the rules. If your child is sixteen or younger you can insist s/he go into treatment for chemical dependency and the child cannot refuse, although s/he might not cooperate. If the child is over seventeen, s/he can legally refuse, but parents hold a trump card if they are willing to play it: "get treatment or get out of our house." This tactic definitely should not be an early consequence. Dr. Kleber says this is a very, very difficult decision because if something tragic happens to the child as a result, there may be tremendous guilt. However, if a child has a serious drug problem and doesn't get treatment, there could be tragic results as well.

Family Support Groups

It is impossible to say whether so-called tough love should be explored before professional treatment begins. It depends largely on the youngster. If you can satisfy yourself that s/he's a first-time or a twice-a-month user and you have the fortitude to lay down laws and the discipline to enforce them, go to work on the problem as a family.

Jean P., who voluntarily staffs the telephone at the Southern California headquarters of Families Anonymous (FA), a 12-step treatment program patterned after Alcoholics Anonymous (AA), insists on "house rules with a contract." Parents set a short list of rules that their children must follow to the letter. Example: no smoking, drinking, swearing, or drugs in this house and you have to go to school full-time or go part-time and get a job. The kid agrees to these stipulations and signs a letter of agreement confirming that s/he understands the terms for living under the family's roof. S/he also voluntarily attends a 12-step treatment program offered by FA, AA, or Narcotics Anonymous (NA), preferably with the parent.

How tough is the love? Jean, an FA member for 10 years, tells of one family's strategy. A 13-year-old girl caught using alcohol and trying marijuana with a boy at school, rebelled and refused to abide by house rules. She cursed her mother, and her stereo was removed from her room. She was late coming home from school and every picture in her bedroom was stripped off the wall and her personal phone was disconnected. She sipped her dad's beer when she thought he wasn't looking, and he took her bedroom door off the hinges. "Two weeks of this and she voluntarily agreed to establish house rules and abide by them," recounts Jean.

Don't expect overnight changes. Teens under the microscope will get easily provoked and irate. You can expect to hear "you don't trust me." A firm but appropriate response: "You've been lying to me for the last year. You've been stealing from us. Why should we trust you?" The process of change is painful for everyone in the family, but when you crack down twenty-four hours a day on a youngster who's been using and impose new standards of behavior, you put the kid on notice. You've started an intervention. Mom and dad are no longer oblivious or ignorant to what is happening under their nose.

Toughlove International

The tough love can get even tougher. Toughlove International, like Families Anonymous, is a family support group with chapters worldwide. Cofounder David York, a former high-school biology teacher who woke up the day one of his sons was arrested for cocaine possession, says "Parents who come to Toughlove are past denial, guilt, or blame and just feel helpless. They need to follow someone else's structured program because they can't manage the problem on their own."

Toughlove takes an important first step used by most professional treatment programs: families complete a crisis assessment sheet (what are the specific problems that brought them to Toughlove?) and set family goals. Other families set up "nurturing teams," visit each others' children, and help a new family meet their goals. Each week a family takes another "action step" toward their goal.

York, who cofounded Toughlove with his wife in 1979, does not believe in kids and parents entering into contracts. "Absolutely not. That's treating a kid who is using drugs like he's an equal. They're not paying the rent. They're not responsible for the living conditions. They're still a kid. Kids in trouble need someone to take charge of their lives and make it safe for them to make changes."

Parents have to change and learn new parenting skills, too, and that can be as difficult and painful as the changes a kid must make to get clean and sober. York tells of the single mother whose 16-year-old son got suspended from school because he was drunk in class. "She was going to kick him out of the house, but other families [in the group] said no: 'He's underage and you would be committing a crime.'" To defuse the crisis, one family took her son home for three days, then another family took him for the next three days.

Do not coddle him. If a youngster who has been put on notice breaks the law, insists York, "you call the police. If the kid is drunk or stoned, you call the police." Don't blame yourself or the youngster—take action instantly.

Professional Treatment

If a youngster is using alcohol or drugs and a family intervention or family support groups are not enough to persuade the youngster to change—or s/he simply cannot—the next option is to seek professional treatment. For some families, this may be the first step.

When to Call a Pro

Specialists use the following criteria in assessing chemical/substance dependency. If three or more behaviors occur within twelve months, seek referrals to a respected treatment program.

1. Tolerance Level. The user needs increased amounts of the substance to get intoxicated or high or achieve a desired pleasurable effect. The pleasure wanes if the user does not increase the substance amounts.
2. Withdrawal effects. The user suffers physical changes if s/he does not use the substance regularly. This could range from nausea, cramps, and sweats to physical pain. The user has to take the substance, or a closely related one, to avoid these withdrawal effects.
3. The user takes the substance in larger amounts or over a longer period than originally intended.
4. The user wants to stop and/or is unsuccessful in cutting down or controlling substance abuse.
5. The user spends a lot of time obtaining the substance (plotting how to obtain alcohol, meeting with a dealer), using it, or recovering from its effects.
6. The user gives up or cuts back on social, recreational, or occupational activities in order to use the substance or because of its effects.
7. Users continue the drug in spite of the fact that it is causing persistent or recurring physical and psychological problems. For instance, using cocaine in spite of having cocaine-induced depression. Or continuing to drink even though the alcohol is causing headaches.

Selecting a Counselor

1. Check your health insurance policy to see what kind of coverage you have. Most provide coverage for psychological services. If not, consult community agencies that might be able to refer you to free or low-cost counseling centers.
2. Ask friends who have been through counseling to give you referrals or look in the Yellow Pages under such headings as "Psychologists" or "Family Counselors."
3. Know the different counselors available and select a

licensed or credentialed practitioner, whether a psychiatrist, psychologist, a Certified Addiction Counselor, or Credentialed Alcoholism Counselor.

Look for addiction specialists or M.D.s who have completed courses from the American Society of Addiction Medicine (ASAM) or the American Academy of Addiction Psychiatrists (AAA).

4. Do you and your child have rapport with and confidence in your counselor? Does s/he make the child feel at ease?
5. Does the counselor offer a well thought-out plan? Does s/he clearly and patiently explain the approach to be used, including both short- and long-term goals and estimated length of treatment?
6. Is the counselor aware of and sensitive to your financial circumstances? M.D.s are usually more expensive than non-M.D. therapists; outpatient programs are less costly than inpatient programs.

What to Expect

Programs usually consist of the following:

♦ Evaluation and assessment interview
♦ Family history
♦ Physical exam (may not occur in outpatient program)
♦ Periodic drug-use screening
♦ Individual, group, and/or family therapy (not all may be offered)

Sundown Ranch is a 28-day intensive inpatient alcohol and drug treatment and educational facility for kids 12 to 18 years old. It has had chemically dependent patients as young as 10 years old. The ranch is no recreational getaway to simply dry out kids. "We break through their denial and delusions [that they don't have a problem]," says Scott Munson, executive director. The daily regimen is intense for anyone, especially teens. A typical day consists of three hours of group therapy, followed by three hours of education on chemical dependency and recovery, including an in-house 12-step program. Next, the kids spend two hours on general education—reading, writing, math, physical education. After that comes one-on-one sessions with drug and alcohol counselors, homework, and room cleaning. "There is no television, no fun and games and only forty-five minutes of free time during the day for seven days a week," Munson explains. "There's no idle time. Therapy happens around the clock."

Selecting an Inpatient Treatment Program

1. Look for one that takes a medical approach to addiction.
2. If your child needs to go through detox, find a center that offers both detox and treatment in one facility.
3. Be sure that the center offers adequate treatment time, generally four weeks for alcoholism and six weeks or longer for drugs. (Note: Managed healthcare plans may only cover some portion.)
4. Select a professional environment where the person knows s/he is a patient, not a resort-like setting.
5. There should be adequate and quality staffing. There should be a mix of trained professionals as well as recovering addicts. There should be full-time staffing and a good counselor to patient ratio. Counselors should have different areas of expertise.
6. The curriculum should include education and a variety of educational methods—lectures, video- and audiotapes, books, movies. Materials should be available to both patients and family members.
7. Look for a mix of individual as well as group counseling. Individual counseling should be provided at least twice weekly and group counseling should occur daily.
8. An after-care program should be part of the overall treatment plan.
9. Family involvement should be an important element of the treatment and recovery process.

The assessment procedure is at the heart of a professional chemical dependency treatment program. It tells you, with surprising accuracy and in considerable detail, the risk factors and needs that could be causing your youngster to drink, do drugs, or otherwise abuse illegal substances. It is also a blueprint for a treatment action plan. In most cases, you order the assessment, but if your kid runs afoul of the law before s/he gets into a treatment program, the court could mandate it.

John Marr, a former Clark County, Nevada, probation officer, who runs private outpatient drug treatment programs in Las Vegas and Reno, says the juvenile justice system is toughening up on kids who abuse drugs. "It used to be 'warn and release.' Kids and parents would see an intake officer at the booking desk who would yell at the youngster for a few minutes and send them home," says Marr. It would take four offenses before the court would consider any type of intervention, he adds, "so, as a result, kids always thought of juvenile court as a joke." No longer. In the last three years the court system has clamped down. Now first offenders—and their parents—may be ordered to attend four to eight hours of drug education. For a second or subsequent arrest, the child will appear before a magistrate or a referee who most likely will order an assessment for the child. Says Marr, "The courts are working with kids and their families to break the cycle of substance abuse."

Assessment: the Crucial First Treatment Step

Hopefully, you will not wait until your child has a brush with the law to order an assessment or evaluation to start drug abuse treatment and recovery. But what does it involve? Dr. David Moore, executive director of Olympic Counseling Service in Tacoma, Washington, and a nationally recognized expert in adolescent assessment for chemical dependency, looks for attitudes and stress levels.

The meat of the assessment is an examination of the youngster's attitudes, biochemistry, and family history and lifestyle, especially their stress levels, explains Dr. Moore. Are their attitudes and reactions resilient or risk factors? By way of example, Dr. Moore relates the different behaviors of ten teens sitting around the table having beers. By the time their blood-alcohol level reaches .08 percent, (which is deemed a legal level of intoxication in some states), seven of the teens will stop drinking or will have quit earlier. "Their body is sending their brain biofeedback that says 'no more,'" says the assessment specialist. These are "resilient" youngsters and they will, in general, go through life able to cope without chemicals or addictions. "But three kids around the table will be wide-eyed, want to go out partying and will try to persuade the other seven to join them. They don't know when to stop." These three are "at risk" for all types of chemical and emotional dependencies and problems.

A child from an alcoholic family or a family where one parent drinks daily and to excess lives with much more stress than a kid from a nondrinking family. Alcohol transforms a parent's mood or personality, and kids study their mom or dad or both so they do not further inflame an angry father or do not get the silent treatment from a mom who shuts down when she is intoxicated. They walk on eggshells; they live with stress. "Kids who live in a protracted state of stress," explains Dr. Moore, "are at great risk for chemical dependency because drugs relieve the stress and make them feel good."

Treatment may require a family reconfiguration. Assessment specialists take a hard line. If a kid is arrested for drug abuse or possession of illegal substances and the parents blame the police or treat it as if it is no big deal, the problem may be mom and dad. The parents are too permissive or in denial, and to send the youngster back into that setting is guaranteeing an instant replay. The first step in treating the problem may involve placing the kid with a relative. It is a bitter pill for families to swallow, but it is also a wake-up call to begin facing reality. The question to ask: How will you, or did you, react if your child is arrested and booked?

The assessment specialist and the adolescent addiction treatment counselor may recommend several strategies:

* Family support group program
* An out-patient program where the parent and the kid work at solving the problem with therapists and hands-on help from specialists in the community.
* A residential treatment program from four to six weeks or longer.
* Rigidly enforced treatment options.

These decisions should not be made lightly. A growing number of communities have juvenile drug courts that are not just a waystation for sentencing in the justice system but instead offer an incredibly intensive outpatient treatment program. One of the most successful is run by Judge John Parnham in Pensacola, Florida, who says "substance abuse moves very rapidly from experimentation with gateway drugs to regular recreational use to the dependency stage. We treat the entire family, not just the kid."

His program is to hold the child responsible for his behavior and his recovery but to keep the parent involved to open up the communication channels in the home. Judge Parnham rules that a kid who appears in drug court and who agrees to a recovery plan must spend four hours a day four times a week in intense treatment, submit to two random urinalysis tests, and come to court weekly. And at least one, but preferably both parents take part in every minute of the program. Next, a family therapist visits the home to size up the setting and stress levels and works with the drug treatment counselor. Judge Parnham's program lasts eighteen months.

One of the most successful residential drug treatment programs in the country is Phoenix House with facilities nationwide. Martha Gagne, director of the American Council for Drug Education, an affiliate of Phoenix House, says sometimes "the choice is jail or Phoenix House, and both parents must be totally supportive of the decision to send the child here. This is the kid's last chance [before entering the juvenile or adult justice system] and the kid needs to know it." Gagne does not believe in sugarcoating. Phoenix House's six- to nine-week program teaches kids life skills they should be learning at home. "We give them back to society with a positive self-image and a sense of responsibility so they can fit in without reverting back to their old ways of coping."

15

Strategies and Smart Ideas for Raising Drug-Free Kids

There is no one drug awareness program, no one strategy, no one foolproof formula for keeping kids drug free. Many kids will experiment with drugs as part of growing up. They're curious. In this final chapter, we review key points from throughout the book and we introduce a few novel ideas for fighting drugs, such as harnessing the power of the Internet or starting an antidrug program in your community.

Key Points

Mary Jo Porreca, a certified addiction specialist in Bryn Mawr, Pennsylvania, says there is no way to predict whether a young-ster will experiment with drugs, but there are factors that could predispose a kid to try them and get addicted. Among them:

♦ A history of drug or alcohol addiction in the family or over several generations
♦ Ongoing physical and emotional abuse in the family or in previous generations
♦ Loss of a parent or a beloved family member
♦ A reluctance among family members to show emotions and discuss feelings, which forces kids to "stuff" their own fears, feelings, and problems and to shut down emotionally

- Rigid, dogmatic religious upbringing
- Poor self-esteem, lack of self-confidence, feeling they are inadequately equipped for the real world
- An unsafe or frightening environment

While any of these factors could indicate a predisposition, they do not guarantee that your child is going to use or get hooked. "If these risk factors are present, do not think you are going to erase them from your and your child's life like cleaning a blackboard. But you can counterbalance them," says Porreca. "It's all about spending time with your kids."

Be Available, Get Involved, Listen

Porreca suggests parents take this test. Ask yourself what are the best things you remember about your own childhood, about growing up. "If you remember what was special or meaningful in your life, you'll usually say it was when people you loved spent time with you," she contends. "That's what most people remember." Your youngsters will remember the same thing, insists Porreca. So schedule time—whether it is every night for a half hour or every Saturday morning—then use it to start listening to your kid and doing things with him or her.

- What are their interests?
- What are they curious about?
- What's on their mind?
- What do they want to see?
- What's bothering them?
- What is happening at school?
- Are there friends they would like to invite for dinner?
- Have you had a chance to visit the new museum exhibit?

The objective here is simply to be available, to be involved. Even if it is only ten minutes a day or every other day, the goal for a parent is to be engaged with their child and not disengaged or watching TV or bringing work home and getting buried in it.

Workaholics can be just as psychologically abusive to their children as alcoholics and addicts. It may be more socially acceptable, but the damage is the same: A kid does not feel like s/he is worth your time.

Even if you are harried, harassed, overworked, or sharing your child with an ex-spouse, you can find "teachable moments" for instilling positive, character-building values in your child that will help him or her rebuff drugs. One Orange County, California, woman does it during carpooling.

"My 13-year-old daughter is in the car, the radio is off, there is no television, no phone, and I have her total attention before we pick up her girlfriends and go to school," says Adrianne L., a home healthcare nurse. "We talk about the fact that she is discovering boys, and that some are drinking beer and offering it to her and her friends and egging them on to try it." Adrianne varies the message. "Some days we talk about weight and diet pills. Some days we talk about dating. I try not to use scare tactics, but I'm tempted. At least we're talking."

Porreca's suggests that you find out your children's dreams and encourage them in every way possible to realize their hopes, their interests. If kids find and pursue their passions, "negative, harmful substances like alcohol and drugs will be less seductive."

Use Real-Life Examples

Being a single parent with a heavy workload and little free time is not an excuse for depriving your child of personal attention. If you do not honestly think you can free up even an hour or two on a regular basis, ask a relative or a trusted, concerned friend for help. There are also excellent organizations like Big Brothers and Big Sisters where responsible adults will spend their time with your youngsters.

Dan Page, a Boulder, Colorado, marketing consultant, is a Big Brother to a 14-year-old boy. Page is on the board of directors of Positive Air, a group of world-class gymnasts who use gymnastic routines as a way to teach kids self-esteem, discipline, and the importance of a healthy, well-toned body. "We send positive messages to kids," says Page. "Our work is to convince youngsters that life is difficult, but they can do anything if they put their mind to it." In gymnastics kids know that winning and losing is up to the individual. A gymnast cannot depend on his teammates to win for him—a sound life lesson.

Page helps his "little brother" with his homework, takes him whitewater rafting, and spends quite a bit of time discussing the pitfalls of drugs. Page uses these opportunities to relate what his little brother sees back to his message of self-reliance and anti-drugs. "I ask him what does he see at school? In middle school, he definitely sees kids smoking dope, and I know when he goes into high school next year he'll see more drugs." The marketing consultant says their conversations are very candid. "I don't beat around the bush. He gets straight answers and I don't talk down to him and I don't preach. I know it will only distance him and he'll shut down to all my messages." Those messages include the importance of honesty, integrity, and ethics in dealing with people of all ages. We talk about all the characteristics of a healthy, successful person."

Just as the most vivid learning experiences are outside the classroom, Page takes his little brother on field trips to bring his anti-drug message to life. "I'll take him to shelters to see how less fortunate people live." But they do not just gawk; they work together organizing clothing drives and toy drives at Christmas and team up on other community projects. Says Page: "We get involved—together."

Provide Parental Support

As parents, all of us want to protect what we love and cherish. Since the dawn of civilization, man has built moats and walls around his castle to keep out the enemy. Today, many people build fences around their homes to keep out intruders and to protect their family and property. When it comes to drugs, you can't build a fence around your kids, but you can provide parental support that goes beyond just talking to your kids. We've already made these points, but they bear repeating.

Set firm ground rules and establish consequences for violating them

Youngsters will always test rules to see if what they can get away with. If rules are not enforced, they will keep trying something new; drugs are often one of these "new experiences." So if a 9 p.m. curfew is established, enforce it and explain why.

Be authoritative

Don't be too permissive or lax because youngsters will think you don't care or you're not serious. Yet, do not be rigid, demanding, inflexible, and intolerant—a "my way or the highway" approach. No question: kids will rebel. Although you should not tolerate drug use by a youngster, the dictatorial approach causes more problems than it cures. Help children make intelligent, healthy choices by encouraging them within limits and standards.

Encourage academic excellence

Not every youngster is a straight-A student. But younsters respond when parents encourage kids to excel, work with them on homework, and take a genuine interest in their schoolwork. They also tend to make friends with other kids who prize learning and discovery and good grades as a way of winning respect and attention. Poor performance at school—bad grades, disruptive behavior—is a reliable predictor of negative behavior. These kids almost always gravitate toward other underachievers and are at a much higher risk of adopting negative behaviors. Poor school performance is correctable.

Get to know their friends and acquaintances

Regardless of whether your child is bringing home As or Ds, you need to know who their friends are and what they and their parents are like. Are their parents attentive and involved or permissive? What are their attitudes toward drugs and alcohol? If your child spends a lot of time with one or two "best friends," meet their parents and go out for an informal meal with all the kids and talk. Your instincts will tell you whether this is a healthy environment for your kids.

Don't be afraid to disapprove of your child's friends

If you sense that your kids' friends could be the type to tease or taunt or generally pressure them into doing things that go against what they know is right, sit down and talk to them. Naturally, they're going to resist, but if you explain your feelings rather than just laying down a law, you'll be surprised that your youngster might agree. Just don't wait until there is a real bonding between the kids.

Raising healthy kids with positive attitudes and good self-esteem is a full-time job. You need to help your child grow from a dependent young person into an independent and successful adult. This involves learning how to accept responsibility, create friendships and relationships, and make the right choices. Using drugs is one of the choices they have to make.

Safeguarding the Internet for Kids

Not that long ago, youngsters went to the library or to a set of encyclopedias to gather information and reference material for a classroom report or a term paper. Now they can switch on a computer, insert a CD-ROM, or go online and search the equivalent of a continually updated global library. The world is literally at their fingertips. But too often parents or responsible adults are at work or busy and are either not present or not Net-savvy enough to be aware of the dangers of this powerful new medium or to help their kids navigate it. At the same time, kids are amazingly computer literate and are becoming increasingly familiar with the Net, which puts them more at risk for encountering offensive Web sites and electronic bulletin boards designed for adults, yet accessible to anyone.

Jupiter Communications, a New York based Internet research company, says 4.1 million youngsters went online in 1996. And that number is supposed to grow fivefold in the next four years. By the year 2000, some 19.2 million kids will be online, predicts Jupiter, while 30.3 million youngsters will be traveling in cyberspace regularly by 2002. Indeed, with powerful home PCs selling for under $1,000, it is forecast that 53 percent of American households will have a home computer by the year 2001.

Today, computer-savvy youngsters trade addresses of unblocked Web sites. Internet watchdogs contend that many parents are in denial when it is suggested that their youngster may be surfing for offensive or obscene Web sites. "Lots of people tell me 'it's not my kid who looks at this stuff,'" says Salomon of SurfWatch. "But then when parents look into the cache [a history file on your computer listing precisely which Web sites have been browsed], lo and behold they find their youngsters are going places they shouldn't be." You should be aware of and steer your child away from Internet sites devoted to alcohol, tobacco, and other drugs; pornography; pedophilia; violence; terrorism; racial hatred and other antisocial forums. Indeed, the Internet is essentially an electronic forum of free speech, as it should be, and it is largely unregulated. Therefore, you can and will find data, documents, and discourse that represent the views of the entire spectrum of morality. The vast majority of the content on the Net is positive and instructive, with educational information and balanced opinion.

Drugs and the Internet

There are a large number of antidrug sites, including ones sponsored by such organizations as D.A.R.E. America, the Partnership for a Drug Free America, and the American Council For Drug Education. These sites offer comprehensive information on drug awareness and prevention. However, when it comes to drugs and the Net, the pro-drug voice is definitely the loudest.

In a June 20, 1997, article in *The New York Times,* an Internet consultant estimates that three-quarters of the online voices speaking about drugs favor some kind of legalization. "They definitely control the discussion on the Internet. The pro-legalization people are light years ahead of the anti-legalization people."

There are nearly 1,000 Internet sites pushing prodrug information, and any kid with a computer, a modem, and Internet access can visit them. These are not just online propaganda pitches from organizations bent on legalizing marijuana or weakening drug laws. Many are far more menacing. Children can log on to the Net and find:

- How to cook up a batch of crack
- A guide for taking an acid trip
- Online "chat rooms" where people recall their "really cool trips" on LSD or other experiences with illegal drugs
- Sources for ordering marijuana seeds and drug paraphernalia
- Sites promoting the pleasures of dangerous substances

All the more reason that parents need to be aware of what's out there and guide them through the available information.

This is a big worry of information professionals. "Our most important partners are the parents of children who are using interactive technology," says Barbara Ford, president of the American Library Association. Tools for monitoring, blocking, and filtering the net can be designed, she notes, "but they can never take the place of adult supervision." Just as you help your children choose appropriate television shows or movies, parental guidance is also needed in the online world.

How the Net Works

Before parents can fully appreciate the problem, they must understand some basics. The Internet, originally the province of educators and government defense officials, is what is now called the Information Superhighway. Anyone can get on it. The most heavily traveled thoroughfare is the World Wide Web, where most of the Web sites are located. Think of Web sites as electronic billboards. Anyone can build a Web site or Web page at virtually no cost. Anyone can design their own "home page" or Web site and display their uncensored message to the world, a right constitutionally guaranteed under the First Amendment. People and organizations can also create electronic bulletin boards where anyone can post and read messages, and no one has control over what is said or read.

And anyone with a Web browser (usually included with an Internet access provider such as America Online, CompuServe, or Prodigy) can visit any Web site by typing in the address that usually starts with http://www. It is that simple. From there, Net surfers can get other addresses and link up to other sites. As users surf the Net, they can download or print out hard copies of information from any of the sites visited.

Blocking Pro-Drug and Objectionable Web Sites

Parents do not need to feel powerless about the Internet. There are a number of inexpensive, effective, and easy-to-use tools that can make the Net and the Web family friendly and safe for children. Virtually every Internet access provider recognizes that child-inappropriate content is a problem and encourages parents to get involved. Steve Case, America Online's founder/president says, "Just like you wouldn't drive without buckling up your kids in seat belts, you shouldn't let them travel in cyberspace without technology safeguards."

Filtering Software

Parents can purchase filtering software to install on their home computers that will do some or all of the following:

♦ Screen user-defined sites (often according to words, phrases, or content that you have determined is inappropriate) to block out offensive Web sites

- Block access to incoming, unsolicited electronic mail
- Block instant messaging or one-to-one communiqué
- Block access to chat rooms and news groups

Typically, a parent inserts the filtering software disk, creates a password, and runs the "install" command. Only a parent knows the password; without it the blocking software cannot be deactivated. The largest Internet access providers all offer filtering software to their subscribers. Fees and features vary according to the provider. Some popular software programs that let parents filter the online material coming into their homes are Cyber Patrol, CYBERsitter, Net Nanny, and SurfWatch. Denny Matteucci, president of CompuServe, warns that "Internet filter software could possibly be circumvented, so active parental involvement is essential."

Even the software companies that filter Internet sites walk a fine line. For instance, software does not block all Web sites under the broad category of drugs because these could include sites sponsored by pharmaceutical companies discussing legal prescription drugs. SurfWatch software will block sites detailing how to achieve "legal highs" or how to sniff glue or misuse prescription drugs. SurfWatch does not simply ban all sites that mention words like "marijuana." "We do not block sites discussing medicinal drug use, industrial hemp use, or public debate on the issue of legalizing certain drugs," says Alexandra Salomon, content services manager for SurfWatch. Sites that provide educational information on drug use are not filtered either.

"We encourage parents to surf the net with their children and visit chat rooms so they can realize the scope of the online community," suggests Ginny Wydler, AOL's Strategy Director for Kids, Families, and Teens. Just as companies that specialize in software and services to filter Web sites are constantly monitoring the Web for offensive sites, parents should continually discuss the information their kids get and need for school. As they mature, constraints can be changed and some sites might be unblocked. Do not just set parental controls and forget them.

Suggestions for Safe Surfing

Using an Internet service provider that blocks antisocial sites or installing filtering software at home is a good first step. The next step is to set some family rules for using the Internet. There is a staggering amount of information—and misinformation—out there. The Internet is a valuable and fun resource when used wisely. When you establish family rules for using the computer and the Internet, explain what you are doing.

Another way to explain your concerns to a youngster is to continue the metaphor that if the Internet is indeed the information superhighway, anyone who drives it needs to know the rules of the road. Tell your child, "You wouldn't get in an automobile without knowing how to drive. The same holds true for the Net." On the other hand, your youngsters may know more about the online world than you do. Do not be embarrassed to let them show you what they do know or to ask them to teach you how to access various services. In short, learn together, but as the parent, you set the rules.

Rules for the Road

Discuss the following rules with your children as common-sense protection to help them be "street smart."

◆ Place the home computer in the family room or in a central location rather than in the child's bedroom. Kids are less likely to get into trouble if they know you are watching.

◆ Limit computer time. Set up regular hours for using it. A home computer linked to the Internet, like the television, can easily be abused. Keep an eye on your phone bills, online service fees, and credit card statements.

◆ Be specific about what sites can and cannot be visited.

◆ Passwords are private and should not be shared.

◆ Never give your password to your youngster so s/he can access your account and log-on to an unfiltered site.

- Discuss the dangers of this medium:
  - It is difficult to assess the intentions and character of people you cannot see.
  - Unless you are e-mailing back and forth to a friend, you have no idea who you are communicating with.
- Do not send or receive e-mail from anyone except for family and friends. Do not converse with or contact anyone online that you have not previously established a relationship with.
- Usenet sites and chat rooms are off limits.
- If you receive offensive e-mail, do not respond. It is not bad manners or being rude to ignore an online communication. If messages get obnoxious, tell your parent or an adult. If they become threatening, have your parents notify law enforcement authorities.
- Do not respond to anyone who even suggests drugs, sex, or anything that makes you feel uncomfortable or frightened.
- Never give out personal information about you or your family. For example, home address; telephone number; school name and location; teacher's name; parents' first names, work address, or work telephone numbers; names or ages of siblings. This is private and personal information.
- Never agree to a meeting with someone you meet online. If you follow the previous rule about restricting e-mail to family and friends, this should not be a problem. Kids should be aware of this rule in case their friends are in contact with strangers. Never have anyone come to your house or meet you before or after school. Even if they say they are a friend of a friend or mention the name of an acquaintance or relative, do not meet a "cyber stranger."
- Do not send your picture or anything else to someone you meet on line, no matter how sincere they sound.
- Never give a credit card number to anyone requesting it. If someone asks you to find an old credit card receipt and type in the number, that is wrong. Even if what is being offered is tempting, never give out a credit card number.

- Never click on a Web site that says "adults only" or asks if you are 18 years of age or older.
- If you find those sites or receive e-mail that you know is intended for adults, let your parents know immediately.
- Participate in and supervise your child's use of the Internet.

Join them at the keyboard. In fact, going online and exploring the Net and the Web together gives you a great opportunity to develop a dialogue with your children. You are spending uninterrupted time together. It is no different than tossing a baseball around in the backyard or working on an after-school project together. The best drug prevention message you can send your youngster is this, and it doesn't have to be spoken: "I'm here with you. You have my full attention and I'm really listening to what you have to say."

Joining your child on a journey through cyberspace is more than an opportunity to play computer games together or simply discover new and interesting Web sites and avoid offensive ones. It is yet another way you can help instill personal and family values in your kid that will influence his or her behaviors—now and in the future. These values help kids make good decisions, give them reasons to say "no" and mean it, and stick to their decisions in the face of peer pressure. This sounds almost too simplistic, too elementary, but it cannot be reinforced enough. It is all about connecting with your kid and building, if you will, a conversational superhighway.

How to Start an Anti-Drug Program

If you are frustrated and want to get involved in confronting drug abuse in your community, you and other motivated individuals can take action on your own.

Your project can be as simple or as involved as you want to make it. Evaluate what resources you have and decide how the project will be funded and maintained. Some projects might be funded by the program's founder (yourself and/or a few others), while others might require volunteers. If your project is really ambitious, you should look into grants available from federal, state, and local government grant sources as well as from private foundations. It is not within the scope of this book to cover the dynamics of applying for and obtaining grants, but your local librarian ought to be able to direct you to necessary resources if you choose to pursue this route.

Another avenue for personal activism is through existing organizations that share your concerns, goals, and objectives. Consult the Resource Directory in the back of this book for the names of local organizations or for national organizations that can direct you to groups operating within your community.

Some projects you might consider:

- Putting together an educational program to raise awareness about drug abuse. Your program could cover a wide spectrum of drugs or focus on one aspect such as pregnancy, alcohol abuse, and fetal alcohol syndrome.
- Creating a network of trained peer counselors to work with teenagers and young adults in your neighborhood.
- Holding an auction of donated goods as a fund-raiser for a women's shelter or a community counseling center.
- Establishing parent and youth support groups to refer members to job training, counseling, and educational resources.
- Coordinating like-minded parents to set up supervised after-school care and activities.
- Sponsoring a workshop with a guest speaker on domestic violence.

Here are some basic project management steps to help you realize your goal.

1. Define a long-term goal and break it down into a series of achievable steps. If your goal is something like "eliminating drug abuse in our neighborhood," you will need to define the problem by gathering information that will support the fact that you are seeking a solution to a well-defined problem. In this case, sources of information are as varied as

school and public health officials, church groups, and local law enforcement.

2. If you have not already, enlist the support of others and form an advisory group or board of directors. Your core group should be comprised of responsible and respected members of the community. Since you will most likely be dealing with issues that effect your children, consider enlisting the support of community youth.

3. Once you have a well-defined problem, you can begin to create a plan of action that will include both short-range goals (eliminate drug abuse in the community's schools) and long-range goals (eliminate drug abuse in the community). Try not to set too many goals because each one will have objectives and corresponding action items.

4. Develop a list of objectives under each goal and be sure to thoroughly outline resources, needs, and action items required to accomplish each objective. One objective for the short-range goal above could be community education.

5. Identify methods to support your objectives.

6. Develop activities that support the methods.

It goes without saying that you should never take the law into your own hands, but there are many things that you can do as concerned parents. As with any community activity, talk to local authorities to be sure that you have any necessary permits.

ACTIVITY

Where to Go Site Seeing

Is your youngster curious about drugs? Are you looking for looking for more continually updated information on drug prevention? There are number of Internet sites you can visit online, either by yourself or with your child.

The National Institute of Drug Abuse (NIDA) is part of the U.S. Department of Health and Human Services. This Web site is worth a visit to keep abreast of current research on drug prevention. Visitors can order a free copy of an informative booklet, "Preventing Drug Use Among Children and Adolescents."
Address: http://www.nida.nih.gov

The American Council For Drug Education has a cool new Web site that takes children, adolescents, and their families on an animated voyage through the human body. The tour illustrates the effects of drugs such as alcohol, nicotine, cocaine, and marijuana. Scientifically accurate, the data is designed to counteract the misleading information on substance abuse now clogging up the Net.
Address: http://www.acde.org

Partnership For a Drug Free America has a must-visit Web site called Drug-Free Resource Net. Solid, no-nonsense information is nicely packaged with clean, attractive graphics. It offers good guidelines for parents.
Address: http://www.drugfreeamerica.org

D.A.R.E. has a comprehensive, antidrug, antiviolence Web site aimed directly at kids, parents, educators, and D.A.R.E. officers. Interactive, it lets all four groups e-mail questions, comments, and stories and get direct feedback. Kids can take part in games, contests, and trivia questions and can get news and views from D.A.R.E. officers and communities around the country.
Address: http://www.dare-america.com

Appendix A
Glossary of Drug Terms

The ability to understand current drug-related street terms is an invaluable tool for law enforcement, public health, and other criminal justice professionals who work with the public. This document contains over 2,000 street terms that refer to specific drug types or drug activity.

All terms are cross-referenced where possible. A single term or similar terms may refer to various drugs or have different meanings, reflecting geographic and demo-graphic variations in slang. All known meanings and spellings are included. No attempt was made to determine which usage is most frequent or widespread. Different definitions for a single term are separated by semi-colons (;). The use of commas (,) and the connective "and" indicates that the term refers to the use of the specified drugs in combination.

For source information, please contact White House Office of National Drug Control Policy, Drug Policy Information Clearinghouse, at 1-800-666-3332 or on the Internet at: askncjrs@ncjrs.org

242

A

A LSD; amphetamine
Abe $5 worth of drugs
Abe's cabe $5 bill
Abolicy veterinary steroid
Acapulco gold marijuana from S.W. Mexico
Acapulco red marijuana
Ace marijuana; PCP
Acid LSD
Acid cube sugar cube containing LSD
Acid freak heavy user of LSD
Acid head LSD user
AD PCP
Adam MDMA
African black marijuana
African bush marijuana
African woodbine marijuana cigarette
Agonies withdrawal symptoms
Ah-pen-yen opium
Aimies amphetamine; amyl nitrite
AIP heroin from Afghanistan, Iran, & Pakistan
Air blast inhalant
Airhead marijuana user
Airplane marijuana
Alice B. Toklas marijuana brownie
All lit up under the influence of drugs
All star user of multiple drugs
All-American drug cocaine
Alpha-ET alpha-ethyltyptamine
Ames amyl nitrite
Amidone methadone

Amoeba PCP
Amp amphetamine
Amp joint marijuana cigarette laced with some form of narcotic
Amped-out fatigue after using amphetamines
Amping accelerated heartbeat
AMT dimethyltryptamine
Amys amyl nitrite
Anadrol oral steroid
Anatrofin injectable steroid
Anavar oral steroid
Angel, Angel dust, Angel hair, Angel mist, Angel Poke PCP
Angie cocaine
Angola marijuana
Animal LSD
Animal tranq PCP
Animal tranquilizer PCP
Antifreeze heroin
Apache fentanyl
Apple jacks crack
Aries heroin
Aroma of men isobutyl nitrite
Artillery equipment for injecting drugs
Ashes marijuana
Astro turf marijuana
Atom bomb marijuana and heroin
Atshitshi marijuana
Aunt Hazel heroin
Aunt Mary marijuana
Aunt Nora cocaine
Aunti opium
Aunti Emma opium
Author a doctor who writes illegal prescriptions

B

B amount of marijuana to fill a matchbox
B-bombs amphetamines
B-40 cigar laced with marijuana and dipped in malt liquor
B.J.'s crack
Babe drug used for detoxification
Baby marijuana
Baby bhang marijuana
Baby habit occasional use of drugs
Babysit guide through first drug experience
Baby T crack
Backbreakers LSD and strychnine
Back door pipe residue
Backjack injecting opium
Back to back smoking crack after injecting heroin or heroin used after smoking crack
Backtrack allow blood to flow back into a needle during injection
Backup prepare vein for injection
Backwards depressant
Bad bundle inferior quality heroin
Bad crack
Bad go bad drug reaction
Bad seed peyote; heroin; marijuana
Bag container for drugs
Bag bride crack-smoking prostitute
Bag man person who transports money
Bagging using inhalant
Bale marijuana

Ball crack
Balling vaginally implanted cocaine
Balloon heroin supplier
Ballot heroin
Bam depressant; amphetamine
Bambalacha marijuana
Bambs depressant
Bang to inject a drug; inhalant
Bank bandit pills depressant
Bar marijuana
Barb depressant
Barbies depressant
Barbs cocaine
Barrels LSD
Bart Simpson heroin
Base cocaine; crack
Baseball crack
Base crazies searching on hands and knees for crack
Base head person who bases
Bash marijuana
Basuco cocaine; coca paste residue sprinkled on marijuana or regular cigarette
Bathtub speed methcathinone
Batt IV needle
Battery acid LSD
Batu smokable methamphetamine
Bazooka cocaine; crack; crack and tobacco combined in a joint
Bazulco cocaine
Beam me up Scottie crack dipped in PCP
Beamer crack user
Beans amphetamine; depressant; mescaline
Beast LSD
Beat artist person selling

bogus drugs
Beat vials vials of sham crack to cheat buyers
Beavis & Butthead LSD
Beautiful boulders crack
Bebe crack
Bedbugs fellow addicts
Beedies cigarettes from India (resemble marijuana joints/vehicles for other drugs)
Beemers crack
Behind the scale to weigh and sell cocaine
Beiging chemically altering cocaine to make it appear a higher purity
Belladonna PCP
Belt effects of drugs
Belushi cocaine and heroin
Belyando spruce marijuana
Bender drug party
Bennie amphetamine
Bens amphetamine
Benz amphetamine
Benzedrine amphetamine
Bernice cocaine
Bernie cocaine
Bernie's flakes cocaine
Bernie's gold dust cocaine
Bhang marijuana
Big bag heroin
Big bloke cocaine
Big C cocaine
Big 8 1/8 kilogram of crack
Big D LSD
Big H heroin
Big Harry heroin
Big flake cocaine
Big man drug supplier
Big O opium

Big rush cocaine
Bill Blass crack
Billie hoke cocaine
Bikers coffee methamphetamine and coffee
Bindle small packet of drug powder; heroin
Bing enough of a drug for one injection
Bingers crack addicts
Bingo to inject a drug
Bings crack
Biphetamine amphetamine
Bird head LSD
Birdie powder heroin; cocaine
Biscuit 50 rocks of crack
Bite one's lips to smoke marijuana
Biz bag of drugs
Black opium; marijuana
Black acid LSD; LSD and PCP
Black and white amphetamine
Black bart marijuana
Black beauties depressant; amphetamine
Black birds amphetamine
Black bombers amphetamine
Black dust PCP
Black ganga marijuana resin
Black gold high potency marijuana
Black gungi marijuana from India
Black gunion marijuana
Black hash opium and hashish
Black mo highly potent marijuana
Black mollies amphetamine

Black mote marijuana mixed with honey
Black pearl heroin
Black pill opium pill
Black rock crack
Black Russian hashish mixed with opium
Black star LSD
Black stuff heroin
Black sunshine LSD
Black tabs LSD
Black tar heroin
Black whack PCP
Blacks amphetamine
Blanco heroin
Blanke marijuana cigarette
Blanks low quality drugs
Blast to smoke marijuana; to smoke crack
Blast a joint to smoke marijuana
Blast a roach to smoke marijuana
Blast a stick to smoke marijuana
Blasted under the influence of drugs
Blizzard white cloud in a pipe used to smoke cocaine
Block marijuana
Block busters depressant
Blonde marijuana
Blotter LSD; cocaine
Blotter acid LSD
Blotter cube LSD
Blow cocaine; to inhale cocaine; to smoke marijuana
Blow a fix injection misses the vein and is wasted in the skin
Blow a shot injection misses the vein and is wasted in the skin
Blow the vein injection misses the vein and is

wasted in the skin
Blow a stick to smoke marijuana
Blow blue to inhale cocaine
Blowcaine crack diluted with cocaine
Blow coke to inhale cocaine
Blow one's roof to smoke marijuana
Blow smoke to inhale cocaine
Blowing smoke marijuana
Blowout crack
Blow up crack cut with lidocaine to increase size, weight, and street value
Blows heroin
Blue depressant; crack
Blue acid LSD
Blue angels depressant
Blue barrels LSD
Blue birds depressant
Blue boy amphetamine
Blue bullets depressant
Blue caps mescaline
Blue chairs LSD
Blue cheers LSD
Blue de hue marijuana from Vietnam
Blue devil depressant
Blue dolls depressant
Blue heaven LSD
Blue heavens depressant
Blue madman PCP
Blue microdot LSD
Blue mist LSD
Blue moons LSD
Blue sage marijuana
Blue sky blond high potency marijuana from Columbia
Blue tips depressant
Blue vials LSD
Blunt marijuana inside a

cigar; marijuana and cocaine inside a cigar
Bo marijuana
Bo-bo marijuana
Boat PCP
Bobo crack
Bobo bush marijuana
Body packer person who ingests crack or cocaine to transport it
Body stuffer person who ingests crack vials to avoid prosecution
Bogart a joint salivate on a marijuana cigarette; refuse to share
Bohd marijuana; PCP
Bolasterone injectable steroid
Bolivian marching powder cocaine
Bolo crack
Bolt isobutyl nitrite
Bomb crack; heroin; large marijuana cigarette; high potency heroin
Bomb squad crack-selling crew
Bomber marijuana cigarette
Bombido injectable amphetamine; heroin; depressant
Bombita amphetamine; heroin; depressant
Bombs away heroin
Bone marijuana; $50 piece of crack
Bonecrusher crack
Bones crack
Bong pipe used to smoke marijuana
Bonita heroin
Boo marijuana
Boom marijuana
Boomers psilocybin/psilocin

Boost to inject a drug; to steal
Boost and shoot steal to support a habit
Booster to inhale cocaine
Boot to inject a drug
Boot the gong to smoke marijuana
Booted under the influence of drugs
Boppers amyl nitrite
Botray crack
Bottles crack vials; amphetamine
Boubou crack
Boulder crack; $20 worth of crack
Boulya crack
Bouncing powder cocaine
Boxed in jail
Boy heroin
Bozo heroin
Brain damage heroin
Brain ticklers amphetamine
Breakdowns $40 crack rock sold for $20
Break night staying up all night until day break
Brewery place where drugs are made
Brick 1 kilogram of marijuana; crack
Brick gum heroin
Bridge up or bring up ready a vein for injection
Britton peyote
Broccoli marijuana
Broker go-between in a drug deal
Bromo 2C-B
Brown heroin; marijuana
Brown bombers LSD
Brown crystal heroin
Brown dots LSD

Brown rhine heroin
Brown sugar heroin
Brownies amphetamine
Browns amphetamine
Bubble gum cocaine; crack
Buck shoot someone in the head
Bud marijuana
Buda a high-grade marijuana joint filled with crack
Buffer crack smoker; a woman who exchanges oral sex for crack
Bugged annoyed; to be covered with sores and abscesses from repeated use of unsterile needles
Bull narcotics agent or police officer
Bullet isobutyl nitrite
Bullet bolt inhalant
Bullia capital crack
Bullion crack
Bullyon marijuana
Bumblebees amphetamine
Bummer trip unsettling and threatening experience from PCP intoxication
Bump crack; fake crack; boost a high; hit of ketamine ($20)
Bundle heroin
Bunk fake cocaine
Burese cocaine
Burn one to smoke marijuana
Burn the main line to inject a drug
Burned purchase fake drugs
Burned out collapse of veins from repeated injection; permanent impairment from drug

abuse
Burnese cocaine
Burnie marijuana
Burnout heavy abuser of drugs
Bush cocaine; marijuana
Businessman's LSD dimethyltryptamine
Businessman's special dimethyltryptamine
Businessman's trip dimethyltryptamine
Busted arrested
Busters depressant
Busy bee PCP
Butt naked PCP
Butter marijuana; crack
Butter flower marijuana
Buttons mescaline
Butu heroin
Buzz under the influence of drugs
Buzz bomb nitrous oxide

C

C cocaine
C joint place where cocaine is sold
C & M cocaine and morphine
C.S. marijuana
C-dust cocaine
C-game cocaine
Caballo heroin
Cabello cocaine
Caca heroin
Cactus mescaline
Cactus buttons mescaline
Cactus head mescaline
Cad/Cadillac 1 ounce
Cadillac PCP
Cadillac express methcathinone
Cakes round discs of crack
Caine cocaine; crack

California cornflakes cocaine
California sunshine LSD
Cam trip high potency marijuana
Cambodian red marijuana from Cambodia
Came cocaine
Can marijuana; 1 ounce
Canadian black marijuana
Canamo marijuana
Canappa marijuana
Canceled stick marijuana cigarette
Candy cocaine; crack; depressant; amphetamine
Candy C cocaine
Candy flipping combining or sequencing LSD with MDMA
Cannabinol PCP
Cannabis tea marijuana
Cap crack; LSD
Caps crack
Cap up transfer bulk form drugs to capsules
Capital H heroin
Caps heroin; psilocybin/psilocin
Carburetor crack stem attachment
Carga heroin
Carmabis marijuana
Carne heroin
Carnie cocaine
Carpet patrol crack smokers searching the floor for crack
Carrie cocaine
Carrie Nation cocaine
Cartucho package of marijuana cigarettes
Cartwheels amphetamine
Casper the ghost crack

Cat methcathinone
Cat valium ketamine
Catnip marijuana cigarette
Caviar crack
Cavite all star marijuana
Cecil cocaine
Cest marijuana
Chalk methamphetamine; amphetamine
Chalked up under the influence of cocaine
Chalking chemically altering the color of cocaine so it looks white
Chandoo/chandu opium
Channel vein into which a drug is injected
Channel swimmer one who injects heroin
Charas marijuana from India
Charge marijuana
Charged up under the influence of drugs
Charley heroin
Charlie cocaine
Chase to smoke cocaine; to smoke marijuana
Chaser compulsive crack user
Chasing the dragon crack and heroin
Chasing the tiger to smoke heroin
Cheap basing crack
Check personal supply of drugs
Cheeba marijuana
Cheeo marijuana
Chemical crack
Chewies crack
Chiba chiba high potency marijuana from Columbia
Chicago black

marijuana, term from Chicago
Chicago green marijuana
Chicken powder amphetamine
Chicken scratch searching on hands and knees for crack
Chicle heroin
Chief LSD; mescaline
Chieva heroin
China cat high potency heroin
China girl fentanyl
China town fentanyl
China White fentanyl
Chinese molasses opium
Chinese red heroin
Chinese tobacco opium
Chip heroin
Chipper occasional Hispanic user
Chipping using drugs occasionally
Chippy cocaine
Chira marijuana
Chiva heroin
Chocolate opium; amphetamine
Chocolate chips LSD
Chocolate ecstasy crack made brown by adding chocolate milk powder
Choe cocaine
Cholly cocaine
Chorals depressant
Christina amphetamine
Christmas rolls depressant
Christmas tree marijuana; depressant; amphetamine
Chronic marijuana; marijuana mixed with crack
Chucks hunger following withdrawal from heroin

Churus marijuana
Chystal methadrine amphetamine
Cid LSD
Cigarette paper packet of heroin
Cigarrode cristal PCP
Citrol high potency marijuana, from Nepal
CJ PCP
Clarity MDMA
Clear up stop drug use
Clicker crack and PCP
Cliffhanger PCP
Climax crack; isobutyl nitrite; heroin
Climb marijuana cigarette
Clips rows of vials heat-sealed together
Clocking paper profits from selling drugs
Closet baser user of crack who prefers anonymity
Cloud crack
Cloud nine crack
Cluck crack smoker
Co-pilot amphetamine
Coasting under the influence of drugs
Coasts to coasts amphetamine
Coca cocaine
Cocaine blues depression after extended cocaine use
Cochornis marijuana
Cocktail cigarette laced with cocaine or crack; partially smoked marijuana cigarette inserted in regular cigarette
Cocoa puff to smoke cocaine and marijuana
Coconut cocaine
Coco rocks dark brown crack made by adding chocolate pudding
Coco snow benzocaine

used as cutting agent for crack
Cod large amount of money
Coffee LSD
Coke cocaine; crack
Coke bar bar where cocaine is openly used
Cola cocaine
Cold turkey sudden withdrawal from drugs
Coli marijuana
Coliflor tostao marijuana
Colorado cocktail marijuana
Columbian marijuana
Columbo PCP
Columbus black marijuana
Comeback benzocaine and mannitol used to adulterate cocaine for conversion to crack
Come home end an LSD trip
Conductor LSD
Connect purchase drugs; supplier of illegal drugs
Contact lens LSD
Cook mix heroin with water; heating heroin to prepare it for injection
Cook down process in which users liquify heroin in order to inhale it
Cooker to inject a drug
Cookies crack
Coolie cigarette laced with cocaine
Cooler cigarette laced with a drug
Cop obtain drugs
Copping zones specific areas where buyers can purchase drugs
Coral depressant

Coriander seeds cash
Corine cocaine
Cork the air to inhale cocaine
Corrinne cocaine
Cosa marijuana
Cotics heroin
Coties codeine
Cotton currency
Cotton brothers cocaine, heroin and morphine
Courage pills heroin; depressant
Course note bill larger than $2
Cozmo's PCP
Crack cocaine
Crack attack craving for crack
Crack back crack and marijuana
Crack cooler crack soaked in wine cooler
Crack kits glass pipe and copper mesh
Cracker jacks crack smokers
Crackers LSD
Crack gallery place where crack is bought/sold
Crack spot area where people can purchase crack
Crank methamphetamine; amphetamine; methcathinone
Cranking up to inject a drug
Crankster person who uses or manufactures methamphetamine
Crap/crop low quality heroin
Crash sleep off effects of drugs
Crazy coke PCP
Crazy Eddie PCP

Crazy weed marijuana
Credit card crack stem
Crib crack
Crimmie cigarette laced with crack
Crink methamphetamine
Cripple marijuana cigarette
Cris methamphetamine
Crisscross amphetamine
Criss-crossing the practice of setting up a line of cocaine next to a line of heroin. The user places a straw in each nostril and snorts about half a line each. Then the straws are crossed and the remaining lines are snorted.
Cristina methamphetamine
Cristy smokable methamphetamine
Croak crack and methamphetamine
Cross tops amphetamine
Crossroads amphetamine
Crown crap heroin
Crumbs tiny pieces of crack
Crunch & Munch crack
Cruz opium from Veracruz, Mexico
Crying weed marijuana
Crypto methamphetamine
Crystal PCP; amphetamine; cocaine; methamphetamine
Crystal joint PCP
Crystal meth methamphetamine
Cystal T PCP
Crystal tea LSD
Cube 1 ounce; LSD
Cubes marijuana tablets
Culican high potency

marijuana from Mexico
Cupcakes LSD
Cura heroin
Cushion vein into which a drug is injected
Cut adulterate drugs
Cut-deck heroin mixed with powdered milk
Cycline PCP
Cyclones PCP

D

D LSD, PCP
Dabble use drugs occasionally
Dagga marijuana
Dama blanca cocaine
Dance fever fentanyl
Dawamesk marijuana
Dead on arrival heroin
Debs amphetamine
Decadence MDMA
Deca-duabolin injectable steroid
Deck 1 to 15 grams of heroin, also known as a bag; packet of drugs
Deeda LSD
Delatestryl injectable steroid
Demo crack stem; a sample-size quantity of crack
Demolish crack
Dep-testosterone injectable steroid
DET dimethyltryptamine
Detroit pink PCP
Deuce $2 worth of drugs; heroin
Devil's dandruff crack
Devil's dick crack pipe
Devil's dust PCP
Devilsmoke crack
Dew marijuana
Dews $10 worth of drugs

Dex amphetamine
Dexedrine amphetamine
Dexies amphetamine
Diablito combination of crack cocaine and marijuana in a joint
Diambista marijuana
Diamonds amphetamine
Dianabol veterinary steroid
Dice crack cocaine
Diesel heroin
Diet pills amphetamine
Dihydrolone injectable steroid
Dimba marijuana from West Africa
Dime crack; $10
Dime bag $10 of drugs
Dime special crack cocaine
Dime's worth amount of heroin to cause death
Ding marijuana
Dinkie dow marijuana
Dinosaurs heroin users in their forties or fifties
Dip crack
Dipper PCP
Dipping out crack runners taking a portion of crack from vials
Dirt heroin
Dirt grass inferior quality marijuana
Dirty basing crack
Dirty joints combination of crack cocaine and marijuana
Disco biscuits depressant
Disease drug of choice
Diss show disrespect
Ditch marijuana
Ditch weed marijuana inferior quality, Mexican
Djamba marijuana
DMT Dimethyltryptamine

Do a joint to smoke marijuana
Do a line to inhale cocaine
Do it Jack PCP
DOA PCP; crack
Doctor MDMA
Dog good friend
Dog food heroin
Dogie heroin
Dollar $100 of drugs
Dolls depressant
Domes LSD
Domestic locally grown marijuana
Domex PCP and MDMA
Dominoes amphetamine
Don jem marijuana
Dona Juana marijuana
Dona Juanita marijuana
Doobee marijuana
Doobie marijuana
Doogie/doojee heroin
Dooley heroin
Dope heroin; marijuana; any other drug
Dope fiend crack addict
Dope smoke to smoke marijuana
Dopium opium
Doradilla marijuana
Dors and 4's combination of Doriden and Tyenol 4
Dots LSD
Doub $20 rock of crack
Double breasted dealing dealing cocaine and heroin together
Double bubble cocaine
Double cross amphetamine
Double dome LSD
Double rock crack diluted with procaine
Double trouble depressant

Double up when a crack dealer delivers an extra rock as a marketing ploy to attract customers
Double ups a $20 rock that can be broken into two $20 rocks
Double yoke crack
Dove $35 piece of crack
Dover's powder opium
Downer depressant
Downie depressant
Draf weed marijuana
Drag weed marijuana
Draw up to inject a drug
Dream cocaine
Dream gum opium
Dream stick opium
Dreamer morphine
Dreams opium
Dreck heroin
Drink PCP
Drivers amphetamine
Dropper to inject a drug
Drowsy high depressant
Drug slinging selling
Dry high marijuana
Dub when a crack dealer delivers an extra rock as a marketing ploy to attract customers
Dube/Dubbe marijuana
Duby marijuana
Duct cocaine
'Due residue of oils trapped in a pipe after smoking base
Dugie/Duji heroin
Dummy dust PCP
Durabolin injectable steroid
Durog marijuana
Duros marijuana
Dust heroin; cocaine; PCP; marijuana mixed with various chemicals
Dust joint PCP

Dust of angels PCP
Dusted parsley PCP
Dusting adding PCP, heroin, or another drug to marijuana
Dymethzine injectable steroid
Dynamite heroin and cocaine
Dyno heroin
Dyno-pure heroin

E

Earth marijuana cigarette
Easing powder opium
Eastside player crack
Easy score obtaining drugs easily
Eating taking orally
Ecstasy MDMA
Egg crack
Eight ball 1/8 ounce
Eightball crack and heroin
Eighth heroin
El diablito marijuana, cocaine, heroin and PCP
El diablo marijuana, cocaine and heroin
Electric Kool Aid LSD
Elephant PCP
Elephant tranquilizer PCP
Elvis LSD
Embalming fluid PCP
Emergency gun instrument used to inject other than syringe
Emsel morphine
Endo marijuana
Energizer PCP
Enoltestovis injectable steroid
Ephedrone methca-thinone
Equipose veterinary

steroid
Erth PCP
Esra marijuana
Essence MDMA
Estuffa heroin
ET alpha-ethyltyptamine
Eve MDEA
Explorers club group of
LSD users
Eye opener crack;
amphetamine

F

Factory place where drugs
are packaged, diluted, or
manufactured
Fake STP PCP
Fall arrested
Fallbrook redhair
marijuana, term from
Fallbrook, CA
Famous dimes crack
Fastin amphetamine
Fantasia dimethyltrypta-
mine
Fat bags crack
Fatty marijuana cigarette
Feed bag container for
marijuana
Felix the Cat LSD
Ferry dust heroin
Fi-do-nie opium
Fields LSD
Fiend someone who
smokes marijuana alone
Fifteen cents $15 worth
of drugs
Fifty-one crack
Finajet/finaject veteri-
nary steroid
Fine stuff marijuana
Finger marijuana cigarette
Finger lid marijuana
Fir marijuana
Fire to inject a drug; crack
and methamphetamine

Fire it up to smoke
marijuana
First line morphine
Fish scales crack
Five cent bag $5 worth
of drugs
Five C note $500 bill
Five dollar bag $50
worth of drugs
Fives amphetamine
Fix to inject a drug
Fizzies methadone
Flag appearance of blood
in the vein
Flake cocaine
Flakes PCP
Flame cooking smoking
cocaine base by putting the
pipe over a stove flame
Flamethrowers cigarette
laced with cocaine and
heroin
Flash LSD
Flat blues LSD
Flat chunks crack cut
with benzocaine
Flea powder low purity
heroin
Florida snow cocaine
Flower marijuana
Flower tops marijuana
Fly Mexican airlines to
smoke marijuana
Flying under the
influence of drugs
Following that cloud
searching for drugs
Foo foo stuff heroin;
cocaine
Foo-foo dust cocaine
Foolish powder heroin;
cocaine
Footballs amphetamine
Forget pill Rohypnol
Forget me drug
Rohypnol
45 Minute Psychosis

Dimethyltryptamine
Forwards amphetamine
Fraho/frajo marijuana
Freebase smoking
cocaine; crack
Freeze cocaine; renege on
a drug deal
French blue
amphetamine
French fries crack
Fresh PCP
Friend fentanyl
Fries crack
Frios marijuana laced
with PCP
Frisco special cocaine,
heroin and LSD
Frisco speedball cocaine,
heroin and LSD
Friskie powder cocaine
Fry crack
Fry daddy crack and
marijuana; cigarette laced
with crack
Fu marijuana
Fuel marijuana mixed
with insecticides; PCP
Fuete hypodermic needle
Fuma D'Angola
marijuana Portugese term

G

G $1000 or 1 gram of
drugs; term for an
unfamiliar male
G.B. depressant
GHB gamma hydroxy
butyrate
G-rock one gram of rock
cocaine
G-shot small dose of drugs
used to hold off with-
drawal symptoms until full
dose can be taken
Gaffel fake cocaine
Gaffus hypodermic

needle
Gage/gauge marijuana
Gagers methcathinone
Gaggers methcathinone
Galloping horse heroin
Gamot heroin
Gange marijuana
Gangster marijuana
Gangster pills
depressant
Ganja marijuana from
Jamaica
Gank fake crack
Garbage inferior quality
drugs
Garbage heads users
who buy crack from street
dealers instead of cooking
it themselves
Garbage rock crack
Gash marijuana
Gasper marijuana
cigarette
Gasper stick marijuana
cigarette
Gato heroin
Gauge butt marijuana
Gee opium
Geek crack and marijuana
Geek joints cigarettes or
cigars filled with tobacco
and crack
Geeker crack user
Geeze to inhale cocaine
Geezer to inject a drug
**Geezin a bit of dee
gee** injecting a drug
Georgia home boy
gamma hydroxy butyrate
George smack heroin
Get a gage up to smoke
marijuana
Get a gift obtain drugs
Get down to inject a drug
Get high to smoke
marijuana
Get lifted under the

influence of drugs
Get off to inject a drug;
get "high"
Get off houses private
places heroin users can
purchase & use heroin for a
fee
Get the wind to smoke
marijuana
Get through obtain
drugs
Getting roached using
Rohypnol
Ghana marijuana
Ghost LSD
Ghost busting smoking
cocaine; searching for
white particles in the belief
that they are crack
Gick monster crack
smoker
Gift-of-the-sun cocaine
Giggle smoke marijuana
Giggle weed marijuana
Gimmick drug injection
equipment
Gimmie crack and
marijuana
Gin cocaine
Girl cocaine; crack; heroin
Girlfriend cocaine
Giro houses non-bank
financial institutions
frequently used by drug
traffickers to launder drug
proceeds
Give wings inject
someone or teach someone
to inject heroin
Glacines heroin
Glad stuff cocaine
Glading using inhalant
Glass hypodermic needle;
amphetamine
Glass gun hypodermic
needle
Glo crack

Gluey person who sniffs
glue
Go amphetamines
Go-fast methcathinone
Go into a sewer to inject
a drug
Go loco to smoke
marijuana
Go on a sleigh ride to
inhale cocaine
Goblet of jam marijuana
God's flesh psilocybin/
psilocin
God's medicine opium
God's drug morphine
Gold marijuana; crack
Gold dust cocaine
Gold star marijuana
Golden marijuana
Golden Dragon LSD
Golden girl heroin
Golden leaf very high
quality marijuana
Golf ball crack
Golf balls depressant
Golpe heroin
Goma opium; black tar
heroin
Gondola opium
Gong marijuana; opium
Gonj marijuana
Goob methcathinone
Good PCP
Good and plenty heroin
Good butt marijuana
cigarette
Good giggles marijuana
Good go proper amount
of drugs for the money
paid
Good H heroin
Good lick good drugs
Goodfellas fentanyl
Goody-goody marijuana
Goof butt marijuana
cigarette
Goofball cocaine and

heroin; depressant
Goofers depressant
Goofy's LSD
Goon PCP
Goon dust PCP
Gopher person paid to pick up drugs
Goric opium
Gorilla biscuits PCP
Gorilla pills depressant
Gorilla tab PCP
Got it going on fast sale of drugs
Graduate completely stop using drugs or progress to stronger drugs
Gram hashish
Grape parfait LSD
Grass marijuana
Grass brownies brownies containing marijuana
Grasshopper marijuana
Grata marijuana
Gravel crack
Gravy to inject a drug; heroin
Grease currency
Great bear fentanyl
Great tobacco opium
Green inferior quality marijuana; PCP; ketamine
Green buds marijuana
Green double domes LSD
Green dragons depressant
Green frog depressant
Green goddess marijuana
Green gold cocaine
Green goods paper currency
Green leaves PCP
Green single domes LSD
Green tea PCP
Green wedge LSD
Greenies amphetamine

Greens/green stuff paper currency
Greeter marijuana
Greta marijuana
Grey shields LSD
Griefo marijuana
Griefs marijuana
Grievous bodily harm GHB
Grifa marijuana
Griff marijuana
Griffa marijuana
Griffo marijuana
Grit crack
Groceries crack
Ground control guide or caretaker during a hallucinogenic experience
Gum opium
Guma opium
Gun to inject a drug; needle
Gunga marijuana
Gungeon marijuana
Gungun marijuana
Gunja marijuana
Gutter vein into which a drug is injected
Gutter junkie addict who relies on others to obtain drugs
Gyve marijuana cigarette

H

H heroin
H & C heroin and cocaine
H Caps heroin
Hache heroin
Hail crack
Haircut marijuana
Hairy heroin
Half 1/2 ounce
Half-a-C $50 bill
Half a football field 50 rocks of crack
Half G $500

Half load 15 bags (decks) of heroin
Half moon peyote
Half piece 1/2 ounce of heroin or cocaine
Half track crack
Hamburger helper crack
Hand-to-hand direct delivery and payment
Hand-to-hand man transient dealers who carry small amounts of crack
Hanhich marijuana
Hanyak smokable speed
Happy cigarette marijuana cigarette
Happy dust cocaine
Happy powder cocaine
Happy sticks PCP
Happy trails cocaine
Hard candy heroin
Hard line crack
Hard rock crack
Hard stuff opium; heroin
Hardware isobutyl nitrite
Harry heroin
Harsh marijuana
Hats LSD
Has marijuana
Have a dust cocaine
Haven dust cocaine
Hawaiian very high potency marijuana
Hawaiian sunshine LSD
Hawk LSD
Hay marijuana
Hay butt marijuana cigarette
Haze LSD
Hazel heroin
HCP PCP
Head drugs amphetamine
Headlights LSD
Heart-on inhalant
Hearts amphetamine

Heaven and Hell PCP
Heaven dust heroin;
cocaine
Heavenly blue LSD
Heeled having plenty of
money
Helen heroin
Hell dust heroin
He-man fentanyl
Hemp marijuana
Henpicking searching on
hands and knees for crack
Henry heroin
Henry VIII cocaine
Her cocaine
Herb marijuana
Herb and Al marijuana
and alcohol
Herba marijuana
Herms PCP
Hero heroin
**Hero of the
    underworld** heroin
Heroina heroin
Herone heroin
Hessle heroin
Highbeams the wide eyes
of a person on crack
Hikori peyote
Hikuli peyote
Him heroin
Hinkley PCP
Hippie crack inhalant
Hiropon smokable
methamphetamine
Hit crack; marijuana
cigarette; to smoke
marijuana
Hit the hay to smoke
marijuana
Hit the house house
where users go to shoot up
and leave the the owner
drugs as payment
Hit the main line to
inject a drug
Hit the needle to inject a

drug
Hit the pit to inject a
drug
Hitch up the reindeers
to inhale cocaine
Hitter little pipe designed
for only one hit
Hitting up injecting
drugs
Hocus opium; marijuana
Hog PCP
Holding possessing drugs
Hombre heroin
Hombrecitos psilocybin
Homegrown marijuana
Honey currency
Honey blunts Marijuana
cigars sealed with honey
Honey oil ketamine;
inhalant
Honeymoon early stages
of drug use before
addiction or dependency
develops
Hong-yen heroin in pill
form
Hooch marijuana
Hooked addicted
Hooter cocaine;
marijuana
Hop/hops opium
Hopped up under the
influence of drugs
Horn to inhale cocaine;
crack pipe
Horning heroin; to
inhale cocaine
Horse heroin
Horse heads ampheta-
mine
Horse tracks PCP
Horse tranquilizer PCP
Hot dope heroin
Hot heroin poisoned to
give to a police informant
Hot ice smokable
methamphetamine

Hot load/hot shot
lethal injection of an
opiate
Hot rolling liquefying
methamphetamine in an
eye dropper and then
inhaling it
Hot stick marijuana
cigarette
Hotcakes crack
House fee money paid to
enter a crackhouse
House piece crack given
to the owner of a
crackhouse or apartment
where crack users
congregate
**How do you like me
    now?** crack
Hows morphine
HRN heroin
Hubba crack
Hubba, I am back crack
Hubba pigeon crack user
looking for rocks on a floor
after a police raid
Hubbas crack, term from
Northern CA
Huff inhalant
Huffer inhalant abuser
Hulling using others to
get drugs
Hunter cocaine
Hustle attempt to obtain
drug customers
Hyatari peyote
Hydro amphetamine
Hype heroin addict; an
addict
Hype stick hypodermic
needle

I

I am back crack
Iboga amphetamine
Ice cocaine;

methamphetamine; smokeable amphetamine; MDMA, PCP
Ice cream habit occasional use of drugs
Ice cube crack
Icing cocaine
Idiot pills depressant
Ill PCP
Illies beedies dipped in PCP
Illy momo PCP
In connected with drug suppliers
Inbetweens depressant; amphetamine
Inca message cocaine
Indian boy marijuana
Indian hay marijuana from India
Indica species of cannabis, found in hot climate, grows 3.5 to 4 feet
Indian hemp marijuana
Indica species of cannabis, found in hot climate, grows 3.5 to 4 feet
Indo marijuana, term from Northern CA
Indonesian bud marijuana; opium
Inns money
Instaga marijuana
Instagu marijuana
Instant zen LSD
Interplanetary mission travel from one crackhouse to another in search of crack
Isda heroin
Issues crack

J

J marijuana cigarette
Jab/job to inject a drug
Jack steal someone else's drugs
Jackhammer amyl nitrite
Jackpot fentanyl
Jack-Up to inject a drug
Jag keep a high going
Jam amphetamine; cocaine
Jam cecil amphetamine
Jamaican gold marijuana
Jane marijuana
Jay smoke marijuana
Jay marijuana cigarette
Jee gee heroin
Jefferson airplane used match cut in half to hold a partially smoked marijuana cigarette
Jellies depressant
Jelly cocaine
Jelly baby amphetamine
Jelly bean amphetamine; depressant
Jelly beans crack
Jet ketamine
Jet fuel PCP
Jim Jones marijuana laced with cocaine and PCP
Jive heroin; marijuana; drugs
Jive doo jee heroin
Jive stick marijuana
Johnson crack
Joint marijuana cigarette
Jojee heroin
Jolly bean amphetamine
Jolly green marijuana
Jolly pop casual user of heroin
Jolt to inject a drug; strong reaction to drugs
Jones heroin
Jonesing need for drugs
Joy flakes heroin
Joy juice depressant
Joy plant opium

Joy pop to inject a drug
Joy popping occasional use of drugs
Joy powder heroin; cocaine
Joy smoke marijuana
Joy stick marijuana cigarette
Ju-ju marijuana cigarette
Juan Valdez marijuana
Juanita marijuana
Juggle sell drugs to another addict to support a habit
Juggler teen-aged street dealer
Jugs amphetamine
Juice steroids, PCP
Juice joint marijuana cigarette sprinkled with crack
Juja marijuana
Jum sealed plastic bag containing crack
Jumbos large vials of crack sold on the streets
Junk cocaine; heroin
Junkie addict
Junkie kits glass pipe and copper mesh

K

K PCP
Kabayo heroin
Kabuki crack pipe made from a plastic rum bottle and a rubber sparkplug cover
Kaksonjae smokable methamphetamine
Kali marijuana
Kansas grass marijuana
Kangaroo crack
Kaps PCP
Karachi heroin
Kate bush marijuana

Kaya marijuana
K-blast PCP
Kee marijuana
Kentucky blue marijuana
Key marijuana
KGB (killer green bud) marijuana
K-hole periods of ketamine-induced confusion
Khat amphetamine; methcathinone
Ki marijuana
Kibbles & Bits small crumbs of crack
Kick getting off a drug habit; inhalant
Kick stick marijuana cigarette
Kiddie dope prescription drugs
Kiff marijuana
Killer marijuana; PCP
Killer green bud marijuana
Killer joints PCP
Killer weed (1980s) marijuana and PCP; **(1960s)** marijuana
Kilo 2.2 pounds
Kilter marijuana
Kind marijuana
King bud marijuana
King ivory fentanyl
King Kong pills depressant
King's habit cocaine
Kissing the exchange of plastic wrapped rocks (crack) by kissing or mouth to mouth transfer
Kit equipment used to inject drugs
KJ PCP
Kleenex MDMA
Klingons crack addicts

Kokomo crack
Koller joints PCP
Kools PCP
Kryptonite crack
Krystal PCP
Krystal joint PCP
Kumba marijuana
KW PCP

L

L LSD
L.A. long-acting amphetamine
L.A. glass smokable methamphetamine
L.A. ice smokable methamphetamine
L.L. marijuana
Lace cocaine and marijuana
Lady cocaine
Lady caine cocaine
Lady snow cocaine
Lakbay diva marijuana
Lamborghini crack pipe made from plastic rum bottle and a rubber sparkplug cover
Las mujercitas psilocybin
Lason sa daga LSD
Late night cocaine
Laugh and scratch to inject a drug
Laughing gas nitrous oxide
Laughing grass marijuana
Laughing weed marijuana
Lay back depressant
Lay-out equipment for taking drugs
LBJ LSD; PCP; heroin
Leaky bolla PCP
Leaky leak PCP

Leaf marijuana; cocaine
Leapers amphetamine
Leaping under the influence of drugs
Legal speed over-the-counter asthma drug; trade name MiniThin
Lemon 714 PCP
Lemon drop methamphetamine with a dull yellow tint
Lemonade heroin; poor quality drugs
Lenos PCP
Lens LSD
Lethal weapon PCP
Lettuce money
Lib (Librium) depressant
Lid 1 ounce of marijuana
Lid proppers amphetamine
Light stuff marijuana
Lightning amphetamine
Lima marijuana
Lime acid LSD
Line cocaine
Lipton Tea inferior quality drugs
Liquid ecstasty GHB
Lit up under the influence of drugs
Little bomb amphetamine; heroin; depressant
Little ones PCP
Little smoke marijuana; psilocybin/psilocin
Live ones PCP
Llesca marijuana
Load 25 bags of heroin
Loaded high
Loaf marijuana
Lobo marijuana
Locker room isobutyl nitrite
Loco marijuana
Locoweed marijuana

Log PCP; marijuana cigarette
Logor LSD
Loony toons LSD
Loused covered by sores and abscesses from repeated use of unsterile needles
Love crack
Love affair cocaine
Love boat marijuana dipped in formaldehyde; PCP; blunts mixed with marijuana and heroin
Love drug MDMA; depressant
Love pearls alpha-ethyltyptamine
Love pills alpha-ethyltyptamine
Love trip MDMA and mescaline
Love weed marijuana
Lovelies marijuana laced with PCP
Lovely PCP
LSD lysergic acid diethylamide
Lubage marijuana
Lucy in the sky with diamonds LSD
Ludes depressant
Luding out depressant
Luds depressant
Lunch money drugs rohypnol

M

M marijuana; morphine
M.J. marijuana
M.O. marijuana
M.S. morphine
M.U. marijuana
M&M depressant
Machinery marijuana
Macon marijuana

Maconha marijuana
Madman PCP
Mad dog PCP
Magic PCP
Magic dust PCP
Magic mushroom psilocybin/psilocin
Magic smoke marijuana
Main line to inject a drug
Mainliner person who injects into the vein
Make up need to find more drugs
Mama coca cocaine
Manhattan silver marijuana
MAO amphetamine
Marathons amphetamine
Mari marijuana cigarette
Marshmallow reds depressant
Mary marijuana
Mary and Johnny marijuana
Mary Ann marijuana
Mary Jane marijuana
Mary Jonas marijuana
Mary Warner marijuana
Mary Weaver marijuana
Maserati crack pipe made from a plastic rum bottle and rubber sparkplug cover
Matchbox 1/4 ounce of marijuana or 6 marijuana cigarettes
Matsakow heroin
Maui wauie marijuana from Hawaii
Max gamma hydroxy butyrate dissolved in water and mixed with amphetamines
Maxibolin oral steroid
Mayo cocaine; heroin
MDM MDMA
MDMA methylenedioxy-methamphetamine

Mean green PCP
Medusa inhalant
Meg marijuana
Megg marijuana cigarette
Meggie marijuana
Mellow yellow LSD
Merchandise drugs
Merck cocaine
Merk cocaine
Mesc mescaline
Mescal mescaline
Mese mescaline
Messorole marijuana
Meth methamphetamine
Meth head regular user of methamphetamine
Meth monster person who has a violent reaction to methamphetamine
Meth speedball methamphetamine combined with heroin
Methatriol injectable steroid
Methedrine ampheta-mine
Methlies Quik amphetamines
Methyltestosterone oral steroid
Mexican brown heroin; marijuana
Mexican crack methamphetamine with the appearance of crack
Mexican green marijuana
Mexican horse heroin
Mexican locoweed marijuana
Mexican mud heroin
Mexican mushroom psilocybin/psilocin
Mexican red marijuana
Mexican reds depressant
Mexican valiums rohypnol

Mezc mescaline
Mickey Finn depressant
Mickey's depressant
Microdot LSD
Midnight oil opium
Mighty Joe Young
depressant
Mighty mezz marijuana
cigarette
Mighty Quinn LSD
Mind detergent LSD
Mini beans amphetamine
Minibennie amphetamine
Mint leaf PCP
Mint weed PCP
Mira opium
Miss to inject a drug
Miss Emma morphine
Missile basing crack
liquid and PCP
Mission trip out of the
crackhouse to obtain crack
Mist PCP; crack smoke
Mister blue morphine
Mixed jive crack cocaine
Modams marijuana
Mohasky marijuana
Mojo cocaine or heroin
Monkey drug
dependency; cigarette
made from cocaine paste
and tobacco
Monkey dust PCP
Monkey tranquilizer
PCP
Monoamine oxidase
amphetamine
Monos cigarette made
from cocaine paste and
tobacco
Monte marijuana from
South America
Mooca/h marijuana
Moon mescaline
Moon gas inhalant
Moonrock crack and

heroin
Mooster marijuana
Moota marijuana
Mooters marijuana
cigarette
Mootie marijuana
Mootos marijuana
Mor a grifa marijuana
More PCP
Morf morphine
Morning shoot
amphetamine
Morning wake-up first
blast of crack from the pipe
Morotgara heroin
Morpho morphine
Mortal combat high
potency heroin
Mosquitos cocaine
Mota/moto marijuana
Mother marijuana
Mother's little
helper depressant
Mouth worker one who
takes drugs orally
Movie star drug cocaine
Mow the grass to smoke
marijuana
Mu marijuana
Mud opium; heroin
Muggie marijuana
Muggles marijuana
Mujer cocaine
Mule carrier of drugs
Murder one heroin and
cocaine
Murder 8 fentanyl
Mushrooms psilocybin/
psilocin
Musk psilocybin/ psilocin
Muta marijuana
Mutha/h marijuana
Muzzle heroin

N

Nail marijuana cigarette

Nailed arrested
Nanoo heroin
Nebbies depressant
Nemmies depressant
New acid PCP
New addition crack
cocaine
New magic PCP
New Jack Swing heroin
and morphine
Nexus 2C-B
Nice and easy heroin
Nickel bag $5 worth of
drugs; heroin
Nickel deck heroin
Nickel note $5 bill
Nickelonians crack
addicts
Niebla PCP
Nigra marijuana
Nimbies depressant
Nineteen amphetamine
Nix stranger among the
group
Nod effects of heroin
Noise heroin
Nontoucher crack user
who doesn't want affection
during or after smoking
crack
Nose heroin
Nose candy cocaine
Nose drops liquified
heroin
Nose stuff cocaine
Nose powder cocaine
Nubs peyote
Nugget amphetamine
Nuggets crack
Number marijuana
cigarette
Number 3 cocaine,
heroin
Number 4 heroin
Number 8 heroin

O

O opium
O.J. marijuana
O.P. opium
O.P.P. PCP
Octane PCP laced with gasoline
Ogoy heroin
Oil heroin, PCP
Old Steve heroin
On a mission searching for crack
On a trip under the influence of drugs
On ice in jail
On the bricks walking the streets
On the nod under the influence of narcotics or depressant
One and one to inhale cocaine
One box tissue one ounce of crack
One on one house where cocaine and heroin can be purchased
One-fifty-one crack
One plus one sales selling cocaine and heroin together
One way LSD
Oolies marijuana cigarettes laced with crack
Ope opium
Optical illusions LSD
Orange barrels LSD
Orange crystal PCP
Orange cubes LSD
Orange haze LSD
Orange micro LSD
Orange wedges LSD
Oranges amphetamine
Outerlimits crack and LSD

Owsley LSD
Owsley's acid LSD
Oyster stew cocaine
Oz inhalant
Ozone PCP

P

P peyote, PCP
PCP phencyclidine
PCPA PCP
P.R. (Panama Red) marijuana
P-dope 20-30% pure heroin
P-funk heroin; crack and PCP
Pack heroin; marijuana
Pack a bowl marijuana
Pack of rocks marijuana cigarette
Pakalolo marijuana
Pakistani black marijuana
Panama cut marijuana
Panama gold marijuana
Panama red marijuana
Panatella large marijuana cigarette
Pancakes and syrup Combination of glutethimide and codeine cough syrup
Pane LSD
Pangonadalot heroin
Panic drugs not available
Paper a dosage unit of heroin
Paper acid LSD
Paper bag container for drugs
Paper blunts marijuana within a paper casing rather than a tobacco leaf casing
Paper boy heroin peddler
Parabolin veterinary

steroid
Parachute crack and PCP smoked; heroin
Paradise cocaine
Paradise white cocaine
Parlay crack
Parsley marijuana, PCP
Paste crack
Pat marijuana
Patico crack (Spanish)
Paz PCP
Peace LSD, PCP
Peace pill PCP
Peace tablets LSD
Peace weed PCP
Peaches amphetamine
Peanut depressant
Peanut butter PCP mixed with peanut butter
Pearl cocaine
Pearls amyl nitrite
Pearly gates LSD
Pebbles crack
Peddlar drug supplier
Pee Wee crack; $5 worth of crack
Peep PCP
Peg heroin
Pellets LSD
Pen yan opium
Pep pills amphetamine
Pepsi habit occasional use of drugs
Perfect High heroin
Perico cocaine
Perlas street dealer (heroin)
Perlas street dealer (heroin)
Perp fake crack made of candle wax and baking soda
Peter Pan PCP
Peth depressant
Peruvian cocaine
Peruvian flake cocaine
Peruvian lady cocaine
Peyote mescaline
Phennies depressant

Phenos depressant
Pianoing using the fingers to find lost crack
Piece 1 ounce; cocaine; crack
Piedras crack (Spanish)
Pig Killer PCP
Piles crack
Pimp cocaine
Pimp your pipe lending or renting your crack pipe
Pin marijuana
Pin gon opium
Pin yen opium
Ping-in-wing to inject a drug
Pingus rohypnol
Pink blotters LSD
Pink hearts amphetamine
Pink ladies depressant
Pink Panther LSD
Pink robots LSD
Pink wedge LSD
Pink witches LSD
Pipe crack pipe; marijuana pipe; vein into which a drug is injected; mix drugs with other substances
Pipero crack user
Pit PCP
Pixies amphetamine
Plant hiding place for drugs
Pocket rocket marijuana
Pod marijuana
Poison heroin; fentanyl
Point a needle
Poke marijuana
Pole mixture of heroin and motion sickness drug
Pollutants amphetamine
Polvo heroin; PCP
Polvo blanco cocaine
Polvo de angel PCP
Polvo de estrellas PCP
Pony crack

Poor man's pot inhalant
Pop to inhale cocaine
Poppers isobutyl nitrite; amyl nitrite
Poppy heroin
Pot marijuana
Potato LSD
Potato chips crack cut with benzocaine
Potlikker marijuana
Potten bush marijuana
Powder heroin; amphetamine
Powder diamonds cocaine
Power puller rubber piece attached to crack stem
Pox opium
Predator heroin
Prescription marijuana cigarette
Press cocaine; crack
Pretendica marijuana
Pretendo marijuana
Primo crack; marijuana mixed with crack
Primobolan injectable and oral steroid
Primos cigarettes laced with cocaine and heroin
Proviron oral steroid
Pseudocaine phenylprop anolamine, an adulterant for cutting crack
Puff the dragon to smoke marijuana
Puffer crack smoker
Puffy PCP
Pulborn heroin
Pullers crack users who pull at parts of their bodies excessively
Pumping selling crack
Pure heroin
Pure love LSD
Purple ketamine

Purple barrels LSD
Purple haze LSD
Purple hearts LSD; amphetamine; depressant
Purple flats LSD
Purple ozoline LSD
Purple rain PCP
Push sell drugs
Push shorts to cheat or sell short amounts
Pusher one who sells drugs; metal hanger or umbrella rod used to scrape residue in crack stems

Q

Q depressant
Qat methcathinone
Quad depressant
Quarter 1/4 ounce or $25 worth of drugs
Quarter bag $25 worth of drugs
Quarter moon hashish
Quarter piece 1/4 ounce
Quartz smokable speed
Quas depressant
Queen Ann's lace marijuana
Quicksilver isobutyl nitrite
Quill methamphetamine; heroin; cocaine
Quinolone injectable steroid

R

R2 Rohypnol
Racehorse charlie cocaine; heroin
Ragweed inferior quality marijuana; heroin
Railroad weed marijuana
Rainbow LSD
Rainbows depressant

Rainy day woman marijuana
Rambo heroin
Rane cocaine; heroin
Rangood marijuana grown wild
Rap criminally charged; to talk with someone
Raspberry female who trades sex for crack or money to buy crack
Rasta weed marijuana
Raw crack
Raw fusion heroin
Raw hide heroin
Rave party designed to enhance a hallucinogenic experience through music and behavior
Razed under the influence of drugs
Ready rock cocaine; crack; heroin
Recompress change the shape of cocaine flakes to resemble "rock"
Recycle LSD
Red under the influence of drugs
Red and blue depressant
Red bullets depressant
Red bud marijuana
Red caps crack
Red cross marijuana
Red chicken heroin
Red devil depressant, PCP
Red dirt marijuana
Reds depressant
Red eagle heroin
Red lips LSD
Red phosphorus smokable speed
Redneck cocaine methamphetamine
Reefer marijuana
Regular P crack

Reindeer dust heroin
Rest in peace crack cocaine
Reynolds rohypnol
Rhine heroin
Rhythm amphetamine
Rib rohypnol
Riding the wave under the influence of drugs
Rig equipment used to inject drugs
Righteous bush marijuana
Ringer good hit of crack
Rip marijuana
Rippers amphetamine
Ritalin central nervous system stimulant
Roach butt of marijuana cigarette
Roach clip holds partially smoked marijuana cigarette
Roaches rohypnol
Road dope amphetamine
Roapies rohypnol
Roasting smoking marijuana
Robutal rohypnol
Roca crack (Spanish)
Rochas dos rohypnol
Roche Rohypnol
Rock attack crack
Rock house place where crack is sold and smoked
Rock(s) cocaine; crack
Rocket caps dome-shaped caps on crack vials
Rocket fuel PCP
Rockets marijuana cigarette
Rockette female who uses crack
Rocks of hell crack
Rock star female who trades sex for crack or money to buy crack

Rocky III crack
Roid rage aggressive behavior caused by excessive steroid use
Roller to inject a drug
Rollers police
Rolling MDMA
Roofies Rohypnol
Rooster crack
Root marijuana
Rope marijuana
Rophies rohypnol
Rophy rohypnol
Rohypnol a sedative that makes users feel very drunk
Roples rohypnol
Rosa amphetamine
Rose marie marijuana
Roses amphetamine
Rough stuff marijuana
Rox crack
Roxanne cocaine; crack
Row-shay rohypnol
Royal blues LSD
Roz crack
Ruderalis species of cannabis, found in Russia, grows 1 to 2.5 feet
Ruffies Rohypnol
Ruffles Rohypnol
Runners people who sell drugs for others
Running MDMA
Rush isobutyl nitrite; amyl nitrite
Rush snappers isobutyl nitrite
Russian sickles LSD

S

Sack heroin
Sacrament LSD
Sacre mushroom psilocybin
Salt heroin
Salt and pepper

marijuana
Sam federal narcotics agent
Sancocho to steal (Spanish)
Sandoz LSD
Sandwich two layers of cocaine with a layer of heroin in the middle
Santa Marta marijuana
Sasfras marijuana
Satan's secret inhalant
Satch papers, letter, cards, clothing, etc., saturated with drug solution (used to smuggle drugs into prisons or hospitals)
Satch cotton fabric used to filter a solution of narcotics before injection
Sativa species of cannabis, found in cool, damp climate, grows up to 18 feet
Scaffle PCP
Scag heroin
Scat heroin
Scate heroin
Schmeck cocaine
Schoolboy cocaine, codeine
Schoolcraft crack
Scissors marijuana
Scooby snacks MDMA
Scoop GHB
Score purchase drugs
Scorpion cocaine
Scott heroin
Scottie cocaine
Scotty cocaine; crack; the high from crack
Scramble crack
Scrape and snort to share crack by scraping off small pieces for snorting
Scratch money
Scruples crack

Scuffle PCP
Seccy depressant
Second to none heroin
Seeds marijuana
Seggy depressant
Sen marijuana
Seni peyote
Serial speedballing sequencing cocaine, cough syrup, and heroin over a 1-2 day period
Sernyl PCP
Serpico 21 cocaine
Server crack dealer
Sess marijuana
Set place where drugs are sold
Sevenup cocaine; crack
Sewer vein into which a drug is injected
Sezz marijuana
Shabu ice
Shake marijuana
Shaker/baker/water materials needed to freebase cocaine; shaker bottle, baking soda, water
Sharps needles
She cocaine
Sheets PCP
Sheet rocking crack and LSD
Shermans PCP
Sherm sticks PCP
Sherms PCP; crack
Sh*t heroin
Shmeck/schmeek heroin
Shoot heroin
Shoot/shoot up to inject a drug
Shoot the breeze nitrous oxide
Shooting gallery place where drugs are used
Shot to inject a drug
Shot down under the

influence of drugs
Shrooms psilocybin/psilocin
Siddi marijuana
Sightball crack

Silly Putty psilocybin/psilocin
Simple
Simon psilocybin/psilocin
Sinse marijuana
Sinsemilla potent variety marijuana
Sixty-two 2 1/2 ounces of crack
Skee opium
Skeegers/skeezers crack-smoking prostitute
Sketching coming down from a speed induced high
Skid heroin
Skied under the influence of drugs
Skin popping injecting drugs under the skin
Skuffle PCP
Skunk marijuana
Slab crack
Slam to inject a drug
Slammin'/Slamming amphetamine
Slanging selling drugs
Sleeper heroin; depressant
Sleet crack
Sleigh ride cocaine
Slick superspeed methcathinone
Slime heroin
Smack heroin
Smears LSD
Smoking PCP
Smoke heroin and crack; crack; marijuana
Smoke a bowl marijuana
Smoke Canada

marijuana
Smoke-out under the influence of drugs
Smoking gun heroin and cocaine
Snap amphetamine
Snappers isobutyl nitrite; amyl nitrite
Sniff to inhale cocaine; inhalant; methcathinone
Sniffer bags $5 bag of heroin intended for inhalation
Snop marijuana
Snort to inhale cocaine; use inhalant
Snorts PCP
Snot residue produced from smoking amphetamine
Snot balls rubber cement rolled into balls and burned
Snow cocaine; heroin; amphetamine
Snowball cocaine and heroin
Snow bird cocaine
Snowcones cocaine
Snow pallets amphetamine
Snow seals cocaine and amphetamine
Snow soke crack
Snow white cocaine
Soap dope methamphetamine with a pinkish rose tint
Society high cocaine
Soda injectable cocaine used in Hispanic communities
Softballs depressant
Soles hashish
Soma PCP
Somali methcathinone
Somatomax GHB

Sopers depressant
Spaceball PCP used with crack
Space base crack dipped in PCP; hollowed out cigar refilled with PCP and crack
Space cadet crack dipped in PCP
Space dust crack dipped in PCP
Spaceship glass pipe used to smoke crack
Spark it up to smoke marijuana
Sparkle plenty amphetamine
Sparklers amphetamine
Special "K" ketamine
Special la coke ketamine
Speed methamphetamine; amphetamine; crack
Speedball methylphenidate (ritalin) mixed with heroin
Speedballs-nose style the practice of snorting cocaine
Speed boat marijuana, PCP, crack
Speed freak habitual user of methamphetamine
Speed for lovers MDMA
Speedball heroin and cocaine; amphetamine
Spider blue heroin
Spike to inject a drug; needle
Spivias amphetamines
Splash amphetamine
Spliff marijuana cigarette
Splim marijuana
Split half and half or to leave
Splivins amphetamine
Spoon 1/16 ounce of heroin; paraphernalia used to prepare heroin for

injection
Spores PCP
Sporting to inhale cocaine
Spray inhalant
Sprung person just starting to use drugs
Square mackerel marijuana bales thrown overboard by smugglers
Square time Bob crack
Squirrel smoking cocaine, marijuana and PCP; LSD
Stack marijuana
Stacking taking steroids with a prescription
Star methcathinone
Stardust cocaine, PCP
Star-spangled powder cocaine
Stash place to hide drugs
Stash areas drug storage and distribution areas
Stat Methcathinone
Steerer person who directs customers to spots for buying crack
Stem cylinder used to smoke crack
Stems marijuana
Step on dilute drugs
Stick marijuana, PCP
Stink weed marijuana
Stoned under the influence of drugs
Stones crack
Stoppers depressant
Stove top crystal methamphetamine
STP PCP
Straw marijuana cigarette
Strawberries depressant
Strawberry female who trades sex for crack or money to buy crack; LSD
Strawberry fields LSD

Strung out heavily addicted to drugs
Stuff heroin
Stumbler depressant
Sugar cocaine; LSD; heroin
Sugar block crack
Sugar cubes LSD
Sugar lumps LSD
Sugar weed marijuana
Sunshine LSD
Super PCP
Super acid ketamine
Super C ketamine
Super Grass PCP
Super ice smokable methamphetamine
Super joint PCP
Super kools PCP
Super weed PCP
Supergrass marijuana
Superman LSD
Surfer PCP
Sweet Jesus heroin
Sweet Lucy marijuana
Sweet stuff heroin; cocaine
Sweets amphetamine
Swell up crack
Swishers cigars in which tobacco is replaced with marijuana
synthetic cocaine PCP
synthetic THT PCP

T

T cocaine; marijuana
T.N.T. heroin; fentanyl
Tabs LSD
Tail lights LSD
Taima marijuana
Taking a cruise PCP
Takkouri marijuana
Tango & Cash fentanyl
Tar opium; heroin
Tardust cocaine

Taste heroin; small sample of drugs
Taxing price paid to enter a crackhouse; charging more per vial depending on race of customer or if not a regular customer
T-buzz PCP
Tea marijuana, PCP
Tea party to smoke marijuana
Teardrops dosage units of crack packaged in the cut-off corners of plastic bags
Tecate heroin
Tecatos Hispanic heroin addicts
Teenage 1/16 gram of methamphetamine
Teeth cocaine; crack
Tension crack
Tex-mex marijuana
Texas pot marijuana
Texas tea marijuana
Thai sticks bundles of marijuana soaked in hashish oil; marijuana buds bound on short sections of bamboo
THC tetrahydrocanna-binol
The beast heroin
The C methcathinone
The devil crack
The witch heroin
Therobolin injectable steroid
Thing heroin; cocaine; main drug interest at the moment
Thirst monsters heavy crack smokers
Thirteen marijuana
Thoroughbred drug dealer who sells pure narcotics

Thrust isobutyl nitrite
Thrusters amphetamine
Thumb marijuana
Tic PCP in powder form
Tic tac PCP
Ticket LSD
Tie to inject a drug
Tin container for marijuana
Tish PCP
Tissue crack
Titch PCP
Toilet water inhalant
Toke to inhale cocaine; to smoke marijuana
Toke up to smoke marijuana
Toluene petrochemical inhalant
Toncho octane booster which is inhaled
Tooles depressant
Tools equipment used for injecting drugs
Toot cocaine; to inhale cocaine
Tooties depressant
Tootsie roll heroin
Top gun crack
Topi mescaline
Tops peyote
Torch marijuana
Torch cooking smoking cocaine base by using a propane or butane torch as a source of flame
Torch up to smoke marijuana
Torpedo crack and marijuana
Toss up female who trades sex for crack or money to buy crack
Totally spent MDMA hangover
Toucher user of crack who wants affection

before, during, or after smoking crack
Tout person who introduces buyers to sellers
Toxy opium
Toys opium
TR-6s amphetamine
Track to inject a drug
Tracks row of needle marks on a person
Tragic magic crack dipped in PCP
Trails LSD induced perception that moving objects leave multiple images or trails behind them
Trank PCP
Tranq depressant
Trap hiding place for drugs
Trays bunches of vials
Travel agent LSD supplier
Trip LSD; alpha-ethyltyptamine
Troop crack
Trophobolene injectable steroid
Truck drivers amphetamine
TT1 PCP
TT2 PCP
TT3 PCP
Tuie depressant
Turbo crack and marijuana
Turf place where drugs are sold
Turkey cocaine; amphetamine
Turnabout amphetamine
Turned on introduced to drugs; under the influence
Tutti-frutti flavored cocaine developed by a Brazillian gang

Tweak mission on a mission to find crack
Tweaker crack user looking for rocks on the floor after a police raid
Tweaking drug-induced paranoia; peaking on speed
Tweek methamphetamine like substance
Tweeker methcathinone
Twenty $20 rock of crack
Twenty-five LSD
Twist marijuana cigarette
Twists small plastic bags of heroin secured with a twist tie
Twistum marijuana cigarette
Two for nine two $5 vials or bags of crack for $9
2-for-1 sale a marketing scheme designed to promote and increase crack sales

U

Ultimate crack
Uncle Federal agents
Uncle Milty depressant
Unkie morphine
Up against the stem addicted to smoking marijuana
Uppers amphetamine
Uppies amphetamine
Ups and downs depressant
Utopiates hallucinogens
Uzi crack; crack pipe

V

V the depressant Valium
Vega a cigar wrapping refilled with marijuana
Viper's weed marijuana
Vodka acid LSD

W

Wac PCP on marijuana
Wack PCP
Wacky weed marijuana
Wake ups amphetamine
Wasted under the influence of drugs; murdered
Water methamphetamine, PCP
Wave crack
Wedding bells LSD
Wedge LSD
Weed marijuana, PCP
Weed tea marijuana
Weightless high on crack
West coast methylphenidate (ritalin)
West coast turn-arounds amphetamine
Wet blunts mixed with marijuana and PCP
Whack PCP and heroin
Wheat marijuana
When-shee opium
Whicked heroin
Whippets nitrous oxide
White amphetamine
White ball crack
White boy heroin
White cloud crack smoke
White cross methamphetamine; amphetamine
White dust LSD
White ghost crack
White girl cocaine; heroin
White-haired lady marijuana
White horizon PCP
White horse cocaine
White junk heroin
White lady cocaine; heroin

White lightning LSD
White mosquito cocaine
White nurse heroin
White Owsley's LSD
White powder cocaine; PCP
White stuff heroin
White sugar crack
White tornado crack
Whiteout isobutyl nitrite
Whites amphetamine
Whiz bang cocaine and heroin
Wild cat methcathinone and cocaine
Window glass LSD
Window pane LSD
Wings heroin; cocaine
Winstrol oral steroid
Winstrol V veterinary steroid
Witch heroin; cocaine
Witch hazel heroin
Wobble weed PCP
Wolf PCP
Wollie rocks of crack rolled into a marijuana cigarette
Wonder star methcathinone
Woolah a hollowed out cigar refilled with marijuana and crack
Woolas cigarette laced with cocaine; marijuana cigarette sprinkled with crack
Woolies marijuana amd crack or PCP
Wooly blunts Marijuana and crack or PCP
Working selling crack
Working half crack rock weighing half gram or more
Works equipment for injecting drugs

Worm PCP
Wrecking crew crack

X

X marijuana; MDMA; amphetamine
X-ing MDMA
XTC MDMA

Y

Yahoo/yeaho crack
Yale crack
Yeh marijuana
Yellow LSD; depressant
Yellow bam methamphetamine
Yellow bullets depressant
Yellow dimples LSD
Yellow fever PCP
Yellow jackets depressant
Yellow submarine marijuana
Yellow sunshine LSD
Yen pop marijuana
Yen Shee Suey opium wine
Yen sleep restless, drowsy state after LSD use
Yerba marijuana
Yerba mala PCP and marijuana
Yesca marijuana
Yesco marijuana
Yeyo cocaine, Spanish term
Yimyom crack
Ying Yang LSD

Z

Z 1 ounce of heroin
Zacatecas purple marijuana from Mexico
Zambi marijuana
Zen LSD

Zero opium
Zig Zag man LSD; marijuana; marijuana rolling papers
Zip cocaine
Zol marijuana cigarette
Zombie PCP; heavy user of drugs
Zombie weed PCP
Zooie holds butt of marijuana cigarette
Zoom PCP; marijuana laced with PCP
Zoomers individuals who sell fake crack and then flee

Appendix B
Resource Guide

Hotlines

Cocaine Helpline 1-800-COCAINE
Offers guidance and refers callers to local treatment and counseling centers. Counselors are reformed addicts.

Crisis Hotline 1-800-421-6353/1-800-352-0386 (California)
24-hour-a-day crisis counseling and information

National Child Abuse Hotline 1-800-422-4453
A program of Childhelp USA in Woodland Hills, CA, the hotline handles crisis calls and provides information and referrals.

National Council on Alcoholism Information 1-800-NCA-CALL
Information and referral service to families and persons seeking help with alcoholism and drug problems.

National Domestic Violence Hotline 1-800-333-SAFE

National Drug Abuse Hotline 1-800-622-HELP
Counselors available to discuss drugs, drug treatment, health, or legal problems. Provides confidential information and referrals in your area.

Organizations

African-American Family Services
2616 Nicollet Avenue, Minneapolis, MN 55408
612-871-7878
Services include crisis intervention, home-based services, family preservation, domestic violence, adolescent and adult outpatient, after care, battered women's programs, and assessments.

Al-Anon/Alateen Family Group Headquarters, Inc.
P.O. Box 862, Midtown Station, New York, NY 10018-0862
1-800-344-2666

Referrals to local support groups for adult children of alcoholics (Al-Anon) and teenage children of alcoholics (Alateen).

Alcoholics Anonymous World Services (AA)
475 Riverside Drive, New York, NY 10115
212-870-3400
A shared-help program for men and women wishing to achieve sobriety. Family members receive help through Al-Anon/Alateen.

American Council for Drug Education (ACDE)
164 West 74th Street, New York, NY 10023
1-800-488-DRUG / 212-595-5810 x7860
Nationwide referral service for any zip code in the country for local drug/alcohol support groups. Provides antidrug films and curriculum for preteens.

Big Brothers/Big Sisters of America
230 N. 13th Street, Philadelphia, PA 19107
215-567-7000
Volunteers offer support to single parents and families under stress by working with children in need of friendship and attention.

Center for Substance Abuse Prevention (CSAP)
Center for Substance Abuse Treatment (CSAT)
5600 Fishers Lane, Room 800, Rockville, MD 20857
1-800-729-6686

Children of Alcoholics
611 12th Avenue South, Suite 200, Seattle, WA 98144
1-800-322-5601

Clearinghouse on Family Violence Information
P.O. Box 1182, Washington, D.C. 20013
1-800-394-3366

Community Anti-Drug Coalitions of America (CADCA)
901 North Pitt Street, Suite 300, Alexandria, VA 22314
1-800-54-CADCA

D.A.R.E. (Drug Abuse Resistance Education)
Box 512090, Los Angeles, CA 90051-0090
1-800-223-DARE
Headquarters of world's largest drug prevention program.

Families Anonymous, Inc.
P.O. Box 528, Van Nuys, CA 91408
1-800-736-9805818-989-7841

Offers a 12-step, self-help program for friends and families of people with behavioral and dependency problems.

Girl Power
11426 Rockville Pike, Suite 100, Rockville, MD 20852
Designed to help 11 million 9- to 14-year-old girls turn down drugs and avoid other risky behaviors.
1-800-729-6686

Institute for Black Chemical Abuse
2616 Nicollet Avenue, Minneapolis, MN 55408
612-871-7878
Provides technical assistance and training to programs reaching out to African Americans and other people of color.

International Institute for Inhalant Abuse
450 West Jefferson Avenue, Englewood, CO 80110
303-788-1951
Provides information on the dangers of poppers, glue, paint, and other inhalants.

Just Say No Clubs
1777 North California Boulevard, Suite 200, Walnut Creek, CA 94596
1-800-258-2766
Workshops, newsletters, activities and seminars providing positive peer reinforcement to youngsters.

Mothers Against Drunk Driving (MADD)
511 east John Carpenter Freeway, Irvington, TX 75062
1-800-GET-MADD / 214-744-6233

Nar-Anon Family Group Headquarters
P.O. Box 2562, Palos Verdes Peninsula, CA 90274
213-547-5800
Structured like Al-Anon; supports people who have friends or family members with chemical dependencies.

Narcotics Anonymous
World Service Office, P.O. Box 9999, Van Nuys, CA 91049
1-800-6624357/818-780-3951
Program is for men and women helping each other with drug dependency problems. Similar to AA.

National Asian Pacific American Families Against Substance Abuse (NAPAFASA)
420 East 3rd Street, Suite 909, Los Angeles, CA 90013-1602
213-617-8277
Provides a substance abuse prevention information outreach program for Asian-Pacific Americans.

National Association for Native American Children of Alcoholics
611 12th Avenue South, Suite 200, Seattle, WA 98144
1-800-322-5601 / 206-324-9360

National Clearinghouse for Alcohol and Drug Information (NCADI)
Box 2345 Rockville, MD 20847-2345
1-800-SAY-NOTO
Publications pertaining to prevention, training, treatment, and research aspects of drug and alcohol abuse.

National Coalition Against Domestic Violence
Helps callers locate a shelter in their area.
(202) 293-8860

National Council of La Raza
810 First Street, N.E., Suite 300
Washington, DC 20002
202-289-1380
Substance abuse information to Americans of Latin descent.

National Council on Alcoholism and Drug Dependence
12 West 21st Street, New York, NY 10010
1-800-622-2255
Volunteer organization with over 300 local affiliates providing information on alcoholism.

National Federation of Parents for Drug-Free Youth
P.O. Box 3878, St. Louis, MO 63122
1-800-554-KIDS/314-968-1322
Information and referral service focusing on preventing drug addiction in children and adolescents. Callers are referred to state networkers or member groups in the caller's community. Educates junior and senior high-school students about drug abuse through (REACH) Responsible Educated Adolescents Can Help.

National Inhalant Prevention Coalition
1615 Guadeloupe Street, Suite 201, Austin, TX 78701
1-800-269-4237
Information on the dangers of inhalants.

National Institute of Drug Abuse (NIDA)
5600 Fishers Lane, Room 10A03, Rockville, MD 20857
1-800-638-2045/301-443-4577
Provides technical assistance to individuals and groups that want to start drug prevention programs. A current focus is on establishing "Just Say No to Drugs" clubs.

National PTA Drug and Alcohol Prevention Project
700 North Rush Street, Chicago, IL 60611
312-577-4500
Publications, kits, and posters for PTA organizations.

National Urban League Substance Abuse Program
500 East 62nd Street, New York, NY 10021
212-310-9000

Office of National Drug Control Policy (ONDCP)
Drugs and Crime Clearinghouse
P.O. Box 6000, Rockville, MD 20849
1-800-666-3332, e-mail: askncjrs@aspnsys.com
Operates toll-free 800 number staffed by drug and crime information specialists. Distributes ONDCP and Department of Justice publications about drugs and crime. Answers requests for specific drug-related data.

Partnership for a Drug Free America
1-800-624-0100
Publications, handbook on how to talk to kids about drugs.

Parents' Resource Institute for Drug Education (PRIDE)
50 Hurt Plaza, Suite 210, Atlanta, GA 30303
1-800-853-7867
Refers parents to state or local groups. Offers information for starting a community group, offers telephone consultation and referrals to emergency health centers, and provides a series of free drug information tapes for callers to listen to.

Safe Homes
P.O. Box 702, Livingston, NJ 07039
National organization encouraging drug/alcohol-free parties in parents' homes through contractual agreements.

Toughlove
P.O. Box 1069, Doylestown, PA 18901
1-800-333-1069
Self-help group for parents and children. Emphasizes cooperation, personal initiative, avoidance of blame, and action between parents, children and their community. Publishes newsletter and books, holds seminars.

U.S. Indian Health Service
5600 Fishers Lane, Rockville, MD 20857
301-443-1054
Provides substance abuse literature and information to Native Americans and their families.

Chapter Notes

Introduction: The Threat is Real
1 Multiple Sources:
  a, b. *National Household Survey on Drug Abuse, Population Estimates 1995*, U.S. Department of Health and Human Services, Substance Abuse and Mental Health Services Administration (Rockville, MD: National Clearinghouse for Alcohol and Drug Administration).
  c, d, e, f, i. The University of Michigan Institute for Social Research, *National Survey Results from The Monitoring the Future Study, 1975-1995*. (Washington, D.C.: U.S. Department of Health and Human Services, 1996).
  g. *FBI Uniform Crime Reports*, 1995, p. 21, Table 2.14
  h. *National Summary of Injury Mortality Data, 1987-1994*. (CDC, National Center for Injury Prevention and Control. November 1996).
  j. "White House Proposal Calls Drug Battle Endless," *San Diego Union Tribune* 2/2/97.
2 "Substance Abuse: The Nation's Number One Health Problem," Brandeis University, Institute for Health Policy (October 1993).

Chapter 1 Why Kids Get in Trouble
1 A ten-year study of over 20,000 youths and their families conducted by the U.S. Department of Education

Chapter 3 Parenting to Build Self-esteem
1 Student survey, U.S. Department of Education

Chapter 7 Gateway Drugs: Alcohol and Tobacco, Avoiding the First Serious Steps
1 U.S. Department of Education
2 "Youth and Tobacco," U.S. Department of Education
3 A study released in February 1997, by the National Cancer Institute (Washington, D.C.)
4 U.S. Department of Health and Human Services, a survey of high school seniors
5 Roger E. Vogler, Ph.D., and Wayne R. Bartz, Ph.D., *Teenagers and Alcohol: When Saying No Isn't Enough*. (Philadelphia, PA: Charles Press Publishers, April 1992).

Chapter 9 Inhalants: Danger Right Under Your Nose
1 U.S. Substance Abuse and Mental Health Administration
2 The University of Michigan Institute for Social Research, *National Survey Results from The Monitoring the Future Study, 1975-1995*. (Washington, D.C.: U.S. Department of Health and Human Services, 1996).

Chapter 11 Steroids and "Sports" Drugs: A No-Win, Fast Way to Lose
1 Mark Zeigler, "A Pumped Up World," *The San Diego Union Tribune* (August 17, 1997).
2 An ongoing study conducted by the University of Michigan and funded by The National Institute of Drug Abuse
3 Mark Zeigler, "A Pumped Up World," *The San Diego Union Tribune* (August 17, 1997).

Index

A

Accidents
  alcohol-related, 112
  marijuana use and, 127
"Acid," 189
Active listening, 45, 49
Activities, 43, 56–57
Addiction
  to alcohol, 112, 116–117
  to barbiturates, 145
  to cocaine, 175–176
  counselors, 219
  to heroin, 193, 195–196
  to methamphetamine, 178
  predisposing factors for,
    225–226
  to "roofies," 184
  to stimulants, 172
Addiction stage, 87, 88
Addictive personality,
  earmarks of, 88–89
Advertising, 73–85
AIDS, 165, 195
Alcohol. See also Alcohol
  use; Drunk driving.
  in cough preparations, 144
  as a depressant, 21
  dialogue about, 29-30
  effects of, 114
  family violence and, 63
  as a gateway drug,
    110–118
  guidelines for, 115
  media allure of, 74
  myths, 114–115
  role play for resisting, 67
Alcoholics Anonymous
  (AA), 113, 141, 203, 215
Alcoholism, 116–117, 222
Alcohol use
  early, 111–112
  heredity and, 89
  in high school, 3
  in the home, 37
  preventing, 112–117
American Council for Drug

Education, 189, 223, 240
Amphetamines, 146, 172,
  177–178
Amyl nitrite ("amyl"), 133
Anabolic steroids, 155, 156,
  158, 159, 163, 168
Analogs, 181
Antidepressants, 148
Antidrug programs, starting,
  237–239
Appetite suppressants, 143,
  172
Assertiveness training,
  58–59, 67–72
Assessment, 221–224
Attention, importance of,
  42–43
Attention Deficit Disorder
  (ADD), 147
Authoritarian parenting
  style, 40, 47
Authoritative parenting
  style, 40, 229

B

Barbiturates, 145
Behavior
  addictive, 88–89
  modeling, 30
  moderate vs. excessive, 28
  responsibility for, 223
  symptoms drug use, 90–93
Behavioral choices,
  framework for, 31–32
Benzedrine, 177
Benzodiazepines, 143
Binge drinking, 112
Blood alcohol content
  (BAC), calculating, 115
"Blotter acid," 189, 190
Buddy systems, 55, 56
Butyl nitrite, 133–134

C

Caffeine, 143, 172
Cannabinoids, 120
Cannabis Sativa, 121

"Cat," 186
Children. See also
  Teenagers.
  accepting mistakes, 46
  damaging self-esteem, 37
  drug use by, 4, 12, 38,
    214–215
  educating about
    medicines, 151
  experimentation by,
    98–99, 210–214
  monitoring attitudes of,
    43
  monitoring income, 169
  openness with, 79–80
  rights of, 59
  supervising, 10–11, 55,
    200
Cigarettes
  as a gateway drug, 98–109
  media allure of, 73, 74
Cigarette smoking, 3. See
  also Nicotine.
  consequences of, 101
  dangers associated with,
    100–101, 105–106
  media role in, 99–100
  myths about, 104–105
  parental messages about,
    102, 105
  role play, 68, 70
  rules about, 109
Clenbuterol, 162
"Club" drugs, 171
Cocaine, 79–80, 171, 172,
  204. See also "Crack"
  cocaine.
  powdered, 173–174
  as a stimulant, 22
  synthetic, 178–179
Codeine, 146
Communication. See also
  Self-esteem.
  about alcohol use,
    114–115, 116–117
  about personal behavior,

118
  opening lines of, 43–44
  of personal problems, 11
Community
  effect of drug abuse on, 4
  effect of gangs on, 53
  violence in, 51–72
Concerts, monitoring, 82–83
Confidence, building, 46.
  See also Self-esteem.
Conflict resolution,
  nonviolent, 64–65
Consequences
  activity, 19
  establishing, 212–214
  spelling out, 31–32, 101,
    213–214
Coping skills, 125
Cough medicine, 144, 146
Counselors, selecting,
  218–219
Court intervention, 221
"Crack babies," 176
"Crack" cocaine, 22, 89,
  171, 173, 174
  risks associated with,
    175–177
"Crack" dealers, 175–177
"Crack houses," 174
"Crank," 146, 172, 179
Credentialed Alcoholism
  Counselors, 219
Crime. See also Violence.
  being informed about, 61
  drug abuse and, 4
  heroin use and, 196
  prevention info, 61
  reporting, 62
Criticism, avoiding, 46
"Crystal meth," 178
"Cycling," 165

D

D.A.R.E. (Drug Abuse
  Resistance Education), ix,
  xii, 3, 240, 267
  Alcohol Fact Sheet, 117
  curriculum, 48, 60, 103
  Drug Fact Sheet, 19,
    20–22, 28, 106–107
Date rape drugs, 183–185
"Day-in-the-life" activity, 48

Decision making, poor,
  11–12
Dependency, assessing,
  217–218
Depressants, 20, 145
  alcohol, 21, 111
Designer drugs, 171, 172,
  181–186
Designer steroids, 161
Dexedrine, 143, 146
Dextromethorphan
  hydrobromide (DM), 144
Dianabol (D-Ball), 160
Diet pills, 142–143, 177
Discipline, nonviolent, 65
Domestic violence, 63–64
Drug abuse
  crime and, 4
  impact of, 4
  risk factors for, 9
Drug abusers, versus drug
  addicts, 88–89
Drug culture, 119–120, 206
Drug Enforcement
  Administration (DEA),
  147, 156, 168, 174
Drug-free children, raising,
  225–240
Drug hotlines, 266
Drug paraphernalia, 94
Drug poisoning, 149
Drugs. See also Drug use;
  Gateway drugs; Over-the-
  counter drugs; Prescription
  drugs; Steroids.
  curiosity about, 12
  dependency on, 88
  early education about, 89
  family violence and, 63
  media allure of, 73–85
  music and, 78
  physical effects of, 28
  role play for resisting,
    67–72
  rules, 30–31, 37
  sources of, 17
  in the United States, 3–4
  using, misusing, and
    abusing, 142
Drug terminology, 241–265
Drug testing, 126, 211, 214
Drug use

behavioral symptoms of,
  36, 90–93
dealing with, 198–224
denial about, 198–200
environmental indicators
  of, 94–95
signs and symptoms of,
  87–96
stages of, 87–88
versus drug abuse, 113
Drunk driving, 8, 30, 31–32,
  115

E

"Ecstacy," 182
Education
  early drug, 89
  gang-related behavior, 53
  importance of, 95
  prescription drugs,
    149–151
  supporting, 43
Effexor, 148
El Paso Intelligence Center,
  178
Entertainment, violence-
  free, 65
Environmental indicators
  of drug use, 94–95
  of inhalant use, 138
Erythropoietin (EPO),
  161–162
Excesses, emotional, 91
Experimentation, 87
  dealing with, 210–214

F

Failure, as a learning
  experience, 46
Families Anonymous (FA),
  215, 267
Family activities, loss of
  interest in, 92
Family foundations
  parenting and, 25–38
  reasons children get in
    trouble, 8–24
  self-esteem and, 39–50
  violence and, 51–72
Family reconfiguration, 222
Family support groups,
  215–217, 223, 266

Family therapists, 223
Fear, of saying no, 11
Fentanyl, 186
Fetal alcohol syndrome, 116
Flashbacks, 188, 190
"Forget pill," 183–184
Frankenstein Syndrome, 162
Freebasing, 173
Freon, sniffing, 137
Friends, changes in, 90. See also Peer pressure.

G

Gamma-hydroxy butyrate (GHB), 162–163, 185
Gangs, 51–52
  effect on community, 53
  membership in, 52
  fashions, 53, 54, 76
  reasons for joining, 12
  reporting, 62
  resisting, 3
  resisting abuse by, 71
  risks, 53–56
  warning signs of, 54–55
"Gangsta" music, 78, 81
Gasoline, sniffing, 137
Gateway drugs, 97–118, 201
  inhalants as, 129–142
Geographical location, drug use and, 89
Glue sniffing, 129
  role play for resisting, 69–70
Gonatropyl-c, 162
Graffiti, 53. See also "Tagging"
"Grass," 21, 121
Ground rules, setting, 229

H

Hallucinogens, 20, 122, 144, 186–192
Hashish, 121
Health, changes in, 94
Health consequences
  of cigarette smoking, 106
  of cocaine addiction, 176
  of marijuana use, 124
Heart disease, steroids and, 164
Helium, inhaling, 132

Heroin, 77, 192–195
  fentanyl and, 186
  preventing, 195–196
  smoking, 193–194
  symptoms of, 195
Hip-hop music, 78
Hormones, synthetic, 159
Hostility, drug use and, 92
Household products
  inhaling, 136, 139–140
"Huffing," 22, 24, 129–130, 134, 135–137, 141, 141
  signs and symptoms of, 137–139
Human growth hormone (hGH), 155, 156, 161–162
Hyperactivity, 147
  addiction and, 88

I

Illegal substances, familiarity with, 95
Improvement, as a learning process, 47
Inhalants, 22, 129–142
  consequences of using, 135–137
  as gateway drugs, 97
  prevalence of, 134–135
  symptoms of use, 138–139
  types of, 130–134
Inhalant use
  dealing with, 141
  paraphernalia, 138
  preventative measures for, 139–141
Inpatient treatment programs, 220–221
Internet
  drug education, 95, 240
  drug sites, 240
  drugs and, 231–232
  music information on, 83
  safeguarding, 230–237
Intervention strategies, 214–215

J–K–L

Juvenile justice, 221, 223
Ketamine hydrochloride, 190–191
Librium, 143, 145

Listening, active, 45
LSD (lysergic acid diethylamide), 119, 186 189–190, 204
Lying, drug use and, 91

M

Manipulation, drug use and, 91
Marijuana, 21, 119–128
  cigarette smoking and, 102, 103
  dealing with use, 123–128
  effects of, 122
  facts about, 120–121, 121–123, 128
  as a gateway drug, 97
  health risks of, 124
  in high school, 3
  long-term consequences of, 126–127
  medical use of, 124
  as a mind-altering drug, 21
  role play for resisting, 68–69
  signs of use of, 123
  use, 8, 10–11, 35–36, 203
MDMA, 182–183
Media
  influence of, 73–85
  monitoring, 81–85
  role in cigarette smoking, 99–100, 105
Medicines
  labeling of, 151
  outdated, 149
  responsible use of, 154
  side-effects of, 152
  storing, 149
  supervising, 151–152
Mescaline, 186, 192
Methamphetamines, 89, 178–179
  dangers of, 179–180
Methcathinone, 186
Methedrine, 146
Methylphenidate hydrochloride, 147
Microdots, 190
Monetary extremes, drug use and, 92
Mood control, 87–88

alcohol and, 110, 114
Moral foundations, 81
Movies
 guidelines for, 84–85
 influence of, 74–75
Mushrooms, psychedelic, 191–192
Music
 guidelines for, 82–83
 influence of, 75–80

N

Narcotics, in prescription medicines, 153
Narcotics Anonymous (NA), 141, 215, 268
National Council on Alcoholism, 64, 269
National Drug Control Strategy, 4, 5
National Household Survey on Drug Abuse, 173, 193
National Inhalant Prevention Coalition (NIPC), 130, 135, 269
National Institute of Drug Abuse (NIDA), 101, 135, 157, 240, 269
Nembutal, 145
Nicotine, 20, 99, 172. See also Cigarette smoking.
 addiction to, 100, 105
Nitrous oxides, 131–132, 137
Nonviolent conflict resolution, 64–65

O–P

Office of National Drug Control Policy, 178, 270
Outpatient programs, 223
Overdosing, 68
Over-the-counter drugs, 142–144, 148–154
Pain relievers, 143
Parental authority, exercising, 37–38
Parental involvement, 5, 25–38, 42, 226–227
Parental support, 228–230
Parenting styles, 40
Parents

drug and alcohol abuse by, 37–38
 responsibilities of, 25–26, 38, 81
 as role models, 26–36, 38, 111, 112, 118
 self-education of, 64, 95
 speaking out and action by, 61
 strategies for, 210
 tools for, 95–96
 what children want from, 42–43
Partnership for a Drug-Free America, 175, 196, 240, 270
PCP (phencyclidine hydrochloride), 119, 187–188, 204
Peer pressure, 12
 alcohol and, 112
 experimentation and, 87
 making children aware of, 36
 resisting, 58–59
 steroid use and, 157
 types of, 13–14
Peer-to-peer communication, 167
Perfectionism, 47
 addiction and, 88
Performance-enhancing drugs, 156, 157–158
Permissive parenting style, 40, 41
Personal appearance, steroid use and, 159
Personal problems, communicating, 11
Petroleum distillates, 134
Peyote, 186
Phenylpropanolamine, 143
Phoenix House, 64, 223–224
Physical abuse, 63
Physical effects
 of drug use, 93–94
 of inhalants, 136, 138
"Poppers," 133–134
Positive behavior, focusing on, 47
"Pot." See Marijuana.
Pregnancy and drinking, 116

Prescription drugs, 144–148
 education about, 149–153
Privacy issues, 36
Psilocin/Psilocybin, 186, 191–192
Psychedelic drugs, 186–192
Psychosis
 PCP-induced, 188
 steroids and, 165
Psychotropic medicines, 148
Puberty, changes associated with, 39–40
"Pyramiding," 165, 166

Q–R

Rave events, 131, 185, 191
Regular drug use, 87–88
 dealing with, 214–215
Residential treatment, 223
Resistance techniques, 2, 14–16
 teaching, 58–62
Resource guide, 266–271
Responsible drinking, 114, 116
Rights
 children's, 59–60
Ritalin, 146–147
"Rochas," 183–184
Rock cocaine, 174
Rohypnol, 183–184
"Roid rages," 165
Role models, parents as, 2, 37, 95, 111, 112, 118
Role playing, 2, 14, 67
 active listening, 49
 assertiveness, 58–59, 67–72
Rules
 guidelines for, 31–32, 92
 laying down, 30–31, 214–215

S

Safety, 139–140
"Saying no," 14–16, 77
School achievement, monitoring, 43
School counselors, talking with, 141
School grades, changes in, 90–91
Seconal, 145

Self-behavior, 26–28
Self-centered behavior, 92
Self-esteem, 40
  assertiveness training and, 58–59
  characteristics associated with, 50
  gang membership and, 52
  importance of, 39–40
  parenting to build, 39–50, 45–48
  poor, 13, 226
  role of drugs in boosting, 12
Serotonin, 183
Sexual abuse, 63
Sexually transmitted diseases (STDs), 126
Single parenting, 227–228
Sleep problems, drug use and, 88, 92
Social drinking, 110
"Special K," 190–191
Speech patterns, changes in, 94
"Speed," 146, 177, 180
"Speedballing," 194
"Sports" drugs, 155–170
Spray paint, sniffing, 137
"Stacking," 165
Stealing, 202
Steroids, 155–170
  body chemistry and, 165
  dangers of, 163–165
  dealers of, 158–159
  females, effect on, 164
  males, effect on, 164
  new users of, 157–159
  preventing use, 166–169
  risk/benefit ratio of, 168
  side effects of, 160–161
  signs of, 165–166
Stimulants, 20, 146
  cocaine, 22
  illegal, 171–180
  over-the-counter, 143
Stress
  alcohol and, 110, 114
  causes of, 12
  dealing with, 59
  family, 222
  marijuana and, 125

Stress Level Test, 18
Substance abuse, key reasons for, 13–14
Sudden Sniffing Death Syndrome (SSD), 129
Support networks, 64
Synthetic heroin, 186

T
"Tagging," 9, 54
Teenagers
  abuse of medicines by, 153–154
  LSD use among, 189–190
  steroid abuse by, 169–170
Television
  guidelines for, 83–84
  influence of, 74–75
Testosterone, 159
  synthetic, 163, 164
THC (tetrahydrocannabinol), 119, 120, 126
Tobacco. See also Cigarette smoking
  addictive nature of, 98–100
  as a gateway drug, 98–109
  use, dangers of, 108
Toluene, 134, 140, 199
Tough love, 215–216
Tranquilizers, 145
Treatment, professional, 217–224
Treatment strategies, 214–215, 223
Trichloroethylene, 140
"Tripping," 189
Trouble, reasons kids get into, 8–24

U–V
United States, drugs and violence in, 3–4
"Uppers," 146, 177
Values
  communicating, 2
  practicing, 30
Vandalism, 53
Vigilance, importance of, 140–141
Violence. See also Domestic

violence.
  crack cocaine and, 176–177
  guns and, 62
  in home and community, 51–72
  media allure of, 73–85
  music and, 78
  in the United States, 3–4
Volatile nitrites, 133–134

W
Web sites. See Internet.
Winstrol-V, 162